A DANGEROUS WOMAN

NEW YORK'S FIRST
LADY LIBERTY

*The Life and Times of Lady Deborah Moody (1586-1659?)
- Her search for freedom of religion in Colonial America*

VICTOR H. COOPER

Heritage Books, Inc.

Published 1995 By

HERITAGE BOOKS, INC.
1540E Pointer Ridge Place, Bowie, MD 20716
1-800-398-7709

ISBN 0-7884-0303-6

A Complete Catalog Listing Hundreds of Titles
On History, Genealogy, and Americana
Available Free Upon Request

To Rhona

without whom.......nothing

Give me the liberty to know, to utter, and to argue freely
according to conscience above all liberties -

JOHN MILTON
Areopagitca in
Works, iv. p.346.

TABLE OF CONTENTS

LIST OF ILLUSTRATIONS

Illustrations are reproduced by permission of: Guildhall Library, City of London 8,14,20; British Museum, Department of Prints and Drawings 50,84; Derek Allen 41; Swampscott Historical Society 68.

INTRODUCTION

A DANGEROUS WOMAN outlines the life and times of Lady Deborah Moody (1586-1659?) told against background accounts of leading defenders of freedom of conscience. NEW YORK'S FIRST LADY LIBERTY was the first-mentioned patentee in the Gravesend charter which granted a group of immigrants freedom from external religious interference and the right to enjoy civil liberties. The book commemorates the 350th anniversary of the charter.

Brooklyn, New York has for many years offered sanctuary to aliens desiring religious and political freedom regardless of their racial origin. English, Irish, Italians, Scandinavians, Germans and Africans have in the past settled there preparing the way for today's Haitians, Poles, Russians and refugees from the Near and Far East.

Among the early immigrants who arrived in search of respite was Lady Deborah Moody who had been deprived of her civic liberties and suffered intolerance in her native England. She fled to the New World to which others of her countrymen had come only to discover that the persecuted had in turn become another generation of persecutors. Driven from Puritan Massachusetts because of her religious beliefs she and her followers began a new community at Gravesend, Long Island during the seventeenth-century Dutch colonial era. The Governor granted them a town charter assuring them of freedom of conscience and the right to choose their town officers. It was issued nearly a century and a half before the Bill of

Rights was enacted. The first Quaker meeting in the colony was held in Lady Moody's home.

The settlement reflects the remarkable achievement of a woman in an age when custom indicated that only men engaged in political activities. Gravesend was the first colonial enterprise to be headed by a woman. To maintain her town's rights Gravesend's fearless matriarch acted with resolution.

Five years after her death, Colonel Richard Nicolls conquered Nieuw Amsterdam and renamed it New York in honor of the Duke of York. Gravesend and five Dutch settlements became the City of Brooklyn which in 1898 were incorporated with Greater New York City.

An examination of the bibliography will reveal that the story of Lady Moody's town told against the general search for freedom of religion during her life-time has been built up from many sources both primary and secondary on both sides of the Atlantic. The flavor of Lady Moody's world has been retained in quotations which frequently utilized spellings which differ from today's usage. These not only varied from one author to another but disparate renderings were frequently used within the same document.

As no portrait has come to light, nor any original writings from Lady Moody's pen, much of her life history remains shadowy and unrecorded, but enough has been discovered to exhibit a character of no ordinary courage and integrity.

"SHEE IS A DANGEROUS WOEMAN"

It was the longest and most dangerous journey of her life. Rarely had an Englishwoman of rank travelled so far from home without an accompanying family member. As the small sailing ship bobbed up and down on the wild Atlantic Ocean a middle-aged gentlewoman huddled with other exiles in primitive and cramped accommodations not knowing from one storm to the next when her end would come. Dame Deborah Moody was driven from the Old World not only by high winds but by intimidation.

The middle-aged gentlewoman fled those "arbitrary engines of power," the English courts, which, during the reign of King Charles I, were robbing citizens of civil and religious liberties. Although her ancestors had loyally served the royal family during six reigns she was now accused of failing to comply with the king's proclamation requiring her to dwell in the country rather than in London. The Court of Star Chamber (the ceiling was ornamented with stars) had named her in an action to prevent her from living in the city of her birth.

Incensed that the state denied her basic rights she chose her own path to freedom. The courageous widow set her face toward the New World in order to escape imperious power and, like John Cotton, to "enjoy the liberty, not of some ordinances of God but of all, and in all purity."[1]

Dame Deborah disembarked in the Massachusetts Bay colony in 1636/39. Some 16,000 English settlers had already arrived in New

England during the previous eleven years. Some planned to trade, others to convert natives to the Christian faith; some had been sent as the result of court action over their misdemeanors while others like Dame Deborah had been oppressed by church or state.

Life in New England contrasted sharply with that in London. Dame Deborah's new community was governed by John Winthrop and eleven members who had established the Massachusetts Bay Company. They had royal warrant "to correct, govern, punish, pardon and rule all the King's subjects within the limits of this patent." In order to obtain a share of this civil power 109 of the first two thousand colonists applied within a year of landing for admission as freemen of the Corporation, but discovered that only male church members were accepted which excluded a majority of settlers. Even church membership was insufficient as each petitioner needed a certificate from a minister that his opinions were approved. But as the twelve churchmen were unwilling to share their rights applicants found they were unwelcome. Although the church was a minority, it plainly intended to preserve its strangle-hold on the colony.

Dame Deborah was accommodated in Salem in a primitive log house with flat roof and brick chimney. Nearby was a spring and a congregationalist-type church where Ralph Skelton was pastor. John Higginson had been elected teacher and Ralph Smith was the ordained Separatist minister. The new arrival applied for membership.[2]

Honored to have a person of Dame Moody's standing among them, (they addressed her as Lady Moody) both church-people and traders welcomed her and engaged her in conversation. She abandoned the advice of *A Tablet for Gentlewomen* (designed to encourage female piety), that "there is nothing that becommeth a maid better than silence." As a mature, titled widow her opinions were sought after - and the townspeople listened with interest.[3]

Lady Deborah ventured surprise at the exacting attitudes of some settlers. When anyone expressed a view not in complete agreement with church teaching and government she noticed the distress of church officials. Aware that they insisted on absolute conformity she remarked that this engendered many "petty differences" and much bickering which "did eate out Christian society and starve common humanity." There was "high conceit" among those who "seemed to be godly" and "a greate dejection of spirit" among the rest who felt "diserted and forsaken" by them. Not only did she find inter-Christian relationships poor, church-members acted coolly towards "those without" as the colonists called them, whom she considered were often more "practically godly" than church attenders.

When some disparaged their "native contrey of England callinge it Babilon, Egipt, Rome, the land of idolatry etc." Lady Moody spoke up vigorously for her homeland. She recalled occasions when she had enjoyed Christian communion and this irritated them. She disliked affectation and the valuing of people only for their looks or skills and strongly disapproved of the "censorious custome" of spying on the supposed faults of church people. She discovered that worshippers were required to report to church authorities when they found a variant belief or practice in another member. That made her feel "frustrated."

Richard Sadler, Clerk of the Writs (1640-1641), noted down the comments of "the gentlewoman lately come from England." He agreed with Lady Deborah's reactions and disapproved of the "I am holyer than thou" attitude of church officials. In the case of a woman in Lynn with healing skills who for many years had not been permitted to receive communion, he recorded "they objectinge that she is a woman of a proud and unbrotherlike spirit." When she spoke to the elders, Sadler noted, "they report that she is of a waspish spirit and fumish disposition." When she declined to talk with them she was said to be "stout and proud."

Sadler, a young man of about twenty-two, concurred with Lady Deborah that religious people were too ready to judge one another. And when a newcomer applied to join, the church elders were "full of unnecessary scruples." They made "unwarrantable extrusion" in their examinations, requiring "long and punctuall conffessions and declaracions concerning the time and manner of there (sic) convercions." Church leaders, "prescribinge rules that Christ did not," were "not fit to be vissible members of the vissible church" he said. Sadler condemned their "merciless cruelty" and "rashness in judginge mens hearts by outward appearings."

Pulpit discourses were often rendered with "a fine whyneinge tone and a sowre countenance" and Sadler noted that those who "preacht out of the Revelation about the constitution of churches and church discipline, subvercion of Anti Christ and the Romish Babilon...begot a conceit of themselves." This clerical arrogance disappointed Lady Deborah. "Hopeinge to have spent her dayes without such disturbances as Christians mett with in England" Lady Deborah was "disheartened concerninge her late hazardous journey," wrote Sadler.

On one occasion Lady Deborah asked some of her neighbors why the Salem populace did not observe the fifth of November, the anniversary of the Guy Fawkes' Gunpowder Plot (1605). English clergy were required by Act of Parliament to hold an annual service of thanksgiving "for this most happy deliverance" from the "Papists' Conspiracy." All English citizens were ordered to attend in recognition that divine providence had delivered both church and nation from "the most Traiterous and Bloudy intended Massacre by Gunpowder." Lady Deborah likened the observance to the feast of Purim which commemorated the defeat of Haman's Persian plot to massacre the Jews - a festival celebrated near Easter. At this her listeners refused to answer her. They furtively turned tail and reported to the church authorities that Lady Moody superstitiously observed holy days and was "therefore unfitt to be a member."

F.L. (probably Francis Lightfoot), an inhabitant of nearby Lynn, "an ould buissy man, came to pumpe her with questions about the persons in the Trinity." First he asked Lady Deborah for a definition of what she meant when in her prayers she addressed God. But she "perceaved his drift and answered him accordingly." Then her London-born interrogator posed "other meane questions" and tried to humiliate her. He contemptuously told her she must be very ignorant not to know what a church was and proceeded to catechize her, but she gave him indirect answers to his theological questions. Finally he left, muttering that she was as bad or worse than the report of her.

Then Lady Deborah fell sick. A group of visiting church-members clustered around her bed and like Job's comforters "censured her that it was impossible to escape the judgement of God that had now overtaken her" because of her "idolatrous superstitions." But before divine retribution descended Lady Deborah regained her health and good spirits which effectively stopped the mouths of her critics.

Joining a church was often a stressful exercise. Before being admitted to membership candidates were expected to relate the story of their struggle against the flesh and how they had come to the conviction that faith, entirely unmerited, had been granted to them. This, according to Thomas Lechford, usually took a quarter of an hour, more or less. Sadler says that women were interviewed privately and "for the most part admitted without there publike confessory speech though formerly that was greate in use."

The newcomer's request for church membership had a mixed reception. Francis Lightfoot objected and some who "could scarce have a charitable thought of her" showed it by "muttering." But after discussion "the members were satisfyed." Lady Deborah joined the Salem Church on 2 May 1640. Accepted at the same time were: Samuell Corning and his wife; Jane, wife of Phillip Veren; Jonathan Porter and Thomas Ruck and his wife, some of whom may have been friends or servants accompanying Lady Deborah.[4]

The following November a group of Lynn residents who were unhappy with their religious leaders gathered into a new church group under Abraham Pierson with the intention of establishing a settlement on western Long Island. They left in December but were forced to the eastern shore where they began the town of Southampton. Other members with similar variant beliefs had already left Salem and near-by Lynn because of disagreements with clergy. Roger Williams had gone to Providence and a group followed him. Winthrop noted that at least twelve of those at Providence rejected infant baptism: "the Hutchinson Party at Aquidnay professed Anabaptism [re-baptism for believers] and other distasteful heresies."[5]

For two years no problem is recorded concerning the English matron's attendance at church. Then discussions and disagreements began again. Members questioned her belief and her understanding of Scripture with reference to baptism. Lady Deborah accepted the anabapatist view that baptism was not for children but for believing adults who had become assured through "further light." Her opinions were not shared by the elders.[6]

During the cold winter the English Lady pondered her insecure situation. She huddled by the fire-side as the wolves and icy winds howled their grim warnings. "A goodly maid of the church of Linne, going in a deep snow from Meadford homeward, was lost, and some of her clothes found after among the rocks." But while the thought of being expelled from her home haunted Lady Deborah, she had time to read her Bible and her books (see appendix 2). They confirmed her conviction that belief must precede the ceremony of baptism. It was not meant for babes.[7]

The consequences of her belief could not have been lost on Lady Deborah. Baptists in London were persecuted and European history was full of frightful warnings. Protestants drowned Felix Manz (probably the first Swiss Anabaptist) in the Limmat River though he affirmed that those who killed him were "destroying the very essence of Christianity." Catholic authorities executed their first Anabaptist by burning in May 1525. Anabaptists who escaped death had no security. Menno Simons of the Netherlands was on the run from 1536 until his death in 1561.[8]

Could Lady Deborah expect greater tolerance in the New World? In 1642 information about her variant ideas reached her new minister, Edward Norris, and the Salem authorities. The church elders catechized her on several occasions during the cold winter. Their faces were grim, tight-lipped and unyielding. They solemnly quoted scripture with the false assumption that they could bludgeon a woman into submission. Then they appealed to her loyalty. Surely she could see that church unity was more important than her individual belief. When they failed to find the response they desired, they bombarded her with hostile criticism. But in the educated Lady Deborah they met their match. She could intelligently discuss her view that the Scriptures offer no support to the practice of infant christening. For centuries few women had access to the Scriptures but Lady Deborah could read the Bible for herself. (Will her copy of the Vulgate version ever be found?) For a woman to study and reason was uncommon in a male-dominated society. Far from treating women as equals in worship and polity church dignitaries considered women's views of no value. But Lady Deborah, in advance of her time, did not view gender as a determinant for understanding scripture.

Some of her friends warned her not to persist with her beliefs. They urged her to submit to the elders. Had not Anne Hutchinson aroused the wrath of the Boston clergy and been forced to flee with her children? The story was etched into the settlers' memories. They could picture the scene in the church with the pastor asking if the members were all agreed that "Mistris Hutchinson" should be "cast out", and when no one spoke, denouncing her, excommunicating her and commanding her "to depart out of the Assembly." But such stories did not weaken Lady Deborah's resolve. She refused to discard her faith for a convention though she must have known she was on a collision course with religious and state leaders who considered her opinions a threat to the unity of the church and colony.[9]

Lady Deborah was summoned to court and "charged with belief in anabaptism." "At the Quarterly Court, Dec. 14th 1642, The Lady Deborah Moodie, Mrs. King, and the wife of John Tilton, were presented [charged], for houldinge that the baptizing of Infants is noe ordinance of God."[10]

Gerard Spencer appeared as a witness. Lady Deborah did not attend, it being reported that she was "in a way of conviction before the elders." Lady Deborah certainly had convictions, but the court which concerned itself with both civil and religious matters assumed the right to quash all unapproved beliefs.[11]

The Salem town records state that though she was "dealt with" by many of the elders and others during the winter, and was "admonished" by the court, she "still persisted in her belief."

Anabaptists like Lady Deborah considered infant baptism to be a coercive offence against a child before it could exercise free-will. They insisted that religious constraint is a sin against God: "Christ's people are a free, unforced, and uncompelled people, who receive Christ with desire and a willing heart." It was this view that enabled baptists to espouse religious toleration, a notion the peremptory Salem dignitaries could not admit. Orthodoxy buttressed by authority had closed their magisterial minds to other than the official opinion.[12]

Where could Lady Deborah turn for help? Governor Winthrop respected her as "a wise and anciently religious woman," and though she had been on good terms with him she knew he did not approve of her views or her desire for freedom of religion. He showed his attitude when Goody Sherman's stray sow was impounded by wealthy Robert Keayne. Speaking against the Court which sided with the poor woman, he declared there was no warrant in scripture for democracy which is "amongst most civil nations, accounted the meanest and worst form of government."[13]

The elders of Salem's first church were so sure of their brand of truth they refused to accommodate any alternative view. There was no room in Massachusetts at that time for so progressive a concept as separation of church and state. The Church planned to admonish her on 12 June 1643 but Lady Deborah determined to avoid giving the authoritarian male clergy a chance publicly to display their wrath and humiliate her as they had done with Anne Hutchinson. Refusing to allow them opportunity to view her discomfort when they read their imperious sentence, the gentle but resolute lady quit Salem.[14]

Later Deputy-Governor John Endecott wrote of Lady Moody in a letter to the Governor: "shee is a dangerous woeman." But Lady Moody considered it dangerous to stifle conscience and chose to be open and honest when questioned. Her faith was rooted in her understanding of Scripture and confirmed by her heritage. Family members and friends had faced similar issues. She knew their stories, having heard them from infancy.[15]

Ex dono *Benj. Maddox Barr.ⁱⁱ* Junij 1709.

St Giles Cripplegate

A RICH HERITAGE

Lady Deborah was the first-born daughter of Walter and Debora Dunch. She was christened in London, 3 April 1586.[1]

The ancient church of St Giles, Cripplegate was "a very fayre and large church" which served a parish of eighteen hundred households and four thousand communicants. It stood outside a gate in the northwest corner of the city wall near "a fayre Pool of sweete water" provided by Dick Whittington, the famous Mayor of London. Church services were crowded with haberdashers, waxchandlers and artisans of the weaving, printing and paper-making trades. Artists, writers and players from Edward Alleyne's Fortune Theatre nearby formed a lively part of the parish. The church's most precious possessions were "one great Byble of the largest volume" and "One Booke of Paraphrases uppon the Gospell" by Erasmus, kept behind an iron grill.[2]

Here, surrounded by family and friends the minister held the infant tightly wrapped in swaddling clothes and asked the baby's name. Then he intoned the prescribed words, "I baptize thee, Deborah, in the name of the Father and of the Son and of the Holy Ghost" and in customary fashion dipped her right side, then her left side and finally her face in the cold water of the church font. The baby was given the same name as her mother - a name popular among God-fearing parents who longed for a "Deborah" to save England from her oppressors. Freedom was in danger. Fresh in Londoners' memories was the persecution of Protestants which had marked the reign of Queen Mary Tudor (1553-8) especially those who had been burned to death at Smithfield Market, close to the Dunch's London home. They prayed that Queen Elizabeth I (1558-1603) whom they dubbed "Protestant Deborah" would successfully preserve England from her enemies.[3]

Deborah Dunch's family and friends together with their ministers were eminent, accomplished people distinguished by long service to the State or the Church. Their convictions and achievements constituted a rich heritage for the new baby.

Deborah Dunch's mother was co-heiress of Bishop Pilkington. She had been christened Debora at Bishop Auckland, County Durham on 8 October 1564, the daughter of James Pilkington, the first Protestant Bishop of Durham, and his wife Isabella Natrisse of the Kingsmill family.

Deborah's grandmother, Isabella Pilkington and her nine brothers were part of the Kingsmill family who craved a greater reformation of the Church of England than that established by Queen Elizabeth. Noted for their puritan sympathies and radical religious connections family members had the courage of their convictions. John and his brother Thomas, when students at Oxford, were publicly warned in chapel for uttering heretical opinions about the sacrament (they rejected transubstantiation) and for shaving their heads in derision of the tonsure. John later signed a letter from the fellows of Magdalen to the Archbishop of Canterbury about their dislike of vestments and helped make Magdalen the most puritan of Oxford colleges. Henry Kingsmill bequeathed a special treasure to Isabella, Deborah's grandmother - "a Geneva bible in English of the great print" complete with anti-authoritarian marginal notes and inscribed with the words: "The life of man is short and subject to many displeasures."[4]

Deborah's grandfather, James Pilkington, from his earliest days as a clergyman was ready to speak his mind. He favored the Reformation and spent much of his life struggling against religious intolerance. He publicly disputed with Dr William Glynn, Chaplain to the Bishop of Norwich, over transubstantiation (the nature of the bread and wine in Holy Communion). After Pilkington's appointment as president of St John's College, Cambridge the Marian persecution of Protestants broke out. He fled to the continent with his brother Leonard and a group of like-minded preachers including John Foxe, Robert Crowley, Edmund Grindal and John Knox. They settled in Zurich, Basle, Geneva and Frankfort. Several London merchants supported them. Then Bishop Stephen Gardiner (the chief opponent of the Reformation doctrines in England) imprisoned their benefactors and said he would make these churchmen "eat their finger-ends for hunger." Thanks to Zurich senators and Christopher, Prince of Wittenberg, Pilkington and his friends were able to survive.[5]

On his return to St John's College he was appointed a commissioner to revise the Book of Common Prayer and named bishop-elect of Winchester. He lost the post because of his forthright Protestant sentiments but was later appointed Bishop of Durham. His brother Leonard who succeeded him at St John's College was of similar propensity, described as "unduly biased by his puritan leanings."[6]

The spirited, outspoken Bishop valued truth so far above popularity that he fearlessly expressed his views even if they involved the monarch. Like his vocal friend Edmund Grindal[7], he was unafraid to criticize the policy of the redoubtable Queen Elizabeth:

> We are under authority and can innovate nothing without the Queen; nor can we alter the laws; the only thing left for our choice is, whether we will bear these things, or break the peace of the Church.[8]

He declared:

> It is no rebellion against princes to do that which God commandeth; for princes themselves are bound, as well as other meaner degrees, to serve the Lord God of heaven with all their might and main; and unto the same God they must make account of their doings, as all others must.[9]

It was a brave speech. Pilkington died at Bishop Auckland, some ten years before the birth of his granddaughter, Deborah. In his will he desired to be buried with "as few popish ceremonies as may be, or vain cost." His body was entombed at Bishop Auckland and later re-interred in front of the high altar at Durham Cathedral close to the remains of those famous Christian monks, Cuthbert, Bishop of Lindisfarne and the Venerable Bede.

❖ ❖ ❖ ❖ ❖

Deborah Dunch's paternal grandparents, William and Mary Dunch, moved in royal circles. William (b. 1508) served several monarchs, was highly regarded as "sworn esquire extraordinary of the body of

Queen Elizabeth" and spent most of his time at court. As an official of the royal household in London he drew up *The MS of William Dunche* which provided formulae for ceremonies and menus for court banquets while Catherine Howard was Queen.

Six years later King Henry VIII appointed him Auditor of the Mint, a post he held under King Edward VI until 1551. During this time he built up a considerable fortune which he invested in real estate. He bought Little Wittenham Manor from Mint official Sir Edmund Peckham.   Avebury Manor, in the County of Wiltshire, was conveyed to him in 1552 for £2,200 when its former owner, Sir William Sharington, Master of the Bristol Mint, was arrested for fraudulent practices.[10]

As commissioned escheator for the counties of Berkshire and Oxfordshire, grandfather Dunch collected rents and ensured reversion of property to the Crown when there were no heirs. He represented the Borough of Wallingford in the English Parliament of 1563 and was Sheriff of Berkshire in 1570.[11]

In later years Deborah's grandparents spent more of their time at Little Wittenham, their country home near Dorchester in the Royal County of Berkshire (royal because Windsor Castle, the largest of the royal residences is situated in this county). The Manor with its terraces and a yew-tree walk was near an ancient church on a picturesque bend of the river Thames. The old mansion nestled among luxurious trees and wooded hills. A phantom raven was said to guard the treasure of soldiers who died violently in Saxon times in a fosse or ditch known as the Money Pit. William Dunch, however, created his own lucrative "money pit." An energetic developer, he acquired properties (some on Crown leases) in Berkshire, Somerset, Hampshire and Oxfordshire and moved among the more affluent segment of English society.[12]

William and Mary Dunch had two sons - Edmund, born about 1551 and Walter, (Deborah's father) born about 1552. After attending Magdalen College, Oxford, Walter was "bred a counsellor at Gray's-inn" the lawyer's educational and work complex near Holborn in the City of London. Gray's Inn and the other three Inns of Court acted as a point of contact for puritan gentry and lawyers from all over England. Walter started work at the age of eighteen, was installed barrister-at-law at the age of twenty-seven. Silk stockings and a beaver hat with a white feather were a distinguishing feature of Gray's Inn lawyers dress. In 1584 and 1588 Dunch was Member of Parliament for Dunwich, a coastal town in Suffolk where the family may have originated - indeed the name may be derived from Dunwich. The town no longer exists having slowly been washed away by the encroaches of the North Sea.[13]

Walter married Debora Pilkington in London on 27 July 1581. His father gave him the Priory Manor of Avebury and extensive lands in Wiltshire at this time. The manor was declared to be of the yearly value of £47 13s. 5d "beyond all reprises" (*outgoings*). In July 1585 Walter obtained a 21-year lease from Queen Elizabeth on the rectory parsonage of Avebury at an annual rent of £30. 16s.. Walter took every opportunity to augment his holdings and acquired properties in Leigh Delamere, Sevington (Semington?), Berwick and the manor of Exford in Somerset.

So although Deborah's father was not his father's heir his land accumulations ensured that young Deborah was born with the proverbial silver spoon in her mouth and would want for nothing. So her legacy included a share of both the Dunch fortune and the Pilkington spirit.[14]

The ministers of the church attended by Deborah's parents reflected the family's religious bent. Robert Crowley, "a very forward man for reformation" was rector of St Giles Church, Cripplegate, and a friend of the family at the time of Deborah's christening. Bishop Pilkington had known him well and when he was suspended because of his puritanism, John Foxe, formerly of Boston, Lincolnshire, became Vicar of St Giles Church for ten months. Foxe was the famous author of *Acts and Monuments*, published in 1563, popularly known as "Foxe's Book of Martyrs." It was chained in many churches along with the Bible.[15]

Crowley and Foxe both spent their last years of ministry at St Giles Cripplegate and had similar interests. Both were Fellows of Magdalen College, Oxford and both were ordained deacons by Bishop Ridley who was later martyred for his faith. After fleeing to the continent both spent time in Frankfurt with Deborah's grandfather. Crowley compiled a book called "Ye Unffoldynge of ye Popyshe atyr [attire]" (unpublished). When order was given requiring the wearing of surplices, he refused to minister in the "conjuring garments of popery" and was deprived and imprisoned for resisting the use of the surplice by his choir. Both ministers published books. Crowley appealed for further religious reformation and attacked the capitalist landlords of his day.

Foxe believed in Christian toleration. As a youth he protested against college rules requiring regular attendance at chapel and opposed enforced celibacy. Ordained a priest by Edmund Grindal, Bishop of London, he would have attained high position in the church had it not been for his consistently maintained Calvinistic views. Foxe argued that ever since Joseph of Arimathea brought the gospel to England a spiritual war had been raging between Christ (associated with Protestants and the Word) and Antichrist (associated with Catholics and the mass). He contended that foreigners had imported superstition, persecuted protestants and made repeated attempts to undermine the autonomy of the English Church.

Foxe expected the English people to defend their national independence and looked to Queen Elizabeth to champion freedom and international Protestantism. He revelled in the liberation that the printing press was beginning to provide: "Either the Pope must abolish knowledge and printing or printing at length will root him out."[16]

But in the struggle for freedom of religion neither the clergy nor Deborah's parents could foresee how events would affect the newborn. England was in a state of ferment.

St Giles City Gate

RELIGIOUS TENSION

At the time of Deborah's birth Protestants lived in fear of the re-establishment of Roman Catholicism and a repetition of religious persecution. Queen Elizabeth I was in perpetual danger. For two decades one plot to dethrone her followed another. The English church had been dis-established as the state religion by Elizabeth's father, King Henry VIII and Pope Pius V had declared Elizabeth a heretic. He released Englishmen from allegiance to her and backed a rising in the North which attempted to rescue Mary Stuart from prison and reinstate Catholicism in England. Ridolphi, the Pope's agent, gave 12,000 crowns to the Earls of Westmoreland and Northumberland to support a military coup, but the conspiracy failed. Northumberland's body was put on a scaffold in the City of York and his head impaled on Micklegate Bar as a warning to other traitors.[1]

By 1586 the Spanish were promising aid and the Duke of Alva was preparing to send an army to England. In December Pope Sixtus pledged Philip II of Spain a million gold ducats to be paid when Spanish soldiers first set foot on English soil, and a reward of plenary absolution was offered for the murder of England's Protestant queen. A cardinal speaking for the Pope declared that anyone who assassinated Elizabeth "not only does not sin but gains merit."

Parliament reacted by ordering the expulsion of all Jesuits and Roman Catholic priests trained in continental seminaries. The plots continued but the priestly intrigues of William Allen, Robert Parsons, William Parry and Francis Throckmorton all failed.

Nobles and gentry from many parts of England bound themselves to protect the Queen and fifty gentlemen pensioners armed with gilt battle-axes closely guarded Elizabeth in her splendid, tapestried Presence chamber. Up and down the land there were calls for the death of Mary Queen of Scots (Mary Stuart), the Queen's imprisoned Catholic step-sister and rival to the throne.[2]

While the Dunches were celebrating the arrival of their first-born, a group of Mary Stuart's supporters met secretly in nearby St Giles Fields to devise a scheme to release Mary from prison and put her on the throne. First the conspirators planned to assassinate the reigning monarch. Their leader, Anthony Babington, firmly believed that the Pope's writ of ex-communication made it lawful to murder Elizabeth. He smuggled a letter outlining his plans to Mary at her carefully-watched prison, Chartley Manor in Staffordshire. It was conveyed in a tiny water-tight box inserted in the bung hole of a beer barrel. Mary transmitted her long and enthusiastic reply in support of Babington by the same channel. But neither knew that Elizabeth's Secretary of State, Sir Francis Walsingham and his Catholic informer were party to the beer barrel postal service. They intercepted the letter which indicated Mary's support for the invasion and her readiness to seize her cousin's throne. The document not only damned the traitors and led to the protracted execution of the Roman Catholic plotters at St Giles in the Fields, it also sealed Mary Stuart's death warrant.[3]

Mary was executed at Fotheringay Castle several months after Deborah was born. Londoners rejoiced, rang the church bells, fired salvos and illuminated every street.

But the death of Mary Stuart did not diminish Catholic determination that England should recognize the Pope as the head of the Church. Indeed King Philip of Spain determined to restore the Pope's control. Two years after Deborah was born he set out to break the power of England, the leader of the Protestant cause in Europe.

Elizabeth ordered her admirals and sea-captains to oppose the Spanish fleet and they readied their ships in Plymouth. Lord Charles Howard was in Sir Francis Drake's four-masted galleon, *Ark Royal*, Sir Francis Drake in the *Revenge*, Sir John Hawkyns in the *Victory*, Sir Martin Frobisher in the *Triumph*, and nearly a hundred ships were made prepared for action.

The Queen collected gifts and raised taxes to support them.
Deborah's grandfather, William Dunch, subscribed £100 (twenty
times the equivalent of the average annual salary) to the Armada
Fund while the family joined in nation-wide prayers for the
preservation of protestant England.[4]

Spain's "invincible" Armada of 129 ships of war set sail with the
blessing of Pope Sixtus V on 29 May 1588. On board were 22,000
men, 2360 brass cannon to conquer England and a group of 180
priests and monks to convert her people. They were said to have
taken with them "whips, chains, thumbscrews and other
instruments of torture which the Inquisition had found so useful in
the Netherlands." The story has been denied as no ship's manifest
listing these punitive articles has been found, but there were many
reports of the Inquisition's tortures applied without fair trial to
continental heretics - too many to be all fictitious. And the savage
massacre in Paris of between ten and twenty-thousand Huguenots
on St Bartholomew's Day, 1572, was still fresh in English
memories.[5]

When the Spanish ventured up the English Channel the nimble,
lively English vessels out-manoeuvered them and the crowded,
unwieldy Spanish galleons were turned into slaughter houses.
Unusually strong winds helped rout the armada. The shores of the
Orkneys, the Hebrides and Ireland were strewn with ship
fragments and dead bodies and only fifty-three Spanish vessels
limped painfully home to Corunna. Simultaneously the threat
from the regiments of Parma which had been waiting to cross the
channel and subjugate England evaporated.

Ruth, a sister for Deborah, was christened at St Giles, Cripplegate
on 6 October 1588. On 17 December a new minister arrived at the
church - the famous Lancelot Andrewes. As Vicar of St. Giles for
seventeen years he stressed the importance of ritual and liturgy.
He became court preacher, poet, scholar and master of fifteen
languages.

On 18 March 1589 (our year 1590) Deborah's sister Mary was born
and baptized at the same church. Later still her sister Anne
arrived. Deborah's father, Walter, awaited a son and heir.

✧ ✧ ✧ ✧ ✧

The Dunch's country home, the Priory Manor of Avebury, was
eighty miles west of London, in the county of Wiltshire. The house

was adjacent to a very ancient site, the Avebury Obelisk Circle, the largest stone monument in Britain outrivalling the famed Stonehenge, 18 miles distant. Deborah and her sisters could roam among the 98 curious megalithic stones each weighing up to 60 tons, doubtless wondering (like thousands of visitors before and since) why they were hauled there three thousand years earlier. Were they intended as a temple, observatory or burial ground?[6]

It was in this puzzling place that a Christian community and church was established in Saxon times and later developed around a monastery which eventually became the Dunches' Manor House. The south-facing property surrounded by sweet green fields offered the Dunch family a welcome retreat from the city.

Included in the family acreage was Silbury Hill, the tallest pre-historic mystery mound in Europe from which Deborah and her sisters could see much of their parents' three-thousand-acre farm which included 160 acres of arable land and 1300 sheep.

The farm produced a bountiful supply of food as did the circular brick pigeon-house which still stands between the house and St James' Church where the family worshipped. The stew [fish-pond] contained fish and eels until wanted for cooking. Wiltshire households brewed their own wines in season - cowslip, dandelion, rhubarb, potato, currant, gooseberry, elderberry and parsnip. The well was situated in the brewhouse next to the kitchen and both there and in the cellar there were barrels and ale firkins, with corks attached by string to the handle, so that when they flew off they would not be hard to find again. Life was peaceful at Avebury Manor with its cherry court and gardens set among elm, ash, sycamore and beech trees.[7]

It was equally serene at the Dunches' ancestral home thirty miles over the Ridgeway at Little Wittenham. Here in March 1594 a brother for Deborah was born. William, the long-awaited heir was christened in St Peter's Church where Christians had worshipped for almost a thousand years and where the font at which he was baptized can still be seen.[8]

Only a few weeks later when Deborah was eight years of age her father fell ill in London. "Sick in body but of perfect memory" and praising God Almighty, Walter Dunch made his last will and testament during Whitsun week on Tuesday, 21 May 1594, "trusting to inherit everlasting life by the only merits and passion of my Lord and Saviour Jesus." He died 4 June at the age of forty-two and was buried in the church at Little Wittenham.[9]

In his will, proved 25 June 1595, Walter left his estate to his son William but provided for £1500 (equivalent to $250,000 or more in today's currency) to be paid to each of his four daughters when they reached the age of eighteen or at marriage whichever came first. The dowry money was to be raised by his wife from the leases of his lands and manors in Wiltshire and Somerset over twenty-one years and from "the profits of the parsonage of Avebury" which yielded £100 a year. Walter appointed his wife as executrix and his uncle, Mr Serjeant Kingsmill, (George) and his brother Edmund Dunche as "overseers." Walter's mother, Mary and his brother Edmund placed a brass memorial plate inside the church (there to this day).[10]

Walter's heir, three-months old William, was according to law made a ward of Court. This had painful consequences for Deborah's mother in the form of heavy taxes. The Court of Wards was considered "an odious institution that preyed on families ravaged by the death of a father with minor children." His widow, Debora encountered many financial problems. She also brought legal actions in the Court of Exchequer against a certain Richard Truslowe for intrusion into part of the rectory premises one of several court cases in which she was involved.

Wardship of Deborah's brother eventually passed to Sir John Cooper and Sir Daniel Norton of Southwick, Portsmouth, both of whom lived in the adjacent county of Hampshire. "William Dunch, either then or after his mother's death, went to live with Sir John Cooper at Rockbourne."[11]

When Deborah was eleven years of age her grandfather, William Dunch, aged 89, died 11 May 1597 and was buried near her father in the chapel he had built inside the Church of St. Peter, Little Wittenham. By his will, dated 12 July 1596, and proved three weeks after his death, he left £40 to buy plate or a diamond ring for Queen Elizabeth as he was "a sworn servant to her most noble father and to her brother and sister as also to herself, and hath received good benefit and great princely favours from them." £30 was to be spent on cups for Lord Keeper Thomas Egerton, the Queen's Treasurer, William Cecil (Lord Burghley) and Sir Robert Cecil (William Cecil's younger son), Secretary of State and principal distributor of royal patronage. William Dunch had great respect for the upright statesman, Lord Burghley, whom Queen Elizabeth considered to be honest with his counsel, "not corrupted with any manner of gifts" and "faithful to the State."[12]

Grandfather's rectory estate at Little Wittenham remained in the hands of the Crown until 1604 when it was granted to Mary, "relict of William Dunche." Grandmother Mary survived till 1605 and was buried near her husband.[13]

St Mary Aldermary

DEBORAH MARRIES

Deborah grew up in an age of change. The discovery of the New World gave rise to commerce. The invention of the printing press led to a revival of learning and stimulated dreams of a better life and hope for increased liberty. England's first printer, William Caxton, affirmed "there is no rychesse gretter than lybete for lybete is better than alle the gold of the world."[1]

Changes occurred in lifestyle. Gunpowder rendered bows and arrows useless. Castles gave way to manors made of brick or stone like those occupied by Deborah's parents and grandparents. Glass was cheap and windows numerous. Bay windows and decorated chimneys distinguished the Elizabethan house. Beautiful front terraces reached down to the Thames in front of mansions like the Dunches' Manor at Little Wittenham.[2]

Inside the manors, the reception rooms or "chambers of presence" were wainscotted with carved oak. Rich tapestries hung on the walls. The private rooms were now often divided into "My lord's side" and "My lady's side." Feather beds and soft blankets replaced straw pallets and wooden pillows. Floors were sprinkled with sweet herbs. And the breeze over the herb garden brought the scents of lavender, roses, pinks, holly-hocks and sweet-william into the houses.

Fashions were changing too. Influenced by Queen Elizabeth, people began to dress more expensively. Gold jewels in the hair were in style, rings of precious stones in the ears, starched cambric ruffs around the neck, velvet hats, immense farthingales or whalebone-hooped petticoats, and stomachers or cummerbunds blazing with jewels. Men often wore an Italian cloak, a Spanish mantle, a French cap and a Scottish dagger. Young women of Deborah's standing could afford good clothes, but those of puritan leanings avoided extravagance in dress.

At the age of thirty-four Deborah's widowed mother, now able to inherit as co-heir of James Pilkington, was married to Sir James Marvyn (Mervin), of Fonthill Gifford, Wiltshire. He was Member of Parliament and Sheriff of Wiltshire when in 1598 at the age of 69 he married Debora Dunch. It was a financially astute move which helped preserve the Avebury estate. Sir James extended the east wing of Avebury Manor and built the Great Parlour in stone with oak panelling and a geometric ribbed ceiling. Above it he built the south bedroom with a large ornate fireplace, carved wooden panels on the chimney breast and heraldic plants and animals between the carved ceiling ribs. He constructed an elegant entrance porch which still bears the crest containing the initials: M(arvyn), I(ames) and D(ebora) and the date 1601. (The letter M is raised above the others which together form a rough triangle.) Sir James who had served Queen Elizabeth as "Esquire of the Body" was now prominent in county affairs, Master of the Swans (1561?-1611), "anti-Catholic and loyal" to the crown.

Sir James also "had a London residence in Farringdon-Without, probably in Fetter Lane" and Deborah and her sisters likely spent time in the city with their mother and step-father. Both the Holborn and Fleet Street ends of Fetter Lane were often used as places for execution and other punishments, so Deborah would not be isolated from the harsh realities of life and death.[3]

Few children had opportunity to obtain knowledge. Offspring of poor families had to start earning their living at an early age, some as soon as they were three. Deborah would be more fortunate. In the families of the gentry the mother provided the earliest education and many could also afford a private tutor. Young women like Deborah who inherited wealth and social position were often taught the lute and harpsichord. While society generally expected women to be "chaste, silent and obedient," parents in English manors usually developed in their children the art of conversation and the acquisition of social graces. Deborah would learn to praise without affectation and to reply gracefully to a compliment. Her chief aim would be to please, in preparation for "a good marriage." Her education would lead her to appreciate people without patronizing while her dressing, carriage, curtsies and manner of speaking were all practiced.[4]

Although an Act of 1543 had forbidden women to read the Bible, noble and gentle-women were permitted to read it privately. But by the end of the sixteenth century even tiny children were learning to recite the Psalms in Latin, the *Gloria in Excelsis*, the Nicene Creed and the *Paternoster*. Deborah like other daughters of the gentry would master writing, following "printed instructions to a gentlewoman" on how to cut her quill and shape her letters for the "Roman, Italian and Mixt hands." Great license was allowed in the matter of spelling.[5]

Women were not permitted to enter a university and while a family's oldest male might qualify for an expensive tour of Europe girls were rarely allowed such a privilege unless sent to the house of a great lady.

In 1603, when Deborah was seventeen years of age, King James VI of Scotland came to the throne as James I - King of Great Britain, France, and Ireland. Aware of the injustices meted out to her countrymen Deborah knew that nobody had freedom to use voice or pen to express personal convictions and conscientiously held beliefs, except the king. Deborah was witness to a deep-seated struggle - a major contest for first principles. The question: Was England a constitutional monarchy or a despotism? The painful conflict over the issue was to last eighty-five years, all of Deborah's life and more.

King James believed in the Divine Right of Kings. In his book, *Basilikon Doron*, he claimed that kings are "the breathing images of God" - "God's Lieutenants" and "even by God himself they are called Gods." "I will govern according to the common weal, but not according to the common will," James told the House of Commons. A combination of learning with an absence of common-sense made James "the wisest fool in Christendom." A stranger to democracy, James considered Parliament unnecessary, except to vote him money. He told the Spanish ambassador that he was astonished "that the kings his predecessors had consented to such a thing." He chose his own ministers, the House of Commons having no say in the matter. He called Parliament whenever he pleased, could veto any bill passed by the Commons, and often did so.[6]

At this time there were three main religious groups in tension: the Episcopalians (Church of England), the Roman Catholics and the Puritans [See Appendix I]. Most Puritans were disillusioned Episcopalians, still within the Anglican Church and hoping for its reform. They desired a simpler, purer form of worship without bishops and elaborate ceremonies. But James, claiming ecclesiastical authority, issued "A proclamation enjoyning

conformitie to the form of service of God now established." He
aspired "to worke an universal conformitie."[7]

Soon after his accession to the English throne, King James called a
Conference with the Puritans who were the strongest and most
numerous party in parliament. Deborah was eighteen years of age
and the existence of a copy of the Hampton Court proceedings in
the family library may indicate her interest. The Puritans requested
the king to agree to some relaxation of church ceremonial, but
James gave away nothing.   "I shall make them conform
themselves," he said, "or I will harry them out of the land." Proud
of his treatment of the Puritans, James boasted: "I peppered them
soundly." Ninety ministers lost their livings.

A more useful result of the Conference was a decision that 47
divines should make a new translation of the Bible. The Dunches'
minister, Lancelot Andrewes, now Dean of Westminster, was the
translator largely responsible for the Pentateuch and the historical
books. The Authorized Version of the Bible appeared in 1611 and
eventually was warmly received.

Opposition to James I came not only from Puritans but from Roman
Catholics. On his arrival in England James told Queen Elizabeth's
minister, Robert Cecil, that he would be sorry if the Catholics
multiplied unduly, yet it was against his conscience "that the blood
of any man shall be shed for diversity of opinions in religion."
Cecil believed that Roman Catholics were not merely seeking
freedom from persecution, but to have their religion established by
law.[8]

About this time Deborah met a young soldier, Henricus (Henry)
Moody, son of Richard Moodie, gentleman, and his wife Christina,
of Lee and Whitchurch-cum-Milborne, Wiltshire. His family name
meant *brave*, *bold*, *resolute*, and was spelt variously: Moody,
Moodey, Moodie, Mody, Mowdye or Mudie. Henry, born about
1582, was not a poor man. His father owned extensive real estate
and was the largest taxpayer in the area. When plans for marriage
in London were discussed it was agreed that Henry should take his
bride to live at Garsdon (grassy hill), a small village, two miles east
of Malmesbury.[9]

A few days before registering the wedding a major plot was
uncovered which is still celebrated every year with bonfires and
fireworks. Robert Catesby, a Northamptonshire gentleman and a
small band of Catholic desperados devised a scheme to destroy

both king and Parliament at a single blow. With no hope of help for their cause from abroad, the group hired a vacant cellar under the Houses of Parliament, piled 36 barrels of gunpowder against the wall and covered them with fagots of firewood.

Sir Guy Fawkes, a Yorkshire gentleman planned to carry out the dark deed on 5 November 1605 during the State opening of Parliament. Lord Monteagle, a Roman Catholic peer, received an anonymous letter warning him to keep away from the House on that day as "Parliament shall receive a terrible blow, and shall not see who hurts them." The letter was shown to Robert Cecil who laid it before the Council on November 4. The King guessed that gunpowder was meant and ordered a search to be made. Fawkes and the gunpowder were discovered in the cellar. He was tortured on the rack. The other conspirators were chased; some were caught and sabred at Holbeach House, Worcestershire, while the rest were captured and put to death as traitors.

King James reacted fiercely against the Gunpowder Plot and harsh new statutes were enacted. He enforced an old law against Catholics by which non-attendance at the parish Church was subject to a fine of £20 a month. Catholics, like Catesby, who owned land were required to forfeit it and were deprived of many of their civil liberties. They were not allowed to live in London and no Catholic could be a lawyer or a doctor. The resulting tensions provided Deborah with an early lesson about the ugly consequences of mingling politics with religion and also the effect of denying religious liberty to a segment of society.

Parental agreement on a "portion" (*dowry*) of £2,000 for Deborah was reached on November 23 and her interests were assured by the signatures of Sir John Cooper of Rockbourne, Sir Daniel Norton of Southwick and Richard Moody, the bridegroom's father. Deborah was promised a "jointure" - provision to support her should she survive her husband - the money to be invested in property in Wiltshire. The ratio of jointure to portion was at this time about one in six or seven, that is for every pound of jointure the wife paid six or seven pounds in portion.[10]

"It was on the basis of a little polite conversation that many, perhaps most, noble marriages were concluded." These tete-a-tetes took place only after the parents had agreed on the contract and settlement. Once the deeds were signed public rejoicing began. On 30 November 1605 the marriage of "Henry Modye and Debora Dunche of Wiltshire" was registered at St Mary Aldermary Church in the same Cripplegate parish of London where Deborah had been christened. She may have been living at this time with her mother and father-in-law, James Marvyn, who would have arranged the nuptials. The banns or notice of marriage were proclaimed three times, usually on successive Sundays.

Deborah's wedding was conducted 20 January 1606 at St Mary Aldermary Church, near the Lord Mayor's Mansion. It was the oldest (alder) church in the city dedicated to Mary or as some believe to the alder (other) Mary, Mary Magdalene. Deborah's cousin, Sir William Dunch had married Mary Cromwell of Hitchinbrooke, County Hampshire in the same church in 1598.[11]

Marriage ceremonies were public affairs, usually followed by a huge banquet for the wedding guests:

> The long day of feasting and jollity ended not infrequently in the public bedding of the couple, with all the ancient ceremonies of casting off the bride's left stocking and of sewing into the sheets. And there, naked within the drawn curtains of the great four-poster...the two strangers were left to make their acquaintance.[12]

Avebury Manor

SHRINKING LIBERTIES

Two months after her wedding, Deborah's new husband and devoted champion, Henry Moody, knelt before his monarch at Westminster.

King James had issued a proclamation requiring his tenants-in-chief and all persons with an income of £40 a year to receive the dignity of a knighthood. It was followed by the usual commission for compounding which threatened those who neglected to comply with fines. The honors were a profitable source of income to the crown.[1]

So it was that on 18 March 1606 at the royal palace in Whitehall Deborah's husband offered loyal service and pledged himself to chivalrous conduct as a mounted man-at-arms. As he stooped before his sovereign King James touched his shoulder with his sword and bade him: "Arise, Sir Henry." He stood erect from the investiture a Knight-bachelor, having achieved at the age of 24 "the ambition of youth, the ornament of manhood and the pride of age." The King granted him a coat of arms so that his fighting-men might recognize him in battle. Thus Sir Henry accepted liability for military service along with his followers who farmed his extensive lands in Wiltshire on terms advantageous to himself and his wife. He would now be responsible for making heavy annual payments to the king. Not only was the squire from Wiltshire now Sir Henry Moody, his wife was styled Dame Deborah Moody and often by extended courtesy, Lady Deborah Moody.

Sir Henry and Dame Deborah made their new home at Garsdon Manor, situated in a two-hundred acre estate known as The Parke some twenty-five miles from Avebury. Described in Domesday Book as a three-hide estate (200-300 acres) it had once been the property of Good Queen Maud, wife of King Henry I (1068-1135) who increased her acreage and then granted it by charter for use as a monastery. It is believed that King Henry VIII gave the house to Sir Henry's ancestor, Edmund, as a reward for pulling him out of a ditch and saving his life when he was hunting.

The five-feet thick walls of the Manor's medieval hall supported a fourteenth century hammerbeam roof (still in position with the majority of the original rafters) made of wood from Blaydon Forest. The Elizabethan ceiling was ornamented with terminals of roses and pears. The richly embellished fireplace was decorated with fashionable coupled Corinthian columns at either side. Through the window of their reception room the Moodys could see the morning sun rising over Garsdon Church across the green fields.

Dame Deborah gave birth to their first child, Henry, on 7 February 1607. He was christened 22 February in Garsdon Church. While the church record is lost, remarkably, after nearly four hundred years, a record of Henry's baptism still exists. The worn piece of early seventeenth century parchment was a transcript sent by the minister to the Bishop of Salisbury as required by law. It contains the names of those who were present, though some surnames are unreadable:

Robertus Browne	Minister.
Phillippe _____	
Edmunde B_____	Old Churchwardens
Thomas _____	
_____ Nicholas	New Churchwardens[2]

The following year Catherina, a sister for Henry, was born. Dame Deborah's children grew up peacefully at Garsdon, but social strife broke out here as in other parts of the country. There was local opposition to arbitrary enclosures of land at nearby Malmesbury, demonstrated by riotous levelling. The hedges of a coppice were hacked down under cover of a storm. As the antiquary, John Aubrey (1626-97) explained, the spinners and clothing workers were paid a low wage even in good years and so "were trained up as nurseries of sedition and rebellion." He was of the sour opinion that as the people only milk cows and make cheese, feeding "chiefly on milk meats which cool their brains too much," this resulted in the populace of North Wiltshire being "melancholy, contemplative and malicious" and contributed to many lawsuits.[3]

Riots were not the only indication of the unsettled condition of the population. The dreaded dungeons at the Tower of London filled with those who earned the king's displeasure were horrifying reminders that anyone who dared speak out for human rights against the king's pretended "divine right" was likely to be incarcerated.

The widely-known story of Andrew Melville was an alarming affair. Along with other Presbyterian Scots he resisted King James who refused them the right to gather for a meeting. As Moderator of the Assembly, a reformer and theologian, Melville wrote a treatise on freewill which cost him the loss of the rectorship of St Andrews in 1597.   Later he fearlessly voiced the Presbyterian opinion that King James was not entitled to summon preachers before his Council and charge them with holding unwarranted and seditious meetings.   Finding himself in the king's presence, Melville took him by the sleeve and cautioned him:

> Sir, we will humbly reverence your Majesty always - namely in public. But since we have this occasion to be with your Majesty in private, and the truth is that you are brought in extreme danger both of your life and crown, and with you the country and kirk of Christ is like to wreck, for not telling you the truth and giving you a faithful counsel, we must discharge our duty therein or else be traitors both to Christ and you! And therefore, sir, as divers times before, so now again I must tell you, there are two kings and two kingdoms in Scotland. There is Christ Jesus the King, and his kingdom the Kirk, whose subject James the Sixth is, and of whose kingdom not a king, nor a lord, nor a head, but a member.   And they whom Christ hath called to watch over his kirk and govern his spiritual kingdom have sufficient power and authority so to do both together and severally; the which no Christian king nor prince should control and discharge, but fortify and assist, otherwise (sic) not faithful servants nor members of Christ![4]

Melville, who had also written a Latin poem critical of Anglican worship, was summoned to London in 1606, charged by the Privy Council and confined to the Tower of London for four years. It was a fate not uncommon for persons with courage to speak out for liberty. England would need the support of many more intrepid subjects if simple justice and religious toleration were ever to prevail.

Support came from citizens of noble birth. A group of inter-related gentry constituted a Puritan bloc and championed one another. The Dunches were among these allied families and shared their common concern. Dame Deborah witnessed the struggles of a burgeoning movement that each year grew larger and stronger against efforts to suppress citizens' liberties.[5]

In 1617 Sir Henry and Dame Deborah sent their eleven year old son Henry to begin his education at Magdalen Hall, the famous Oxford grammar school. Henry's father and Uncle Edmund had been to this prestigious school as also had John Moodye of London who matriculated in 1598 and Robert Mooddy of Lincoln in 1607. King James I sent his son, Prince Henry, and the school enjoyed a large share of royal favor. Magdalen, the richest and most beautiful of the colleges, became a Puritan stronghold attracting such famous members as Richard Foxe (Bishop of Winchester), John Colet (Dean of St. Paul's), Thomas Wolsey (Archbishop of Canterbury), John Foxe (the martyrologist), John Mason (founder of New Hampshire) and John Hampden (the famous Buckinghamshire Member of Parliament).

The rising bell woke the boys at five a.m. for Matins and a short homily by one of the Fellows. The Chapel was at this time freshly embellished with new colored glass windows (by Richard Greenbury) depicting saints and martyrs which reminded worshippers of the cost of the Christian faith.[6]

The price of freedom could not escape the Moodys on their visits to Oxford where stories recorded in Foxe's *Acts and Monuments* came alive. It was the Oxford populace who had witnessed the martyrdom of that outstanding preacher of the English Reformation, Hugh Latimer, Bishop of Worcester, along with Nicholas Ridley, Bishop of Rochester and of London. Latimer had understood the separate roles of church and state and contended that while it was the king's duty to correct all transgressors, including offending preachers, with the sword, it was a minister's duty to correct all, including the king, with the spiritual sword "fearing no man...though death should ensue." This bold man of integrity was examined for his "heresies" and then cruelly burnt alive while he encouraged his companion with words that still energize people of conscience: "Be of good comfort, Master Ridley, and play the man. We shall this day light such a candle, by God's grace, in England, as I trust shall never be put out."[7]

Also close to Magdalen at St Mary's Church on The High (High Street), Archbishop Thomas Cranmer had been tried for treason. Students and visitors could visualize him in a thin ragged shirt, taken from Bocardo prison as a "heretic" and declaring "as for the Pope, I refuse him as Christ's enemy and Antichrist." Fastened to an iron stake in The Broad (Broad Street) Cranmer was publicly burnt.[8]

In 1618-19 Dame Deborah's husband was created Sheriff of Wiltshire, responsible for the keeping of the peace and the execution of Court orders. Lawyers were faced with many knotty problems and often created enemies. Would Sir Henry ever need to use the secret priest's hole behind a small door in Garsdon Manor as a refuge?

Sir Henry once alleged in the Star Chamber that certain justices had achieved their ends by holding a private sessions at Malmesbury, but in 1621 a similar allegation was made against him that "he most unlawfully and corruptly keepeth a session in his own chamber, and there at his will and pleasure dischargeth offenders and vexeth innocent persons, who are compelled to attend him there to their intolerable vexation."[9]

The charge was probably not as serious as it may appear. The justices were not paid and were chosen because they were men of good character. They dispensed rough judgment which resulted in frequent allegations against them. Dissatisfied litigants could appeal to a higher court like the Star Chamber. But this tribunal, appointed by royal authority, met in secret session without a jury, used torture to force confessions, and handed down extremely severe and arbitrary judgments. Few believed the Court to be more fair than the local justice of the peace.

Social equity was also the subject of debate in Parliament concerning the restrictive attitudes of James I. The Commons maintained that freedom of speech was their "ancient and undoubted right." James replied that all their rights and privileges were derived from "the grace and permission of his ancestors and himself," which was more than English people were prepared to concede.

And now the Moody family news. King James created Deborah's husband a soldier and a baronet on 11 March 1622: "miles et Baronettus superstes." Baronet is a titled hereditary order, ranking next below a baron, founded to raise money for the settlement of Ulster. The out-of-pocket cost for the honor was then some £200, in addition to which Sir Henry undertook to support for three years 30 foot-soldiers in Ireland "for the Security of the said Kingdom, and especially for the Security of the said Plantation of Ulster." In the great hall of Garsdon Manor Sir Henry added his coat of arms over the beautiful Elizabethan stone fireplace.[10]

Young Henry matriculated (was admitted and enrolled in the University) at the age of fourteen on 2 November 1621. He was awarded a Bachelor's degree on his eighteenth birthday 7 February 1624. Oxford University noted Henry's changed status in the record against his name: "eq. aur. fil." (son of a baronet).

Dame Deborah's sisters had married by this time. Ruth wed Sir William Button of a staunchly royalist family and went to live six miles away at the tall-chimneyed Priory House at Alton Priors. They nurtured four sons and three daughters.[11]

Dame Deborah's sister, Mary, married Ellis Swayne of Blandford Forum, Dorset, and after his death Sir John Philpott, Knight of Compton and Threston, Hampshire. For his views on transubstantiation Sir John's ancestor, John Philpot, Archdeacon of Winchester, narrowly missed the Inquisition in Italy, was imprisoned in the King's Bench prison in London during Mary's reign and then burned at Smithfield.[12]

Dame Deborah's third sister, Anne, married Thomas Lambert of Boyton, County Wiltshire, who became Member of Parliament for Hindon in 1625. Anne had a child almost every year for ten years or more and named her first daughter, born in 1614, Deborah.[13]

And what of Dame Deborah's brother William who lived with Sir John Cooper? At the age of sixteen, he married one of Sir John's daughters, Margaret, who was some three years younger. Following the family tradition William was admitted to Gray's Inn on 5 February 1611. He was fined twenty shillings on 30 June 1617 by the governing body of Gray's Inn for non-attendance at communion for twelve months. The law required that every Englishman attend the services of his parish church once a week and take communion three times a year. Those who refused were considered "recusants" and liable on conviction to a fine of £20 a month or two-thirds of the income from their estates whichever the government preferred. William, like his eldest sister, was not a conformist. Kingsmill Long of Avebury dedicated his translation into English of John Barclay's "Argenis" to "William Dunche of Avebury," and considered him "Truly Noble."[14]

William also had financial troubles. He brought an action in court against George, the brother of Sir John Cooper, and in 1620 conveyed the manor and lordship of Avebury to his brother-in-law

Thomas Lambert. Debts and court cases plagued the family for some years.[15]

Meanwhile the estate of Sir Henry and Dame Deborah grew when Sir Henry's father, Richard Moody died aged seventy on 30 November 1612. His properties passed to his son. This was also the year Dame Deborah's illustrious cousin Sir William Dunch, K.G. who had married into the Cromwell family, died at the early age of thirty-three.[16]

Life expectancy was short. In 1624 Sir Henry's sister Anne died. She was the third wife of Sir John Stafford of Thornbury, Gloucestershire. He had married Anne at St Andrews Holborn, London in February 1622. After only two years of marriage they both died in 1624 within a month of one another. Threatened by pox, plague, rampant disease and unclean drinking water, life hung by a tenuous thread. Every year between one and four thousand English people died of the plague and in 1625 35,417 persons are said to have succumbed to the dread sickness. Widespread fear of the plague grew among travellers among whom Sir Henry, as Member of Parliament for Malmesbury now commuted between Wiltshire and London from 1625 onwards.

During this period Catherina, the Moody's daughter, was married by licence of the Bishop of London to John Snow on 7 February 1627 at the church of St Gregory-by-St-Paul in the City.

Charles I came to the throne after the death of his father, James I in 1625. Parliament immediately called for the removal of the peoples' grievances. But the new king's views of power and royal prerogative were even more severe than his father's. Charles dissolved Parliament after only two weeks, warning the Commons : "parliaments are altogether in my power for their calling, sitting and dissolution; therefore as I find the fruits of them good or evil, they are to continue, or not to be."[17]

When the king needed money he called the members and dismissed them before they passed a single act. He resorted to forced loans, benevolences, and other illegal and arbitrary means of obtaining money. He refused to call the third parliament until 1628. Before granting the king a single penny members drew up the famous Petition of Right with four demands: that no person be compelled to pay loan, benevolence or tax without consent of parliament; that no subject be imprisoned without cause shown; that soldiers and sailors should not be billeted upon people against their will; and that no person in time of peace be tried by martial law. Charles was forced to assent. Then Parliament voted him £400,000.[18]

Dame Deborah and her husband who had been loyalists found themselves in increasing sympathy with the Puritans who strongly opposed the imperious actions of their self-willed king. Charles made known his wishes through his lord-keeper, Sir John Coventry who in November 1628 addressed a meeting of the judges, bishops and justices which Sir Henry would have been ordered to attend. Coventry told them the king demanded strict enforcement of the laws against all non-conforming papists and required a list of all London recusants. Innovations of worship contrary to the Book of Common Prayer would not be permitted and bishops were to maintain "the trewe religion of oure church." He charged all gentlemen "to repaire into the countrye to keepe up hospitallytie."

While no record of Sir Henry's reactions exists Sir Thomas Barrington wrote his mother: "he left us not satisfied in any measure to that expectation which was among us concerning none of those points."[19]

Early the next year several of Dame Deborah's family and acquaintances were elected members of the Third Parliament. They witnessed the history-making episodes that took place in the House of Commons. With her husband, Sir Henry, were her brother-in-law, Sir William Button knt. and bart. (representing Wiltshire County); her second cousin Edmund Dunch (Wallingford); John Fettiplace (Berkshire County) and Sir John Cooper, (Poole Borough).

A bill had been placed before Parliament entitled *Resolutions on Religion* regarding the growth of Roman Catholics in England, Scotland and especially in Ireland which was said to be "almost wholly overspread with Popery." The preamble indicated that in some churches communion tables had been placed at the upper end of the chancel in imitation of the high altar and that the orthodox doctrines set forth in the Articles of Religion were being suppressed. The petition called for the enforcement of laws against Papists, the burning of Popish books, and a program for licensing the printing of books.

John Pym respectfully drew the King's attention to the ancient laws which assured freedom of speech to the people of England. He spoke of the need to maintain "those good Lawes which are prepared for the Establishment of Religion and releife (sic) of our Greivances." The King refused to listen.

The eloquent and fearless Sir John Eliot pointed out in a major parliamentary speech on March 2 that the King had several times violated the terms of the Petition of Right to which he had given his assent.   When a vote was about to be taken the Speaker, Sir John Finch, stated that he had received a royal order to adjourn the House.   Some members got up and locked the door, and laid the keys on the table of the House while two members held the Speaker down by force in his chair.   Denzil Holles read the Protestation of the Commons declaring that any one who should "bring in innovation of religion" or "seek to extend or introduce Popery or Arminianism or other opinion disagreeing from the true and orthodox Church," or advise the payment of money to the king without the consent of Parliament should be regarded as an enemy of the nation, "a betrayer of the liberties of England."[20]

The king sent for the Serjeant of the House but he was not allowed to leave.   Then Charles dispatched the Usher of the House of Lords, but the commons would not let him in. Seething with rage Charles ordered the guard to break open the doors, but by then the members had voted their protest and quietly slipped away.   The king trounced them as "vipers," dissolved Parliament, summoned the Privy Council which committed the active protesters to the Tower of London.   The notable champions of liberty locked in the dungeons of this medieval prison with Sir John Eliot were Denzil Holles, John Selden, Benjamin Valentine, William Coriton, Sir Miles Hobart, Sir Peter Hayman, Walter Long and William Stroud. After three years Sir John contracted consumption and wrote to the king: "I humbly beseech your Majesty you will command your judges to set me at liberty, that for recovery of my health I may take some fresh air."   The vindictive king replied callously: "Not humble enough."   Eliot died in the Tower and was called "the first martyr of English liberty."[21]

Charles I had made a serious mistake. He refused to acknowledge that his "absolute" royal power was limited by parliament. Members believed he was denying the English people their fundamental and ancestral freedoms.   And so thereafter, when Black Rod, the royal messenger from the House of Lords, came to summon the Commons to hear the Sovereign's Speech at the opening of Parliament, they slammed the door of their chamber in his face before admitting him.   The ceremony (which continues to this day) underlined the people's rights in a democracy.

But the autocratic king, still with a swollen concept of the royal prerogative, now even attempted to limit freedom of speech. Foolishly he went so far as to forbid the public even to speak of the reassembling of a parliament.   Such repressive measures drove many out of England, while most including Dame Deborah and her family endured the restraints in silence.

Avebury Church

It is tyrannical to restrain by faggots.   Consciences love to be taught, and religion wants to teach. Moreover the most effective master teacher is love. When this is absent, there is never anyone who can teach aright nor can anyone learn properly -

John Foxe[22]

Garsdon Manor

FACING LIFE ALONE

Sir Henry Moody appears to have fallen sick in London. He ran up a large bill with his apothecary, Thomas Fones to whom he was in debt £73. In addition he owed forty-five pounds, twelve shillings and threepence for supplies from Fones' apothecary shop at the Three Fauns in Old Bailey Street. Fones also became ill at about the same time and Dr William Harvey from St Bartholomew's Hospital, physician to Charles I, was unable to save him. Fones made his will April 14 by which his daughters Elizabeth and Martha became wards of their uncle, John Winthrop. The next day Fones expired. The Moody bill was outstanding.[1]

Nine days later on 23 April 1629 Dame Deborah's husband died at Garsdon at the age of forty-seven.

His widow would now have to meet the coming storm alone. But first Dame Deborah's financial position must be clarified. Sir Henry had left no will! An inquest was held on 4 January 1630 at Marlborough before escheator, James Yateman, and a jury of eighteen persons. It was their task to ensure that property reverted to the crown when there were no legal heirs. The properties in which Sir Henry had an interest were enumerated:

There was the manor house of Lee and Cleverdon with twenty houses, ten cottages, ten homesteads or sites for homesteads, one dovecote, a thousand acres of land, 150 acres of meadow, five hundred acres of pasture, twenty acres of wood, five hundred acres of furze(gorse) and heath.

There was the manor of Garsdon, with its twenty houses, ten cottages, ten homesteads, one dovecote, one water mill, 1500 acres of land, two hundred acres of meadow, a thousand acres of pasture, a hundred acres of wood and five-hundred acres of furze and heath. Sir Henry was entitled to rents from these holdings, the right of tithes of corn, grain and hay and also the prerogative of presenting the vicar of the church in Garsdon.

The thirteenth century manor and farm of Whitchurch-cum-Milburne which Sir Henry had inherited from his father was retained by an elderly Welsh tenant, Sir Matthew Morgann, knt. It included Crabbe Mill and Crabbe Mill Meade, C(S)outhfield, Brode Meade, Garston meadow, Leewards Close pasture, Wanslopp Meade in Milborne, a farm in Whitchurch and several other parcels of land in Lee. Dame Deborah was to have the use of the manor of Whitchurch-cum-Milborne during her lifetime and receive rent from the tenured properties connected with it. This was in respect of her marriage portion of £2,000 and she was to receive a clear income of £26 a year from this investment.

The lands including part of the forest of Breden occupied some 840 acres, but the properties were heavily encumbered. Like a ravenous bird of prey the Crown hovered over the pickings of an estate not included in a will, demanding taxes, fees, fines, confiscations and return of estates. Dame Deborah was forced to surrender her life interest in Whitchurch Manor to her son who inherited his father's property and title and became known at the age of 22 as Sir Henry Moody, 2nd Bart.(Baronet). He in turn sold Whitchurch Manor to Henry Danvers, Earl of Danby.[2]

Sir Henry also sold the rest of the real estate including the family home, Garsdon Manor. It was purchased early in 1631 by Sir Lawrence Washington (cousin to the great, great, great grandfather of George Washington, first president of the United States) who is memorialized in Garsdon Church.[3]

Dressed in her long black mourning veil and black clothes Dame Deborah faced an uncertain future. She had kinsfolk and friends among the Puritan gentry and the common threat to their freedom drew them closer. The old feudal ties linking them were strengthened by their common understanding of the gospel. The Puritan cause which had flowered under James I now flourished under King Charles. The gentry had been monarchy's greatest supporters, but as a tyrannical sovereign attempted to enforce religious conformity they reacted strongly.[4]

The county where Dame Deborah lived had long been a seed-bed of non-conformity. Groups of Wiltshire people dissatisfied with the established church gathered in Bradford-on-Avon, Hilperton, Westbury, Warminster, Chippenham and the county town of

Salisbury. Horningsham Chapel at Longleat, which bears the date 1566, is the earliest standing non-conformist chapel in England. Thomas White of Slaughterford who left the ministry to preach only in private houses, emigrated with others to Amsterdam where he set up a non-conformist church. Members of this group transmitted the first seeds of the Baptist movement, begun by John Smith, back to Salisbury and other Wiltshire towns. In the years 1630-2 a group of anabaptists at Salisbury was several times fined for absence from church but their influence spread.[5]

Many baptists had suffered for their faith and women like Dame Deborah knew that they were not exempt from persecution and even death on account of their religious beliefs. Indeed a majority of continental anabaptist martyrs were women, viz. Elizabeth and Joanna in Holland, helpers of Menno Simons, the Baptist leader. Elizabeth, a young Dutch girl, found a Latin New Testament, in which she read the gospel, escaped from the convent disguised as a milkmaid and lived with a young Baptist woman named Hadewyck. After her baptism as an adult she was arrested at Leeuwarden but refusing to confess the whereabouts of her associates and the reformed teachers she was stretched on the rack while a torture screw bit into her thumbs and forefingers. On 27 March 1549 she was tied in a sack and thrown into the canal in Leeuwarden to drown.

Joanna Van den Hove, a young Dutch Baptist maid-servant to two sisters who lived near Brussels, was buried alive. A picture in Birmingham Art Gallery, England shows her being led to her gruesome death. They laid her down in a grave and poured earth first on to her feet, then on to her body up to the neck. At each stage the Jesuits asked her if she had considered and would ask for mercy. "They that seek to save their life here," she answered, "shall lose it hereafter" and she continued praying to God. Then the executioner covered her head with earth, and packed it down by treading on it.[6]

But Dame Deborah was in England. Could non-conformist Englishwomen expect similar treatment? Leonard Busher, a Baptist of London, wrote in *Religion's Peace: or a Plan for Liberty of Conscience*, (1614): "We that have the truth are most persecuted; and therefore most poor." He contended: "it is not only unmerciful, but unnatural and abominable; yea, monstrous for one Christian to vex and destroy another for difference and questions of religion." He urged that "the King and Parliament may please to permit all sorts of Christians; yea, Jews, Turks, and pagans, so long as they are peaceable, and no malefactors."[7]

The well-known case of the Traskes provided no consolation. The Star Chamber prosecuted John Traske in 1618 for maintaining that the Jewish Sabbath ought to be observed as holy. He had a following in London, and admitted that he had tried to convert people to his opinion. Despite a recantation, he was fined and imprisoned. His wife, Dorothy Traske, a school teacher, was even more determined than her husband to keep Saturday as Sabbath, and was confined for fifteen years in the Maiden Lane prison "appointed for the restraint of several other persons of different opinions from the Church of England."[8]

The Star Chamber with its swollen powers and inquisitor-type activities struck fear into English hearts. There was no appeal from its decisions. A person could be hanged for stealing an article worth more than seven pence. If his life was in danger a man on his first offence, whatever his profession, might take advantage of a medieval law and plead "benefit of clergy," and place his case within a bishop's jurisdiction. But this privilege was never extended to women whether or not they could read or write. In London women were often hanged for first offenses.

There was another threat to freedom - monopolies. Cartels had been abandoned by Elizabeth, extinguished by Act of Parliament under James, and denounced with the assent of King Charles in the Petition of Right. Yet they were now revived on a gigantic scale. Wine, soap, salt and almost all articles for the domestic market were grabbed by monopolists, and rose in price out of all proportion to the profit gained by the Crown. "They sup in our cup," Nicholas Culpepper told the Long Parliament, "they dip in our dish, they sit by our fire; we find them in the dye-fat, the wash bowls, and the powdering tub. They share with the cutler in his box. They have marked and sealed us from head to foot."[9]

Dame Deborah had no freedom to speak out against monopolies or any other unjust power of law. One alderman who bitterly complained that men were worse off in England than in Turkey was ruined by a fine of two thousand pounds and sent to the Tower of London.[10]

So where should freedom-loving people turn? Almost miraculously the king who created the problem helped provide a solution. Just before dissolving his third Parliament Charles granted the charter which established the colony of Massachusetts. The action was regarded by Puritans as providential. They now began to dream of a land in the West where religion and liberty could find a safe and permanent home. Gentry and traders talked of the new colony on the other side of the Atlantic and Puritan families excitedly discussed the advantages of living in Massachusetts. Two hundred people sailed to Salem, followed later by John Winthrop, the Governor, an acquaintance of Dame Deborah. He took with him eight hundred men and seven hundred more followed within a year.[11]

While thousands of emigrants left for New England and the West Indies the lone widow, Dame Deborah, stayed back in old England. Some of her kinsmen were planning a new colony. Members of four families related to the Dunches, including John Hampden and Richard Knightley, formed a group of Adventurers to the Islands of Providence and Henrietta in the Caribbean. Each member invested £500. The group under the chairmanship of the Earl of Warwick, a leading Puritan, established the Providence Company and the first expedition left in February 1631. Soon there were 500 able-bodied persons growing cotton, madder, indigo and flax on a plantation. Then friction among the settlers enabled some Spaniards to raid and take over the tiny island. It was fortuitous that Dame Deborah did not go. These Caribbean islands soon proved no haven for puritans of strong religious conviction.

Garsdon Manor fireplace

Coat of Arms

LONDON: SEED-BED OF DISSENT

After the death of her husband and settlement of his estate Dame Deborah was now free to travel. All major roads in England, like spokes of a wheel, led to London and within thirty-five miles of the city roads were "sandy and very fair." Most aristocrats risked the journey in spite of the danger of attack from highwaymen. A hackney from Wiltshire to George Inn, Aldersgate took only two days and cost approximately twenty shillings. Dame Deborah could use her family coach or, if she chose, travel part of the way by boat down the river Thames.[1]

London "the garden of England, whear wee [sic] may all live together," held the key to advancement and wealth for generations of Dame Deborah's ancestors. Titles, land-ownership, favors and contacts awaiting cultivation were all to be found at the royal court. Persons of rank also went for pleasure and to escape the loneliness and boredom of the country. Women liked to go for the winter to attend plays or ride about the streets in their coaches, people-watching. While crime and disease were rampant, fires frequent and city roads foul, the gentry and their families moved about in sedan chairs without their feet touching the mire. They could buy clothes, furnishings, paintings and the latest in transport. The best doctors were available and there was plenty of good food, the River Thames providing "fat and sweet salmons,.. trouts, perches, smelts, breams, roaches, daces, gudgeons, flounders, shrimps, eels."[2]

Popular in warmer weather was a river cruise on a barge with musical accompaniment. The 25-mile jaunt to Gravesend was by tilt boat (a sailing boat with a covering for passengers) which left at high tide from the wharf at Billingsgate. The Thames, London's highway, with its symbols of a freer life had strong appeal for seventeenth century lovers of liberty. The billowing sails and flags of departing ships beckoned the oppressed and persecuted. Thousands were leaving London and Gravesend (the Gateway to London) for the New World.[3]

On arrival at the Royal Terrace Pier, Gravesend gentry visited popular sights, especially the grave of Pocahontas, an American-Indian princess, the English colonists' first convert to Christianity. Her idol, Captain John Smith, father of Sir Walter Ralegh's Lost Colony, was author of *A Description of New England*, (1616) which advertised Massachusetts as an attractive alternative to life in England, "the paradise of all those parts." Smith told Puritans "could I transport a colony, I would rather live here than anywhere." The prospect attracted those in search of freedom.

In London Dame Deborah was close to relatives and friends. Her son, Sir Henry Moody, 2nd Bart. registered at Gray's Inn, a hostel for lawyers and students on 5 August 1632. He was listed (in 1638) an inhabitant of the "long but very mean" Blackhorse Alley. The narrow street was near the newly restored Church of St Giles, Cripplegate which now had a "handsome towered steeple with spires at each corner and a Lanthorn in the middle with a good Ring of Bells."[4]

Dame Deborah's second cousin, Edmund Dunch, especially shared her free spirit. He was educated at Gray's Inn, married Bridget, a beauty of some renown, and became three times Member of Parliament for Wallingford. On the death of his father-in-law, Sir Anthony Hungerford, Edmund inherited at least twelve manors worth some £60,000 - a prodigious fortune. King Charles determined to wrest the property from him. Edmund resisted royal intrusion and refused to compound for knighthood, but demonstrated his loyalty in supplying horses for the northern army and in serving as captain and county committeeman. There was a series of severe court actions against Edmund - "a strenuous advocate for the liberty of the subject." William Lenthal, the speaker of the Long Parliament, addressing the house, said that as the king had "taken all" from Edmund "it cannot then be wondered at, that his acrimony was great against that prince." To speak up for human rights or for religious freedom during the reign of Charles I involved heavy penalties. But Dunch and Moody consciences were sensitive and courage was strong.[5]

The presence of the gentry in London became a threat to the King. He considered their independence of thought a menace to social peace and justice. There were too many opportunities for conversation and discussion that could lead to insurrection. They spent too much money in London, he said, and ruled that they should live in their country mansions and offer hospitality to those in need rather than live in the capital.[6]

But the capital had many attractions, especially for the devout. Good preachers were hard to find in the provinces while religion was thriving in the city. For Dame Deborah "a nonconformist" who dissented from the doctrine and practice of the established episcopalian church London provided access to groups of variant persuasions. There were also opportunities to buy new books and investigate fresh understandings of scripture. People could now read the Bible for themselves in public places (six copies were placed in the nave of St Paul's Cathedral) and the metropolis became a nursery of new thought and theological dialogue, much to the displeasure of the bishops. Non-conformity spread. London, the seed-bed of separatism, was an exciting world.[7]

Dame Deborah's exact movements went unrecorded but she and her associates were later reported to have unorthodox beliefs regarding baptism, the Sabbath, the mode of worship, church government and the role of the clergy. These were among the main topics of religious discussion in the London of her day. There were many viewpoints. Some non-conformists believed they had direct revelations from heaven, some kept Sabbath on the seventh day of the week instead of the first, while some specialized in the study of the Apocalypse and the Book of Daniel. There were variant ideas about baptism, marriage, property and ecclesiastical rule. The four or five main separatist groups each held to some specific Biblical teaching and were "divided into divers and sundry fellowships and congregations, so that either they will not or cannot come together." These independent assemblies multiplied and gave birth to congregationalism and the Baptist churches.[8]

At first there were few if any non-conformist chapels in the city, only secret gatherings, conventicles, which of course were banned by the the authorities. Dame Deborah could disappear into the shadowy streets and listen to the religious issues of the day at lectures, discussions and clandestine gatherings. There was a conventicle close to the London home of her mother in Fetter Lane while near-by Gray's Inn was the meeting-place for Puritan nobility to hear the passionate Richard Sibbes. At Lincoln's Inn his friend John Preston, chaplain to the Prince of Wales, attracted large crowds. And the more that preachers quoted the Scriptures the more their hearers accepted the right to follow their individual convictions regardless of church or state pressures.[9]

Dame Deborah inclined to the anabaptist belief which was attracting wide interest. But there was no comfort in the story of two Dutch Anabaptists from Aldgate, London, John Wielmacher and Hendrick Ter Woort. They had been unjustifiably and shockingly burnt at the stake in Smithfield during Queen Elizabeth's reign, in spite of a plea for clemency from John Foxe.[10]

Since that time baptists had grown in numbers. The first English Baptist church had been founded at Pinners' Hall, Spitalfields in 1612 by Thomas Helwys a Puritan exile who became convinced in Amsterdam that 'infant baptism' was not baptism at all. His book *A Short Declaration of the Mystery of Iniquity*, printed in Holland (1611-12) contained the first substantive plea by an English divine for universal religious toleration. He repudiated the right of the state to legislate on matters concerning a person's relationship with God.

London's second Baptist church was established near Newgate in 1615. Helwys' friend, John Murton, was pastor and by 1626 there were 150 members. Baptism was performed by affusion (pouring), while immersion was not practiced till 1641. By the time Dame Deborah came to London many Particular Baptist congregations were formed and some had taken over unused church buildings in the city. Members of John Lathorp's congregation of independent dissenters left to form one of these groups on 12 September 1633 because they believed their baptism as infants was invalid and so they received a new baptism. Dame Deborah was acquainted with at least one member of this group and may have attended their meetings.[11]

Baptists insisted that as faith is God's gift, religious compulsion is an offence against him. It was a doctrine for which Englishmen were hungry and Dame Deborah found herself susceptible to this belief. Baptists also relished the themes of the sabbath, church authority, ecclesiastical discipline and the practical content of New Testament teaching.

The origin of the sabbath was a subject of interest to many non-conformists including Dame Deborah. Many books both for and aginst the Biblical day of rest were published during her lifetime and stimulated public discussion. Included in the family library books (listed a year or two after her death) was Joshua Sylvester's long epic, *La Semaine*, (The Week) translated from "The six days work of the Lord" (1578).[12]

In "A Treatise of the Sabbath" puritan minister Richard Greenham maintained that the fourth of the ten commandments which sustains a seventh-day sabbath is a moral law binding on Christians. Six editions of his book were printed between 1599 and 1612. Meanwhile Nicholas Bownde wrote his classic *The True Doctrine of the Sabbath* in 1606 favoring Sunday as a day of rest. [13]

Theophilus Brabourne of Norwich, a minister of the established Church, issued *A Discourse Upon the Sabbath Day* (1628) in which he argued that the seventh-day Sabbath supported "by an express commandment of God" was not abolished but still in force. In 1632 he wrote the second edition of *A Defense of that most ancient and sacred ordinance of God's, the Sabbath day... Undertaken against anti-Sabbatarians, both of Protestants, papists, antinomians, and Anabaptists.* Published in Amsterdam the book was smuggled into England and for this Brabourne was incarcerated for eighteen months in Newgate prison. He later wrote two further books on the Sabbath in answer to his opponents.

Controversy on the Sabbath intensified at the time when Dame Deborah went to live in London. King Charles attempted to secularize Sunday by issuing *The Book of Sports*. This was opposed by the puritan wing of the Church of England which could not accept the validity of the royal prerogative to authorize feasting and rural sports on a day which they considered was set apart for worship and spiritual growth. Then Dr J. Pocklington published his sermon "Sunday No Sabbath" (London: 1636). It was eagerly bought until the Puritan Long Parliament ordered it to be publicly burnt.

Another Saturday Sabbath-keeper was Dr Peter Chamberlen, physician-extraordinary to King Charles I and physician-in-ordinary to several English kings and queens. His tomb at Woodham Mortimer, Malden, Essex indicates he came from a long line of French Huguenot physicians, and "as for his Religion he was a Christian keeping ye Commandments of God and faith of Jesus ...and keeping ye 7th day for ye saboth above 32 years."[14]

So considerable was the impact of the issue raised by Brabourne and others that King Charles charged two of his ministers, Dr Peter Heylin of Westminster and Bishop Francis White of Ely, to refute sabbatarianism. Bishop White defended Sunday as a church ordinance but admitted that Brabourne's arguments were sound and reported that in view of the validity of the fourth commandment "it will be impossible to you, either in English or Latin, to solve Theophilus Brabourne's objections."[15]

Poet-laureate John Milton confirmed this view (in a manuscript which Elzevir of Amsterdam feared to print) that if Christians are to be regulated by the decalogue regarding the time of their worship "it will surely be far safer to observe the seventh day, according to express commandment of God, than on the authority of mere human conjecture to adopt the first."[16]

King Charles examined the evidence and accepted that the Sunday Sabbath and Easter were both established by the authority of the church rather than by Scripture.[17]

Some dissenters and non-conformists like Dame Deborah's kinsman, Sir Henry Vane the Younger, also considered the Sunday Sabbath was "of magisterial institution" and observed it for that reason only. Dame Deborah adopted a similar attitude though later she and her neighbors were noted for their non-acceptance of any scriptural validity for the traditional observance of Sunday.[18]

Dame Deborah respected one group of dissenters which was having an especially difficult time with the authorities. Their members addressed people whatever their rank as "thou" and refused to doff their hats. Their consciences would not allow them to swear with an appeal to God or the Bible, considering it contrary to New Testament teaching. They were threatened by a law passed after the Gunpowder Plot which required all subjects, including Roman Catholics, to acknowledge, profess, testify and swear that the Pope had no power to depose the king.

This group, later dubbed 'quakers' refused to take the oath on Biblical grounds. When their religious beliefs were not respected, court actions often resulted in terrible persecution. The Star Chamber and other judiciaries proceeded against them as though they had confessed to the indictment.[19]

Quakers, dissenters, separatists, non-conformists, baptists and sabbatarians all possessed high moral values, but were considered enemies of both State and Church. Sadly both civil and ecclesiastical authorities harshly treated their enemies. The state had not only burned men alive at Smithfield Market but a number of women also, including Isabel Foster, Joane Warne, Katherine Hut, Joan Horns, Elizabeth Thackvel, Margaret Hide, Agnes Stanley and Margaret Dearing. Their stories, recorded by John Foxe, were conversation-pieces in London.[20]

The firm determination they inspired was further strengthened by sermons and lectures. The weekly sermon at St. Paul's Cross regularly attracted a thousand people in the open air outside the famous Cathedral. The wooden, lead-covered pulpit had long been a rallying place for those interested in religious matters. Dame Deborah's bold grandfather, Bishop Pilkington, had preached there. But the disposition of the bishop with whom she and the Puritans of England now had to reckon was very different from that of her grandfather.[21]

Moody crest

A Gentlewoman

"A WOLF BY THE EARS"

The typical London housewife was said to be "very loving and obedient to her parents, kind to her husband, tender-hearted to her children, loving all who were godly...very ripe and perfect in all stories of the Bible; likewise in all stories of Martyrs." Religion was the primary topic of conversation. She was aware of the cruel persecution during the reign of Queen Mary and believed that if the Catholics returned to power there would be "more martyrs" and "her Bible would be taken from her." Imagine her terror when she heard the rumor that Archbishop William Laud was doing all he could to bring Catholicism back! Imagine Dame Deborah's reactions.[1]

Laud, a clothier's son, of Reading, Berkshire, appointed Bishop of London in 1628 was elevated by Charles I to be Archbishop of Canterbury, England's premier bishop. He was of a moral, noble, pious mind (as shown by his diary) but a stranger to religious liberty. He considered it his duty to create unity (which he equated with uniformity) in the English church and enforce orthodox religious practice. He permitted no divergence in form of worship and severely punished any variant religious opinion through the Courts. With the support of King Charles the Archbishop attempted to foist the Arminian (Anglo-Catholic) version of Anglicanism on all citizens.

Laud directed bishops to exercise tighter control over lecturers and private chaplains and suspend parish clergy for holding unorthodox views - or deprive them of their livings. He ordered altars at the east end of churches, introduced surplices, encouraged archery and other sports on Sunday, all of which angered Puritans who called him a Papist. Indeed, he was offered a cardinal's hat by the Pope and recorded in his diary that he dreamt of becoming a Catholic.[2]

Aided by the high death rate amongst bishops the "Pope of Canterbury," as non-conformists tagged him, appointed divines of his own choosing to the courts of Star Chamber and High Commission and used them to suppress Puritan propaganda. Determined to subjugate all schismatics, he deported some, imprisoned others and extorted heavy fines. He ordered ministers not to preach on controversial subjects. Dissidents found themselves in dire trouble and non-conformists were outraged, including French and Flemish refugees who were denied freedom to worship after their own custom.[3]

One London clergyman called on all Christians "to resist the bishops as robbers of souls, limbs of the Beast, and fathers of Antichrist." Alexander Leighton, a strict Presbyterian, courageously put his opinions into written form. "Sion's Plea Against Prelacy" was a petition calling for the extirpation of bishops, to which he claimed five-hundred signatures. To evade censorship it was printed in Holland. When a copy reached Laud, Leighton was arrested. The Star Chamber sentenced him to whipping and to stand in the pillory - a device with holes in which an offender's head and hands were locked - to be exposed to public abuse. While in the pillory at New Palace Yard Leighton was to have one of his ears lopped off, his nose split, and his face branded with the letters S.S. for "Sower of Sedition." He was also condemned to be whipped and pilloried at Cheapside where his other ear would be cut off. Those were not pleasant days for people of religious conviction!

The penalty of £10,000 which Leighton had no means of paying illustrated the excessive fines imposed by the Courts of Star Chamber and High Commission. The scene on 26 November 1630 was like dozens that followed. "This is Christ's yoke!" Leighton shouted as the pillory was clamped on him. When the executioner lopped off his ear, he exclaimed: "Blessed be God, if I had a hundred, I would lose them all for the cause!"

Laud and liberty were in deadly conflict! "The great censor of other men's conduct, dress and haircuts" (Laud tried to outlaw long hair) assumed control of the press and banned Foxe's Book of Martyrs. A royal proclamation forbad the printing or importation of any book dealing with religion, church government or matters of state until it had been approved. Through the Star Chamber Laud issued a decree warning that any unauthorized printer found establishing a press would be set in the pillory and whipped. Despite this the Puritan barrister, William Prynne, John Bastwick and others wrote books.[4]

Prynne attacked the stage in *Histriomastix* (1632), depicted actors as ministers of Satan and theaters as the Devil's chapels. He opposed hunting, maypoles, cards, music, false wigs and the decking of homes with evergreens at Christmas. The book was denounced for its veiled attacks on Charles I and his Catholic Queen Henrietta Maria who both loved theater and took part in masques. This led to Dr. Prynne's sentence by the Star Chamber of imprisonment for life, a fine of £5,000, expulsion from Lincoln's Inn, the loss of his university degree, the burning of his book in his presence and punishment in the pillory where he was to lose both ears and be exposed to public abuse. The whole judgment, except the length of his imprisonment and the fine, was carried out. Prynne lost one ear at Westminster, the other at Cheapside.

A prisoner in the Tower, Prynne "who had got his ears sewed on that they grew again as before to his head" later found himself again under sentence, standing in the pillory at the Palace of Westminster to have what was left of his ears struck off. Dr Bastwick and the Reverend Henry Burton were with him to endure the same punishment and in the pillory Bastwick declared "Were the press open to us we would scatter [Antichrist's] kingdom." Bastwick gave the hangman a knife and told him how to do his duty quickly and efficiently. But the hangman did a clumsy job with Prynne, slicing off a piece of his cheek as well as the remainder of his ear. Prynne was also branded with S.L. (Seditious Libeller).

> The haingman burnt Prin in both cheekes, and, as I hear, because hee burnt one cheek with a letter the wronge waye hee burnt that againe; presently a surgeon clapt on a plaster to take out the fire.

Prynne fainted in the pillory. When he revived and left Westminster Palace yard thousands of Londoners proudly escorted him, shouting their encouragement and prayers. With great courage Prynne composed a verse in which he made a pun of the "S.L." on his disfigured cheeks, finding Laud's wounds reason for praise:

> Triumphant I returne, my face discryes
> Laud's scorching Scarrs,
> God's gratefull sacrifice
> S.L. Stigmata Laudis.[5]

Henry Burton was of similar dedication. As he approached the pillory, he said "This day will never be forgotten....through these holes (pointing to the pillory) God can bring light to his church." A woman spoke up for the crowd: "There are many hundreds which by God's assistance would willingly suffer for the cause you suffer this day." These were the first English gentry to receive this humiliating and cruel public punishment.

Clergy like John Etzell also suffered. Etzell was indicted by the High Commission Court for "erroneous opinions that God seeth no sin in his elect" and charged with keeping a conventicle (allowing others than his family to attend a chapel in his house). He was censured, held worthy to be imprisoned and pay costs of suit, "to be deprived and degraded if he do not confess and be suspended in the meanwhile."

Archbishop Laud continued to fine and punish his victims in a vicious attempt to stamp out all opposition to the officially held religious dogma. He claimed he was trying to reduce the Church to order and "settle it to the rules of its first reformation" but he attracted bitter antagonism from those who did not share his belief. They nicknamed him "little vermin." and "little hocus pocus" (he was very short). He considered Puritans "as a wolf held by the ears" - as dangerous to hold on to as to let go. Would Laud ever manage to take Dame Deborah "by the ears" in the tender place where he gripped non-conformists - their consciences? The phrase could only have sounded sinister and ominous. The Moody crest was a wolf's head, erased (leaving the severed part jagged), a heraldic device placed above the shield in the coat of arms granted to Sir Henry Moody, and used by Dame Deborah separately on her seal. On the Moody coat of arms there were three wolves represented as walking toward the (viewer's) left side of the shield with the right forepaw raised. The symbols had been granted by the College of Arms to Dame Deborah's soldier-husband, "Henricus Moodye de Garesdon."[6]

Laud provided punishment for a variety of innocent people. One London citizen was severely punished by the court merely for calling a nobleman's crest on the buttons of his livery-servant a goose, instead of a swan. There were public whippings in the market places while others were press-ganged into the army and treated like criminals. Puritans and lawyers, nobility and gentry all smarted under his vicious attacks on them through the courts while the severity of the sentences made Laud, "a fellow of mean extraction and arrogant pride," easily the most unpopular man in England.[7]

When Sir Robert Wiseman was convicted of uttering a libel against William Juxon, Bishop of London, the Star Chamber sentenced him to be degraded from the rank of knight and baronet and to have his ears cropped. The threat of ear-cropping for the aristocracy, though not carried out in this instance, must have induced fear in persons of rank like Dame Deborah. When would her non-conformist views come under review? It was unwise to entertain the thought that the nation's premier court would be unconcerned with a widow's religious beliefs. The Court of the Star Chamber frequently examined petty cases that should have been dealt with by a local magistrate - charges of forgery, perjury, deserting a wife, scandal, making hatbands with base metal, misdemeanors in church, riots in the Fens.

In the latter action Charley Moodey, Richard Strode and other defendants were held on a charge of obstructing an Order in Council to drain the Fenlands. They were accused of demolishing ditches and banks, beating workmen, burning shovels, wheelbarrows and planks, setting up a pair of gallows to terrify the workmen, pushing some of them into the water and holding them under. This enthusiastic East Anglian member of the Moody family was fined £1000. William Moody of Ipswich also found himself in trouble with the authorities and emigrated to the Massachusetts Bay colony on the ship *Mary and John* in 1633.[8]

Sir Richard Knightley of Fawsley, Northamptonshire, who belonged to Deborah's extended family, "a very eminent Christian and a great Countenancer and Protector of the Puritans" resorted to artifice to solve his problem. When Bishop Dove carried out a purge of non-conformity he relieved Sampson Wood of his living. Knightley who was Wood's patron appointed Christopher Spicer, a Puritan minister who was also rector of another parish. In practice Wood continued to serve as minister until his death. Knightley was one of the few gentry who were shrewd enough and lived far enough away from the authorities to escape trouble.[9]

Many saw no prospect of relief. History was repeating itself. The English were still fighting the same battle their ancestors had fought four-hundred years before. They had then been told that with the signing of Magna Carta at Runnymeade in 1215, the rights of barons, churchmen and freemen were secure. King John guaranteed the liberties of the English people in perpetuity. No freeman was to be imprisoned or banished except by the law of the land and money and supplies were not to be exacted without the consent of the Common Council of the realm. The Charter had been confirmed on thirty occasions! But times had now changed.[10]

John Hampden of Great Hampden, Buckinghamshire made a brave stand and provided a new focus of hope. Few Englishmen had larger possessions but he refused on principle to contribute to forced loans and told the Council "I would be content to lend but for fear to draw on myself that curse in Magna Charta which should be read twice a year against those that do infringe it." He was imprisoned in the Tower of London. On his release the fearless Hampden took a prominent part in Parliament, especially in debates on religious issues. Others were not so fortunate.[11]

Two of the leading Puritan squires in Essex, the aged and infirm Sir Francis Barrington and his son-in-law Sir William Masham, both refused on principle to act as commissioners for the forced loan. They were committed to loathsome prisons, the Marshalsea and the Fleet. Sir Francis died soon after his release. They were two of at least six of Dame Deborah's kin from the powerful families of England imprisoned for refusing to subscribe to the forced loan.[12]

In 1634 King Charles attempted to raise funds through an additional tax - ship-money. Some objected because the levy intended for the navy was in support of the army, others because it was a war-tax and England was not now at war. The assessment was eventually demanded from residents of inland counties who had never paid it before, imposed at the will of the king without consent of Parliament. "The libertie of the subjects of England received the most deadlie and fatalle blow it had been sensible of in 500 yeares," wrote Sir Simons D'Ewes. If the king's order to levy money was lawful, then by the same right he could demand any amount from his subjects at any time "soe noe man was in conclusion worth anie thing." People found a voice in Hampden who of course could easily afford the tax but who declined to pay the twenty shillings as ship-money. His case was argued in front of 12 judges. Judge Berkeley told him "I have never read or heard that lex was rex, but it is common and most true that rex is lex." Seven judges gave in favor of the Crown.[13]

Did the king have a divine right to make and enforce whatever laws he pleased? Thousands who disagreed with Berkeley decided to escape to freedom overseas! But in spite of the threats of pain and severed ears a majority, including Dame Deborah, with family, friends and property on English soil, still hoped that liberty, their birthright, would be restored to them in their own land.

AT THE ROYAL COURT

Members of Dame Deborah Moody's family had served the royal court under four monarchs - Henry VIII, Edward VI, Queen Elizabeth, James I - and now Charles I. Dame Deborah's son was appointed to the royal household: "Sir Henry Moody, second Baronet, Gentleman Usher of the Privy Chamber Extraordinary to Charles I." Sir Henry used his gift with words to please the king. He was "in some esteem at court for his poetical fancy."[1]

Sir Henry was an extraordinary (i.e not regular) servant of the king, attending Court periodically, perhaps one month in four. In the royal household "above stairs" known as the Chamber, he gave loyal service in the tradition of his forbears. While "ordinary" (full-time) Gentlemen Ushers were paid a salary or fee (£120 with an allowance of £100 plus £317 for Diet or Board Wages, a total of £537+ per annum) Sir Henry in an unpaid capacity would be less fortunate. Initially he may have received compensation for his expenses but in later years Charles was in great debt to the members of his household.[2]

At the Court in Westminster large retinues of aristocrats and courtiers came and went with great show. Rival groups jockeyed for position. Dame Deborah despised fawning bootlickers, but the three "P"s - Patrimony, Patronage and Purchase - which had always distinguished court life were the recognized path to Position and Promotion. Notorious for conspiracy and intrigue, the system earned Sir Walter Ralegh's condemnation: "Say to the Court it glows and shines like rotten wood."[3]

The elegant court was also costly. When Parliament refused to support it Charles resorted to such dubious methods of raising money as cashing his wife's dowry, exacting forced loans from wealthier subjects, billeting his soldiers without paying for them and illegally levying tonnage and poundage and other taxes without parliamentary sanction. So the king's coffers were amply supplied and life at court went on without a hitch. Charles had a high sense of kingly duty, but he seemed unable to understand that when he practiced political deceit to express his authority public confidence in him diminished.[4]

On 22 June 1632 the peaceful pursuits of Dame Deborah and other persons of rank in London were suddenly interrupted by a royal public notice issued at Greenwich under the Great Seal:

> A Proclamation commanding the Gentry to keepe their Residence at their Mansions in the Countrey, and forbidding them to make their habitations in LONDON, and places adjoyning[5]

Some 248 nobles, clerics and gentlemen of various ranks were subpoenaed before the Star Chamber in 1633. It was claimed that the city was becoming difficult to govern and more vulnerable to infections and the plague. The presence of gentry in town was alleged to bring no benefit to the king and contributed to adverse economic conditions. Charles considered they spent money earned in country areas on "vaine delights and expences" and clothes from "forraigne parts" to the enriching of other nations, so they were now commanded to return to their estates and provide a stimulus to local prosperity. Charles' intention was "not untainted by such concerns as financial advantage for the Crown and the need to restrict political action in London."[6]

As Richard Fanshawe wrote of Charles:

> To roll themselves in envy'd leisure,
> He therefore sends the Landed Heirs,
> Whilst he proclaims not his own pleasure
>   So much as theirs.[7]

Throughout Dame Deborah's life there had been royal proclamations on this theme - more than a dozen of them. What should she do? Leave London?

The crown intended to disperse uncertainty by the case of William Palmer. He owned substantial estates in Somerset and Sussex and was charged by Attorney-General Noy with remaining in town in contravention of the proclamation. An exemplary fine of £1,000 was imposed on him. Later is was reduced to a more reasonable

£25 but few knew about it. D'Ewes who was living in Islington expressed great surprise that Noy, "being accounted a great lawyer" should deny an individual's liberty to live where he would within the kingdom.[8]

Dame Deborah may immediately have gone back to Wiltshire, but if so it was not for long, for her family and friends were in the city. So along with many of the gentry Dame Deborah only made a show of complying with the edict.

The proclamations coming from King Charles were many and varied. But it was not the number of royal pronouncements but the growth of Catholic influence at the Jacobean court which most disturbed loyal citizens. For years Rome had been gaining strength. The Puritan Lucy Hutchinson spoke of "proud encroaching priests" and John Pym had warned as early as November 1621 that James was making a big mistake in tolerating the growth of Catholicism:

> The King may think, by not executing laws against papists, to win their hearts and so procure his own safety....the endeavours of that religion are not idle but active, and will admit no mean. For having gotten favour they will expect a toleration; after toleration they will look for equality; after equality, for superiority; and having superiority they will seek the subversion of that religion which is contrary to theirs.[9]

The respected leader of the House of Commons outlined to Members of Parliament details of the Grand Design - the plan for reunion with Rome. Spanish and other Catholic agents, Pym said, were granting pensions to Englishmen who would work with them to corrupt religion and government, by admitting "popish" tenets not only into court but into the Church of England. Englishmen, greedy for promotion and preferment, were running into "popery."[10]

Catholic infiltration of the court had escalated during the reign of Charles I. Henrietta, his wife, a Catholic princess had brought with her a bishop and an ecclesiastical household. She had been taught to regard herself as the instrument through whom her husband and his kingdom would revert to the papacy. Unknown to the English people King James had signed a secret clause in his son's marriage treaty by which he agreed to relax the penal laws against Catholics. On his accession Charles signed an agreement with the King of Spain which permitted his subjects to have liberty of religion in ships and houses and not be compelled to go to church or perform any other ceremony.[11]

A papal agent was actively working to form a Catholic party at court, frustrating the efforts of the Archbishop of Canterbury to implement the anti-Catholic laws and counselling the king in both foreign and domestic policies. Sir Francis Windebank, Secretary of State, a powerful agent for accelerating the wishes of the Papacy, enjoyed such exemption from penal laws as amounted to toleration.[12]

Cardinal Barberini had commissioned Signor Gregorio Panzani, a secret papal agent, to spy on Church of England bishops. When the Queen informed her husband of this he permitted Panzani to carry on his business in secrecy. Panzani assisted in the growth of Charles' vast hoard of art which was hung in his twenty-four royal residences, palaces and hunting lodges, helping make it one of the finest collections in Europe. Cardinal Barbarini, said he was happy to assist in robbing Rome of her art if in return "we might be so happy as to have the King of England's name among those princes who submit to the holy see."[13]

Puritan writers were not silent during this period. The polemicist John Vicars described Jesuits as perfidious prelates, atheistical courtiers and foreign agents. He accused the "pernicious woven knot of malignant active spirits" of scheming to undermine and demolish the fundamental laws and principles of government.[14]

Dame Deborah and her son were doubtless privy to these court activities. Among the books in the family library (later listed by her son) was the following which if ever found would contribute to our knowledge both of King Charles and the Moodys - "A written book contining [sic] private matters of the King."

Another Moody book was *Ecclesiastica Interpretatio* - *Expositions on the difficult and doubtful passages of the seven epistles called catholic and the Revelation* - collected by John Mayer. The drift of the commentary is epitomized in the heading for Revelation chapter 14:

> Now Antichrist is revealed in such lively colours that none, except the divell blinde his eyes, but may see the Pope to be Antichrist.[15]

Developments at Court could only deepen puritan apprehension. But for freedom-loving Dame Deborah there was strength in the ancient Moodie Motto: "God With Us."[16]

"

10

A FINGER IN THE PIE

It was now six years since the death of Dame Deborah's husband. Life in London was becoming more precarious and uncomfortable. Civil and ecclesiastical authorities were intrusive and over-bearing. Puritans lived in uneasy apprehension, non-conformists in increasing fear. Ministers were faint-hearted. Papists and Jesuits were growing in strength and numbers. Crucifixes and popish pictures appeared in churches. Some pulpits were openly adorned with the Jesuits' badge. Priests were dressed in new vestments: lawn-sleeves, four-cornered caps, copes and surplices, tippets, hoods, canonical coats and bishops' rochets.

Clergy introduced innovative ceremonial for worshippers. Congregations were standing up at *Gloria Patri* and during the reading of the Gospel, turning to the east to pray and bowing to the altar at mention of the name of Jesus. The communion table was changed into an altar and communicants required to go up to receive the sacrament - a precursor of the Mass. As if these Roman characteristics were not enough, there was a rash of sprinkling and consecrating. Clergy pretended that anything unconsecrated was polluted and unclean so they "consecrated" churches and chapels, fonts, tables, pulpits, chalices and churchyards.[1]

John Milton expressed the general misgiving about the clergy:

> ...such as for their bellies' sake
> Creep and intrude and climb into the fold:
> ...
> The hungry sheep look up and are not fed

...
> Besides what the grim wolf with privy paw
> Daily devours apace and nothing said.[2]

The wolf! "The grim wolf!" The ravager of the flock! Both wolves and lambs were lawyers' symbols, as depicted on an inscription at the Inner Temple gateway - the headquarters of London lawyers:

> 'Tis all a trick; these all are shams
>> By which they mean to cheat you:
> But have a care - for *you're* the *lambs*,
>> And they the *wolves* that eat you.[3]

Dame Deborah was silent as a lamb in the face of the surrounding subversion. She wisely made no written statements of her reactions or beliefs. To have done so could have resulted in a heavy price to pay considering the extensive powers of the prerogative courts. The Court of the High Commission (known as England's Little Inquisition) was charged with the responsibility of enforcing the crown's ecclesiastical supremacy and dealing with religious dissent. The Court of the Star Chamber punished with fines, flogging or maiming, imprisonment or deprivation. It eroded the liberties of the king's subjects and became a dreaded threat to persons of conscience and conviction.[4]

Milton depicted the Courts as leeches "that suck and suck the kingdom":

> What a mass of money is drawn from the veins into the ulcers of the kingdom this way; their extortions, their open corruptions, the multitude of hungry and ravenous harpies that swarm about their offices, declare sufficiently.... Their trade being, by the same alchemy that the Pope uses, to extract heaps of gold and silver out of the drossy bullion of the people's sins.... What stirs the Englishmen...sooner to rebellion, than violent and heavy hands upon their goods and purses?[5]

An anonymous author described the disturbing trend:

> To the end that the civil state may be subservient to the ecclesiastical church, these ecclesiastics have their oar in every boat, and their finger in every pie, where anything may be plucked from the subject.... None can be sure that his goods are his own, when all, and more than all, are taken from him at one censure, and that at the will and pleasure of the board, without any and against all law.[6]

The inquisitorial finger suddenly reached into Dame Deborah's pie! Information was supplied to the Star Chamber concerning "Dame

Deborah Mowdye" and other "divers Persons of Quality, for residing in Town contrary to the Kings (sic) Proclamation." London-born Dame Deborah had been in the capital longer than permitted by the law of 20 June 1632 which commanded the gentry "to reside upon their estates in the countrey."

A document addressed to King Charles by the Attorney-General, Sir John Banks, outlined the official action of 21 April 1635. Some 180 members of the gentry and aristocracy were cited: about a hundred esquires, various countesses and "Ladies of Quality," many of whom had puritan or non-conformist leanings. Mentioned by name in Laud's text were: Dame Deborah Mowdye, Dame Jane Lambert, the Countess of Oxford, Dame Ellenor Terrett, Dame Ursula Barty, Dame Christian Maven, Dame Alice Butler and Widow Anne Cotton. Many had left the city but returned and were discovered there after the 40-day grace period. The group was also accused of meeting together on several occasions "to oppose, resist, and withstand" the royal proclamation.

The persons named were required to appear before king and council and answer the charges. Did Dame Deborah respond? Did she compound for the offence, paying a fine? The decree books of the Star Chamber for this period are unfortunately lost as are the details of the suits, citations, fines and censures instituted or imposed by the Court.[7]

The gentry refused to accept the king's right to control the location of their residences and the loyalty of those who were cited took a severe blow. To underline the action another proclamation followed from the king :

> Our Royal Wil and commandement...doe, therefore hereby straitly prohibite and forbid all Our Subjects of this Our Realme...without the speciall licence of Us... [to] pass or depart out of this Our Realme of England...and that no Owners, Masters, or Mariners of any ships or vessels, doe henceforth carry, or transport beyond the Seas, any person or persons whatsoever, without such licence so obtained from Us...upon paine of Our high displeasure, and such forfeitures, and losse of Office, ship or vessel and other penalties.[8]

Dame Deborah quickly disappeared from London society concealing her exact movements. Did she seek a pass from the Customs officers, as did Thomas Mayhew who then headed for Gravesend purposing to take the first opportunity of a passage to the New World? Or did she first go to Holland? Details of how the Wiltshire widow accomplished her purpose remain unknown, but as a result of this obstruction to her personal freedom she gathered some of her belongings and quit England.[9]

What will not all oppressed, rich and religious people do to be delivered from all kinds of oppression, both spiritual and temporal, and to be restored to purity and freedom in religion, and to the just liberty of their persons and estates?[10]

11

THE IMMIGRANT

Rather than submit to the unconscionable demands of the Star Chamber Dame Deborah placed herself and her goods in the care of an unknown sea captain. Like thousands of other courageous pilgrims in search of freedom, she fled old England to begin a new life in New England. exchanging the comfort of her manor for a cramped berth in a sailing boat.

Passengers had to take the oath of allegiance and supremacy. A commissioned minister or knight examined them to ensure their beliefs were in conformity with the Church of England.   Dame Deborah either boarded one of the sixty-nine ships that went to New England during the year 1635 or she may have left later.[1,2]

As her vessel sailed past the coast of Cornwall and looked back at her own dear vanishing country the lone widow's reaction would reflect those of religious refugees who had left before her:

> When they came to Land's End, Mr Higginson calling up his Children and other Passengers unto the Stern of the Ship to take their last sight of England. He said, 'We will not say as the Separatists were wont to say at their leaving of England, Farewel Babylon! Farewel Rome! But we will say, Farewel Dear England! Farewel the Church of God in England, and all the Christian friends there! We do not go to New England as Separatists from the Church of England; though we cannot but separate from the Corruptions in it; But we go to practice the positive Part of Church Reformation, and propagate the Gospel in America.'[3]

Dame Deborah, forsaking her own beloved City of London risked storms, pirates and uncharted rocks to reach an unknown land three thousand miles away from home. She had time to build her castles in the air and make plans for a castle on the ground. A new Garsdon Manor?

A group of Dame Deborah's acquaintances left England for Boston 7 July 1635 aboard the *Abigail* of London. They included John Winthrop, Jr. and his wife Elizabeth; Henry Vane Jr. who travelled incognito and the noted Puritan, the Reverend Hugh Peter, who also was not listed. The Moody and Winthrop families had contact with one another in London. John Winthrop, Snr. of a non-conformist family was an attorney in London at the same time as Dame Deborah's husband. In 1631 Dame Deborah had held £40, part of the dowry of John Winthrop Jr.'s second wife, Elizabeth Reade of Wickford, the step-daughter of Hugh Peter, the minister. John Winthrop Jr. had married the 21-year old Elizabeth in 1635 just before they left England. Elizabeth's mother, also named Elizabeth, did not accompany her husband, Hugh Peter, to the New World. They had been married two years earlier when he was twenty-seven and she fifty, the widow of Edmande Reade. Now, Hugh Peter, identified with congregationalism in Holland and with a reputation for cheerfulness and jesting in his sermons, was going out alone as pastor of the church at Salem, Massachusetts to succeed Roger Williams. It is possible that Dame Deborah sailed with this party without being listed. Some English emigrants did this to avoid detection by the authorities. Passengers on the *Abigail* were listed only from June 4 to July 24 and the ship sailed under Captain Richard Hackwell with Plymouth as her last point of departure, about August 1. There were 220 persons aboard and many cattle.[4]

The Winthrop group was sponsored by Robert Rich, Earl of Warwick, now President of the Council for New England. A Cornish puritan aristocrat, Rich had granted a patent for lands in the lower Connecticut valley to a group that included Lord Saye and Sele, Lord Brooke, Sir Richard Saltonstall (son of a Lord Mayor of London), George Fenwick and John Humphrey. John Winthrop Jr. took with him 50 men to build a fortress and "such houses as may receive men of quality." Henry Vane Jr., said to be one of Dame Deborah's kin, was also on the ship and though his father and Archbishop Laud attempted to dissuade him from going, King Charles I intervened in Henry's favor, suggesting the experience might do the young man good. The *Abigail*, (along with the *Defence*) reached Boston on 6 October infected with smallpox.[5]

A group of immigrants from Dame Deborah's home county of Wiltshire which included a family named Veren, ropers by trade, had arrived June 1635 in the ship *James* of London. Could the lady from Garsdon Manor have travelled with them? Jane Veren joined the Salem Church at the same time as Dame Deborah did.[6]

Whatever the exact date, Dame Deborah crossed the Atlantic without accompanying relative. There is no mention of her son in any Massachusetts document relating to the period 1635-50. Sir Henry was in his London house in 1638 and his name included in a list of Oxford residents between 1641 and 1646. In 1647 he was still writing poems for King Charles so had he accompanied his mother to Massachusetts as some have thought he must immediately have returned to England, which seems unlikely.[7]

Did Dame Deborah have any other relatives in Massachusetts? William Moody of Ipswich, Suffolk may have been known to her though he bore arms that did not resemble those of Sir Henry Moody. Both branches of the family had roots in Wales. There is a tradition that William Moody was by trade a blacksmith and that he was the first person in New England to adopt the practice of shoeing oxen to enable them to walk on ice. Many outstanding personalities descended from this branch of the family including evangelist Dwight L. Moody.[8]

The first historical reference to Dame Deborah's name within North America was made by a Boston lawyer, Thomas Lechford, who made an entry in his note-book: "Received of My Lady Moody - 22.2.39 - £1-11s." Her new friends were charmed to have a woman of her status among them and instead of calling her "Dame Moody" generally gave her the title "Lady" - a custom with which we shall now conform.[9]

Where did Lady Deborah Moody live? She may have stayed some time in Boston but is described as "of Lynn" (10 miles distant) which she reached between 1638 and 1640. The area resembled a garden, which easily provided a 30-60% increase in corn. According to Francis Higgeson 100-200% was expected and realized. By setting corn little children could earn more than the cost of their own maintenance. Green peas were "as good as in England." Gardens grew herbs, leeks, onions, vines, mulberries, plums, currants, cherries, filberts and walnuts. A quart of milk sold for a penny. There was an abundance of sea-food - fresh salmon, bass, skate, lobsters, herring, haddock, mullet, eel, crab, mussels and oysters. Turkeys were plentiful; flocks of pigeons were so dense they "darkened the sky." Spring and autumn were beautiful; winter was colder and summer hotter than in England.

John Cotton confirmed the abundance in Massachusetts. The woods, he wrote, are filled with wild animals: foxes, wolves, deer, moose, beaver, raccoons, rabbits, woodchuck and squirrels. One of the most troublesome animals he encountered was the catamount (now extinct), a cat from three to six feet long that climbed trees and jumped down on the early settlers - doubtless not a gentlewoman's favorite feline![10]

Lady Moody's house, Swampscott

THE LADY OF LYNN

The town of Lynn, incorporated in 1630 and originally called Saugus was renamed in 1637 after Lynn Regis in England. Several tanneries were operating and shoemaking, which later brought prominence to the settlement, was established in 1635.

A contemporary ballad pictures life in Lady Deborah's new home town:

> The place where we live is a wilderness wood,
> Where grass is much wanting that's fruitful and good;
> Our mountains and hills, and our valleys below,
> Being commonly covered with ice and with snow.
>
> And when the northwest wind with violence blows,
> Then every man pulls his cap over his nose;
> But if any is hardy, and will it withstand,
> He forfeits a finger, a foot, or a hand.
>
> And when the spring opens, we then take the hoe,
> And make the ground ready to plant and to sow
> Our corn being planted, and seed being sown,
> The worms destroy much before it is grown.
>
> And while it is growing, some spoil there is made
> By birds and by squirrels, that pluck up the blade;
> And when it is come to full corn in the ear,
> It is often destroyed by raccoon and by deer.

And now our old garments begin to grow thin,
And wool is much wanted to card and to spin;
If we can get a garment to cover without,
Our other in-garments are clout [patch] upon clout.

Our clothes we brought with us are apt to be torn,
They need to be clouted soon after they're worn;
But clouting our garments they hinder us nothing,
Clouts double are warmer than single whole clothing.

If fresh meat be wanting to fill up our dish,
We have carrots and pumpkins, and turnips and fish;
And if there's a mind for a delicate dish,
We haste to the clam banks and take what we wish.

Stead of pottage and puddings and custards and pies,
Our turnips and parsnips are common supplies;
We have pumpkins at morning, and pumpkins at noon,
If it were not for pumpkins we should be undone.

If barley be wanting to make into malt,
We must then be contented and think it no fault;
For we can make liquor to sweeten our lips,
Of pumpkins and parsnips and walnut tree chips.

Now while some are going let others be coming,
For while liquor's boiling it must have a scumming;
But I will not blame them, for birds of a feather,
By seeking their fellows, are flocking together.

Then you whom the Lord intends hither to bring,
Forsake not the honey for fear of the sting;
But bring both a quiet and contented mind
And all needful blessings you surely shall find.[1]

There was plenty to content the new Lady of Lynn, but what was "the sting?" Did this refer to the native Americans about whom terrifying stories were circulating? The English had helped create a problem by offering an award for every Indian killed on production of the victim's scalp. A Puritan group from Connecticut had attacked a Pequot Indian village on 5 June 1637 and slaughtered five-hundred men, women and children. But in spite of the inevitable animosity between native Americans and Europeans, new settlers kept coming and by 1640 some 65,000 English people had emigrated to North America and the West Indies.

New settlers needed land and on 13 May 1640 the General Court granted Lady Deborah four-hundred acres "where it might not hinder a plantation nor any former grant." It was a generous allocation (most immigrants received only fifty acres) doubtless reflecting respect for Lady Deborah's standing in society. But having been used to a farm of several thousand acres she wished for more land and a farmhouse.[2]

There was a well-built property on a five-hundred acre tract of land close by Lynn called Swam(p)scott meaning *the red rock* listed by William Wood in his book *New Englands Prospect* as one of the 32 "Noted Habitations" of the Indians. The estate on the Essex County coast was owned and occupied by the Deputy-Governor, Sir John Humphrey, an educated and godly man who had lived at Dorchester in England in the same county as Lady Deborah. Of considerable wealth, Humphrey had been active in the organization of the Massachusetts Company which had purchased a patent for lands where "non-conformists might enjoy the liberty of their own persuasion in matters of worship and church discipline." He had persuaded many immigrants to come to Massachusetts; indeed he may have encouraged Lady Deborah to join them and is said to have been related to her through his father-in-law.[3]

Humphrey and his third wife, Lady Susan Fiennes, a court beauty, daughter of Thomas the third, Earl of Lincoln, had arrived at Boston in *The Planter* in 1634. He brought with him a good supply of munitions and sixteen heifers sent by a friend, one for every minister. In recognition of his rank and services he was granted the valuable estate at Swampscott and paid the Indians for the land on which he farmed.[4]

Humphrey built his house on the red cliff over-looking the sea attempting to ensure that Lady Susan would be safe and secure from attack. The first winter was so cold that his wife refused to stay in her new home except in summer so Humphrey sent her down to the West Indies each year before the cold weather began.[5]

By 1641 Lady Susan had become weary of life in the barren colony with its little log houses and wigwams, around which Indians roamed by day and wild animals by night. Her sister, Lady Arabella Johnson, (wife of Isaac Johnson) had died soon after they arrived and the lonely Lady Susan pined for England.[6]

So when Humphrey decided to take his wife back to her homeland, Lady Deborah bought "master Humphrey's farme, Swampscott." On 26 October 1641 Lady Susan, her husband and two of her children climbed aboard a ship that came up to the beach in Lynn close to the house. Farewells were said, anchors weighed and the sails set. From what became known as Lady Moody's Beach (now King's Beach), near Monument Square a lonely, isolated figure climbed up Black Will's Cliff to her new home among the trees.[7]

While the original deed of the house is lost Major William Hathorn, one of the appraisers, confirmed to his lawyer, 2 December 1670:

> ...about thirty yeares agoe when my Lady Moody first came ouer & mr Humfryes had receiued of her eleun hundred pounds, as they were both agreed, Capt Turner, Mr. Edward Tomlin & my self were chosen by them to value an estate that was prsented to vs by mr Humfry, pt of which estate was the house & land in which he then liued caled Swampscott, we had an order deliuered to vs, made at new Towne, by the Generall Court directing vs to the bounds which weere by estimation, a mile from the sea side, & run to a great white oake, neere the Rock and soe to the Rockes vpon the same line; the other farme on the north fell som yeares after into my hands, whoe knowing what wee had valued before, I sold to mablehead, & noe further to the southward, & from Rock to the spring, between Georg Farrs & and Thomas Smithes.[8]

Lechford wrote in his notebook: "Lady Moody lives at Lynn....She is a good lady almost undone, by buying Master Humfries' farm, Swampscott."[9]

Was Lady Deborah defrauded in the purchase of her farm? Records indicate the average price received from the sale of houses was less than £25 (c.$50), though most were very simple, primitive dwellings. The high price hardly reflects the fifty per cent fall in land and cattle values which Essex County records indicate took place in October 1640.[10]

So perhaps the rich woman alone in a man's world paid too much for her farmhouse. She could at least comfort herself in the knowledge that she was well established. In control of 900 acres of land and with English restrictions left behind Lady Deborah could begin a new chapter in her life.

IN SALEM

The nearest settlement to Lady Deborah's Swampscott farmhouse was Salem. To reach it she travelled from "Lady Moody's Beach" along a five-mile native trail by the shore through Marblehead. [It became North America's first public highway on 5 July 1659.] Salem had been colonized in 1628 by about a hundred Puritans under Captain Endecott and called Naumkeag (safe haven). These settlers were loyal to the Church of England unlike the early pilgrims who came in 1620. They were also wealthier. They had brought with them aboard the *Talbot*, *Arabella* and *Jewell* all sorts of food, oatmeal, butter, cheese, sugar, bacon, as well as cows, chickens, goats, pigs, tools, nails, extra clothes, blankets, cooking utensils, guns, ammunition and books.

Lady Deborah possessed a small dwelling in Salem at Town House Square, Planter's Row, (now Washington Street). The nine feet tall log cabin was a short walk from a spring which still delivers fresh water in the center of town.[1]

Lady Deborah had distinguished neighbors. Hugh Peter lived next door in a house formerly occupied by Roger Williams. On the other side were the homes of George Corwin, Dr George Emery, Thomas Ruck, Samuel Skelton, John Pickering, Emanuel Downing, William Hathorne and the Deputy-Governor John Endecott. Endecott was a fighter, and not solely on the battlefield. He opposed the wearing of long hair by males and insisted that women should veil their faces in public assembly. He had little patience with any whose religious views differed from the accepted orthodox opinion.[2]

Thomas Savage was the colonist whom Governor Winthrop said had more acquaintance with Lady Moody, however slight it may be, than anyone else.   A tailor from St. Albans, Hertfordshire Savage had left the Port of London on the *Planter* for Boston on 2 April 1635.   He was a member of the Ancient and Honourable Order of the Artillery Company, a prominent center of the secular activities of London Puritans, and he was married to Faith, a daughter of Anne Hutchinson.   So Lady Deborah probably had some association with the Hutchinson family.[3]

Close to Lady Deborah's cabin was the most prominent building in Salem - the church.   Like other early New England houses of worship it had mud walls, a thatched roof and an earthen floor. Before Lady Deborah's arrival church leaders had found the Salem meeting house was too small and decided to extend it twenty-five feet.   A high pulpit was erected which emphasized the authority of the minister.   The galleries were continued from the old part of the building and new stairs were built up to them.   The extension housed a chimney which projected four feet above the top of the building and the timbers were catted to create a draft through the space between them.   The fireplace was about ten and a half feet wide and the bier stood in it when a fire was not needed.   The addition was lit by windows, one on each side and two on the end. It was covered with one and a half inch planks and overlaid with one inch boards.   John Pickering, the builder spent £63 on the extension, which was recovered by levying a rate on the community.[4]

Lady Deborah joined this church in May 1640.   On Sundays men and boys sat on one side; women and girls on the other.   In the unornamented meeting-house the minister wore no symbolic vestments but gravely fostered a vigorous religious life.

> The sermon, learned long and cold
> The psalm in graveyard metre told;
> But piety, right deep and true,
> Each exercise ran through and through.[5]

Psalms were not only "in graveyard metre told" they were sung from the new Cambridge *The Whole Booke of Psalmes* printed by Stephen Day, (1640) known as "the Bay Psalm book."   The 400-page version made for public worship was North America's first publication.   For centuries men had sung psalms while women - until the close of the seventeenth century - were generally expected to keep silent in church.   Whereas her Biblical namesake could publicly voice her sentiments and have her name and song preserved for thousands of years in writings considered sacred by

Jews and Christians, Lady Deborah may have had to stifle her feelings, and refrain from allowing praise of God to part her lips.[6]

But if she was not permitted to sing she would quickly discover that it was necessary for her to attend church - and stay awake! A church official used a long stick with a ball at one end and a fox tail at the other. He rapped slumbering males on the head with the knob and roused sleepy women by gently drawing the fox tail across their faces. One member, Roger Scott, was charged "for common sleeping at the public exercise upon the Lord's day, and for striking him that waked him." In the following December, "not having amended his conduct he was sentenced by the court to be severely whipped."[7]

The whipping post (introduced when the Quakers were considered a menace) was a few yards around the corner from Lady Deborah's cabin next to a pillory and stocks (installed by Isaac Davis, January, 1638) as required by law in Massachusetts settlements. The constable was paid two shillings and sixpence for each person he whipped. He did not fare badly.

The founders of "God's commonwealth" in the new colony used such punishments frequently not merely for criminals, and not only in summertime! On 27 December 1642, William Goult, "for reproachful and unseemly speeches against the rule of the church," was ordered to sit in the stocks for an hour and be severely whipped.[8]

Lady Deborah was horrified to realize that religious toleration was not practiced in the colony and many stories of the treatment of various settlers were in circulation. In the first prosecution for a religious offense in the Massachusetts colony it was ordered "that John Baker shall be whipped for shooting at fowl on the Sabbath day." At this time there were no statutes on the books. So the Court re-enacted the entire Mosaic code of religious, political and sanitary laws in hope of duplicating the ancient theocracy in the New World. Cases were decided "according to the laws and the Word of God," as interpreted by the court which combined the legislative, judicial and executive departments of government in one.[9]

In addition, as Captain Breedon said, the people were "subject both to the written lawes and those in the magistrates' breasts." Some like Roger Williams had opposed court actions that referred to breaches of the first table of the Ten Commandments, believing that religious matters were not the concern of the secular authority. But Church leaders required members to render blind obedience to

God's will as interpreted by them. In their zeal they failed to see
that the attempt to set up the Kingdom of God by legislation would
inevitably produce religious persecution.[10]

Official orders made adultery subject to the death penalty. And
even when the statute was abolished the punishment was replaced
by a public whipping and the wearing of clothes marked "AD." But
there was no opposition in the colony to the slave trade which
became profitable as boats regularly left Boston for raids along the
West African coast.

Colonists were punished for scolding, eavesdropping, meddling,
naughty speeches, profane dancing, making love without the
consent of the congregation, playing cards, pulling hair and
pushing wives. At Salem twenty-nine women appeared before the
Essex County justices a total of 149 times for "contempt of the
authorities, Sabbath absence, or heresy." Nicholas Phelp's wife said
of Salem minister John Higginson that he "sent abroad his wolves
and his bloodhounds amongst sheep and lambs and that the priests
were deceivers of the people."[11]

When the Court heard complaints that some church members were
absenting themselves from church meetings upon the Lord's day it
gave power to any two Assistants to hear and censure members
either by fine or imprisonment (at their discretion) for all
misdemeanors of that nature, the fines not to exceed five shillings
for one offense.[12]

Thus the Church held a firm grip on the lives of its communicants.
Consumed with the idea that they were chosen by God, well-
meaning clerics easily became fanatics and hypocrites. Their laws
mirrored their lives:

> It was forbidden to run or walk on the Sabbath Day, except
> 'reverently to meeting'; to sweep the house, to cook, or to shave;
> mothers were advised not to kiss their children on the Lord's
> Day; adultery, blasphemy, and idolatry were punishable by
> death; heresy and keeping Christmas Day, by fine and the stocks;
> absence from public worship, by fine and whipping; renouncing
> Church membership, or questioning the canonicity of any book
> in the Bible, by fine and banishment; all gaming was prohibited
> and cards and dice forbidden to be imported; dancing anywhere,
> and kissing a woman in the street, 'even in the way of honest
> salutation,' was punished by flogging; women were forbidden
> under penalty of imprisonment to wear clothing beyond their
> station in life, to cut their hair like a man; and for speaking ill of
> the minister, to have their tongues fastened in a split stick.[13]

Nor were the laws idle threats. John Wedgewood, for being in the company of drunkards, was ordered to sit in the stocks; Thomas Pettit, for suspicion of slander and stubbornness, was to be severely whipped; Josiah Plaistowe, for stealing four baskets of corn, to be called by the name "Josias and not Mr.."

A New Hampshire farmer who killed a bear that was tearing up his garden on Sunday was required to make public confession and demonstrate repentance. He narrowly escaped excommunication. A sailor who returned to the colony after a three-year voyage kissed his wife "publiquely" on a Sunday. For this offense he was clamped in the stocks for two hours.

Few were willing to challenge ecclesiastical authority. While women in particular had no voice, some like Deborah Wilson were determined to protest. She went through Salem completely nude as a sign, she said, of the spiritual nakedness of the colony. As a punishment she was tied to a cart along with her mother and sister and all three were dragged and whipped through the town. Her husband Robert tried to soften the whip lashes by placing his hat between the whip and her back.[14]

When Lydia Wardwell of Hampton, New Hampshire was summoned before the church elders to account for her non-attendance at church, she walked naked up the aisle of the Newbury Meeting House in front of the startled congregation. She told the court that because the church was destitute of spiritual life she wished to wake up church members who were "blinded with ignorance and persecution." For this display she was lashed at the whipping post and her husband also for defending his wife's right to appear nude in public. She watched in horror as he was tortured and several women were stripped and beaten.[15]

Women were not unwilling to demur. The educated Lady Deborah was amply fitted for verbal protest but knew only too well how her comments would be received. For more than a year she avoided trouble. She was named in a minor court case involving Francis Ingers and an impounded horse which went in her favor. But her chief concern was to find a refuge from intolerance. She was frustrated to realize that her fellow countrymen who had come to the New World to establish a state were actually, through their legalistic fanaticism, founding a church. The freedom of worship they enjoyed for themselves was not extended to those whose views did not exactly replicate theirs and all too quickly they were repeating even more excessively the persecutions from which so many of them had fled.[16]

The lonely exile was also without the moral support which young Sir Henry Vane, Massachusetts Governor 1636-7 had given to Anne Hutchinson. Vane may have encouraged his distant relative and kindred spirit, Lady Deborah, to go to Massachusetts in the first place, but he returned to England in 1637. The great English puritan poet, John Milton, admired Vane's principled opposition to a state church and wrote of him:

> Both spiritual power and civil, what each means,
> What severs each, thou hast learned, which few have done,
> The bounds of either sword to thee we owe:
> Therefore on thy firm hand Religion leans
> In peace, and reckons thee her eldest son.[17]

Lady Deborah now sorely needed the support of a wise statesman but the Massachusetts rulers were unable to offer the tolerant and discerning attitude of either a Milton or a Vane. It would be many years before the state was willing to recognize its bounds, grant freedom of religion to its inhabitants and adopt its official motto: "Ense petit placidam sub libertate quietem" - "*By the sword we seek peace, but peace only under liberty.*"

For Lady Deborah, peace without liberty was only pain.

NO ROOM IN MASSACHUSETTS

The winter of 1642 was exceptionally cold with very deep snow - the coldest for forty years, the natives said. While the Indians appeared friendly a report that they intended to exterminate the English caused great alarm. So the settlers built a log cabin 40 feet long as a safe retreat in which Salem's women and children could huddle together for warmth and security. And during the long winter there was plenty of time for conversation.

The laws regarding women's apparel could hardly have escaped discussion. Salem's citizens were not permitted to make or buy clothes decorated with lace, gold, silk or thread. Neither could they wear the fashionable slashed clothes being limited to garments with one slash in each sleeve and another in the back. "Embroidered or needle worked caps, bands, and rayles are forbidden hereafter to be made and worn." The Lynn General Court banned short sleeves and regulated the size of long sleeves - not more than an ell wide (twenty-two and a half inches). Other items on the proscribed list included gold and silver girdles, hatbands, belts, ruffs, beaver hats and long hair. Two women were fined for wearing silks and tiffany, while Alice Flint of Salem was arraigned for "succumbing to the vanity of a silk hood."[1]

And the women must have reacted to the offensive comments of Salem males which exacerbated their lot. One ill-mannered chauvinist attacked women as "squirrel-brained" and thought their fashions disfigured them into "bar-geese, ill shapen, Egyptian hieroglyphics or at best into French flirts of pastry."[2]

Conversation would also stray beyond family interests into religious matters and top of the list was the story of Anne Hutchinson, a woman of strong opinions. It was a crime to express sympathy with her but women whispered the details in sober tones to newcomers.

Lady Deborah entertained many of the radical views of Anne Hutchinson. Both women had spent some time in London and may well have been known to one another. Anne Hutchinson left England in 1634 just before Lady Deborah and quickly made her mark in the colony. She advocated a religion based on "a direct knowledge of God's grace" rather than on obedience to state laws. She held meetings, originally with women, that were strongly condemned by clergy who denied her cardinal tenet of the priesthood of all believers. Trained from childhood in Biblical exegesis she dared to ask questions about the immortality of the soul, the resurrection of the dead and the morality of the Sabbath. She insisted that individual conscience was a reliable guide but this conflicted with the carefully guarded right of church leaders to discipline their members. The elders, who generally attempted to suppress discussion, visited Anne Hutchinson but were unable to convince her of any error. So they harassed her in order to collect material for a court case.[3]

They created a statement containing "29 beliefs of Mistris Hutchison" which they considered false. They accused her of believing: that the souls of all men are "mortall like the beasts, *Eccl. 3.8.*"; that the resurrection mentioned in *1 Corinthians 15.44* and *John 5.28* "is not meant of the resurrection of the body, but of our union here and after this life;" that Jesus Christ's disciples were not converted before his death; that "the Law is no rule of life to a Christian;" and that "there is no such thing as inherent righteousness."[4]

Anne Hutchinson quoted Ecclesiastes and the first chapter of Genesis in support of her belief in the mortality of the soul. She said the faith referred to in St Paul's letter to the Galatians was the faith of Christ, and not any faith inherent in us. The elders told her not to be obstinate, but "she was deafe of that eare" and would not acknowledge her beliefs to be unscriptural.[5]

Pastor John Wilson was agitated when she won over to her teachings such men as Governor Harry Vane and most of the men in the congregation. As her following grew Anne Hutchinson became a threat to the authorities. Governor John Cotton, who had gained the dubious distinction of "unmitred pope" of Boston, left it to Pastor Wilson "to deal with her" but declared his own judgment based on Revelation (chapter 22) that "such as make and maintaine a lye ought to be cast of the Church." After "laboring with her to no avail" the pastor decided to take action.

He summoned Anne Hutchinson, mother of several children and expecting another, to the Boston Meeting house on Thursday, 22 March 1638. She arrived only after the sermon and prayer were concluded and immediately asked by what rule an elder could come to her "pretending to desire light, and indeede to entrappe her." There was no answer to that. In front of the whole congregation the minister intoned: "The Church consentinge to it we will proceed to excommunication." Then he paused. Nobody made a sound. Nobody moved.[6]

Turning to Anne Hutchinson he continued:

> Forasmuch as you, Mrs Hutchinson, have highly transgressed and offended...and troubled the Church with your Error and have drawen away many a poor soule, and have upheld your Revelations; and forasmuch as you have made a Lye...Therefor in the name of our Lord Je[sus] Ch[rist]...I doe cast you out and deliver you up to Sathan...and account you from this time forth to be a Hethen and a Publican....I command you in the name of Ch[rist] Je[sus] and of this Church as a Leper to withdraw your selfe out of the Congregation.[7]

Pronounced a heathen, publican and leper by a Christian minister, Anne Hutchinson stood to her feet, walked down the aisle, and was joined by Mary Dyer, also an expectant mother. One of her accusers told her: "You have stepped out of your place, you have rather been a Husband than a Wife, a preacher than a Hearer, a Magistrate than a subject and so you have thought to carry all Things In Church and Commonwealth as you would."[8]

"Mistris Hutchison" was to be banished but as it was wintertime the sentence was not carried out until the season was safe for travelling. Then the prisoner was "released over the river," a simple way of dealing with heretics according to Reverend Hugh Peter, who once tolerant of varying viewpoints became prominent in suppressing antinomian and anabaptist separatists. With her six youngest children Anne Hutchinson journeyed 200 miles to Anne's Hoeck, a lonely place on Pelham Bay, Long Island Sound (now Pelham Neck near New Rochelle, New York).[9]

Lady Deborah who held most of Anne Hutchinson's views, though she did not propagate them, could only expect similar treatment. While the women huddled together and talked during the cold winter some of Lady Deborah's views inevitably emerged. Baptism for infants?   No, she had found no scriptural support for the practice.

Any woman however gifted and well-read who dared to speak of her beliefs was like a child crying in the night.   In Rome an unwanted babe would be taken to the hills and left to die, exposed to the sun and wild beasts.   In Salem it was not dissimilar.   "Babes" who talked were not ignored - they were ousted, denied Christian communion, sent across the river. Proponents of religious liberty were baying for the moon.   Indeed Master Thomas Shephard, the minister of Cambridge, Massachusetts declared it was "Satan's policy, to plead for an indefinite and boundless toleration."   Strict adherance to the prescribed faith was considered necessary for the successful operation of the state.   The colony's clergy and administration feared to lose their positions of authority and required church members to report on neighbors' unorthodox beliefs or practices.[10]

There were eighty-two blasphemous, erroneous, or unsafe opinions that must not be espoused in the colony.   Blasphemy and worship of any other God, were two of fifteen crimes punishable by death within the jurisdiction of Massachusetts.

The Lady of Lynn did not engage in public discussion as did Anne Hutchinson but desired the right to hold a belief she considered Biblical.   Adamant church leaders regarded her opinion on infant baptism as "unsafe."   None admitted the validity of her position. None sanctioned both kinds of baptism.   Lady Deborah was confronted with the reality that there was no more room for heretics in Massachusetts than in Rome or Madrid.

Samuel Maverick expressed this concern on his return to England: "Whereas they went over thither to injoy liberty of Conscience, in how high a measure have they denied it to others...meerly for differing in Judgment from them...witnesse that Honble. Lady, the Lady Deborah Moody and severalle with her, merely for declareing themselves moderate Anabaptists."   Sir Richard Saltonstall who had helped start the colony, complained in a letter to John Cotton: "We had hoped that the Lord would have given you so much light and love there that you might have been eyes to God's people here, and not to practice those courses in a wilderness, which you went so far to prevent."

This affair led Lady Deborah to an acceptance of the Trevelyan postulate that "doctrine of one kind or another has been the cause of half the woes of mankind."   Some may consider her opinion "dangerous" but the moderate Lady Deborah regarded it unsafe to deny her conscience and disavow her understanding of scripture. Rather than cause further conflict she chose to withdraw from her church, from her newly purchased land and expensive farm and from the colony. She would leave it all. Nothing was more valuable than the modest religious toleration she had been denied. "Lean liberty was better than fat slavery."[11]

Salem First Church today

Winter habit / English gentlewoman

A PROVIDENTIAL HAVEN ?

The news was on many lips: "Lady Deborah is leaving Salem," "she is quitting her farm at Swampscott," "she is offended by the church leaders." Having come to the colony to enjoy freedom from church and state interference she was exasperated by the Quarterly Court action in which church and state had united to oppose, fine and evict her.

And she was not alone. Goody (Mary) Tilton "a woman of strong religious convictions, was not afraid to assert them." She resolved with her husband John to leave with Lady Deborah. So did James Hubbard, a supporter who was also brought to court for not believing in baptism and for speaking his views in public.

A few settlers lacked the courage of their convictions. William Bound and his wife were indicted the day after the action against Lady Deborah for holding that baptism of infants was not an ordinance of God. The court accepted that the elders would successfully persuade them to accept the orthodox position, so the complaint was dismissed. Michael Shafflin and the wife of William Bowditch under pressure withdrew from opposition to infant baptism. But William Wilcot bravely refused to have his child baptized.[1]

The Rev. Mr Walton of Marblehead and many others also set out during the year either accompanying or following Lady Deborah. Rather than face the hazards of a 200-mile journey through virgin forest or Pequot-Indian held territory it was considered safer to go by sea. With baggage and farm animals to transport Lady Deborah left by ship - and shipping was available. *The Blessing of the Bay*, 30-ton pioneer of New England commerce, had been launched by Winthrop in 1631. The *Desire* (120 tons) was built at Marblehead. Lady Deborah's neighbor Hugh Peter "procured a ship at Salem of 300 tons, and the inhabitants of Boston, stirred up by his example, set upon building another at Boston of 150 tons." Five boats were built in the summer of 1642, three at Boston, one at Dorchester, and one at Salem. So by the time Lady Deborah was ready to leave there was a choice of shallops, lighters and pinnaces of between a hundred and four hundred tons that had been built from a plentiful supply of good timber, costing only half of England prices. She either used one of the trading vessels that plied up and down the coast or "bought a fairly large sized boat, in which she left Boston with a group of men and women and sailed around the Cape landing at Providence."[2]

Lady Deborah boarded with cattle and pigs which lawyer Solomon Lachaire confirmed that she and her followers took with them. Her party may have left from Boston though some like William Thorne travelled overland to temporary refuge in Plymouth Colony, stopping at Sandwich, or from Scituate as the Tilton family did. A group of like-minded people with unorthodox views on baptism was gathering there under the leadership of Rev. Charles Chauncey.[3]

Meanwhile the clerics back in Salem considered the seriousness of Lady Deborah's crime and voted to excommunicate her from the Church. The ceremony was rarely used except in extreme cases. But for wayward independents who refused to submit to church authority and who influenced others by their actions nothing was too severe. The clerk rang a bell, opened the Church Record and against the name of Lady [Deborah] Moody wrote one foreshortened word: "excommunict.." Then he closed the book, and snuffed out a candle. The censure deprived Lady Deborah of the right to receive communion or to attend public worship. As was customary on such occasions, the minister warned the faithful to have as little social intercourse with Lady Moody as possible as anabaptists were considered "incendiaries of the commonwealth and infectors of persons in main matters of religion."[4]

John Winthrop summarized events in his *Journal*: "The lady Moodye, a wise and anciently religious woman, being taken with the error of denying baptism to infants, was dealt with by many of the elders and others, and admonished by the Church of Salem, (whereof she was a member) but persisting still, and to avoid further trouble, etc. she removed to the Dutch against the advice of all her friends. Many others, infected with anabaptism, removed thither also. She was after excommunicated."[5]

Within months of Lady Deborah's departure a new law was enacted in Massachusetts:

> That if any Christian within this Jurisdiction, shall go about to subvert and destroy the Christian Faith and Religion, by broaching and maintaining any damnable Heresies: as denying the immortality of the soul, or resurrection of the body, or any sin to be repented of in the regenerate, or any evil done by the outward man to be accounted sin,...or shall openly Condemn or oppose the Baptizing of Infants, or shall purposely depart the Congregation at the administration of that Ordinance, or shall deny the ordinance of Magistracy, or their Lawful Authority to make war, or to punish the outward breaches of the first Table, or shall endeavor to seduce others to any of the errors of heresies above mentioned, every such person continuing obstinate therein after due means of Conviction, shall be sentenced to Banishment.[6]

Samuel Gorton commented:

> This Story's strange, but altogether true
> Old England's Saints are banished out of New.[7]

Lady Deborah's ship called at Providence where Roger Williams had founded a community which offered the religious freedom which she valued so highly. But Williams did not respond to repeated hints that he invite her to his liberal Rhode Island colony.[8]

Williams had become a Baptist for a few months in 1639 and then a Seeker, accepting the fundamentals of Christianity but not any creed. He entertained some unusual opinions. He thought it was not lawful to take an oath before a magistrate. He considered that the land patent he received from King Charles was invalid - an instrument of injustice to the natives by a king who had no right to dispose of their lands without their consent. Williams also believed that magistrates had no right to deal with offenses against the first four of the ten commandments, maintaining they applied only to an individual's personal relationship with God. He espoused unlimited toleration for all religions and anonymously published *The Bloudy Tenent of Persecution for Cause of Conscience,* declaring that "forced worship stinks in God's nostrils" - a belief which Lady Deborah shared. He considered any punishment meted out for matters of conscience as persecution. When a report got back to England that the Rhode Island colony did not keep the "Sabbath" Williams was quick to point out that there was no scripture for "abolishing the seventh day" and though he himself was not a sabbatarian, Williams told critics "you know yourselves do not keep the Sabbath, that is the seventh day." So Sabbatarians and other Christian variants all found a home in Providence. It appeared to be a suitable refuge for Lady Deborah.[9]

But Williams was an idealist, impetuous and precipitate in his decisions. Excitable, "divinely mad," often hasty in speech and indiscreet, he quickly reached conclusions and then insisted on his own opinions without compromise. As a result there were tensions in the colony.[10]

Providence seemed to be the most democratic of the Rhode Island towns, but some young single men who had promised to be "subject to the orders made by the consent of the householders" had become "discontented with their estate" and sought the right to vote. A number of other independent thinkers, heads of separate communities strove for local independence and their own chosen forms of worship, while "sober baptists began to explore the implications of separation of church and state."[11]

Sensing that Providence would not suit her, the wanderer in search of freedom chose rather to face the unknown. Providence may have led Williams to Rhode Island but appeared to be leading Lady Deborah elsewhere.[12]

Her ship sailed on into the excellent harbor at New Haven a settlement founded by John Davenport, an Independent Puritan cleric who considered conditions too lax at Boston. Lady Deborah met and may have stayed with the Governor, Theophilus Eaton, and his second wife Anne at their commodious 17-fireplace mansion on the north side of Elm Street. Anne Eaton who already inclined against the baptizing of infants, "spake with Lady Moodey and importuned her to lend her a book made by A.R. which having gotten into her hands she read secretly."

The volume by the mysterious A.R. *A Treatise on the Vanity of Childish [children's] Baptisme* propagated the ideas of Henry Denne, a strict puritan whose beliefs led to his immersion and membership in the Bell Alley Church in London. The book had only just been published (London: 1642) but Lady Deborah had managed to obtain a copy. The author, "Andrew Ritor," attempted to prove, against the teaching of the established church, that dipping is necessary to the right administration of baptism and that this sacrament is not to be given to infants.[13]

The events which took place after Lady Deborah continued her journey show how volatile were reactions to the view of baptism which both women endorsed. Anne Eaton, daughter of the Bishop of Chester and independently wealthy, walked out of church after the morning sermon and before the Lord's Supper was conducted. The same afternoon, when baptism was administered she refused to be present, in the belief that predo-baptism is not scriptural. She was condemned because she did not ask for help from her husband, her pastor or other church members and because she secretly lent her book to one or two members. But New Haven's first lady had a will of her own and publicly flaunted the neglect of marital obligations with which she punished her husband.[14]

When the New Haven elders failed to confound Anne Eaton she was called before the church on 14 July 1644 and publicly admonished by Davenport. She maintained her opinions without yielding and on 20 April 1645, by a unanimous vote and in the presence of elders from neighboring churches, she was excommunicated from "the company of God's elect."[15]

As in Lady Deborah's case it was ironic that this should happen to a woman of means and culture. But Mistress Eaton was not without supporters. Lucy Brewster wanted to complain to the New Haven General Court that Anne Eaton had seduced her, so that both of them would be banished and could then go to Rhode Island. She reported she was "sermon sicke" and told her son to convert into wastepaper some notes taken on John Davenport's sermons.

Mistress Moore, another New Haven churchgoer of independent thought, attacked the "divine" institution of Puritan ministry alleging that though Jesus Christ had once appointed ministers "now pastors and teachers are but the inventions of man."[16]

Governor Eaton did not easily brook these opposing views especially from his own wife. As magistrate, re-elected every year till his death, he ruled with a rod of iron. "He was so reactionary that he brought about the rejection of trial by jury." He also drew up rigorous blue-law Sunday legislation, declaring that anyone who profaned the Lord's day by work or sport "shall be punished by fine, or corporally." And if the court had clear evidence that the sin was "proudly, presumptuously, and even with a high hand, committed against the command and authority of the blessed God, such person... despising and reproaching the Lord shall be put to death."[17]

Protesters described the New Haven jurisdiction as tyrannical. A ruthless, judgmental Puritan of the Endecott type, Eaton's dictum was: "Power of Civil Rule, by men orderly chosen is God's Ordinance." He provided further evidence that colonists who set up independent congregations were unwilling to concede the same liberty they enjoyed to dissenting groups that sprung up among them. The Governor's comments to Lady Deborah went unrecorded but she received "harsh treatment" in Connecticut for stoutly denying that "baptism has come in place of circumcision, and is to be administered unto infants."[18]

Lady Deborah continued her voyage through Block Island Sound like Noah's unsettled dove flying over the waters and finding "no rest for the sole of her foot." She and Anne Eaton were not the only women looking for liberty in a male-dominated society. Many were protesting against the denial of their rights, and played a selfless part in the struggle for freedom of religion.[19]

Sarah Keayne was driven out of the First Church of Boston for "hir Irregular prophesying in mixt Assemblys and for refusing ordinarly to heare in the Churches of Christ." Mrs Oliver of Salem disturbed a church meeting because she was excluded from membership. And in England only a few miles from Lady Deborah's former home Dorothy Hazzard of Bristol in puritan fashion refused to close her shop at Christmas, and walked out of the Anglican church when the Laudian who was preaching dared to justify pictures and images. She was compared to "a he-goat in the flock" and set up a separatist congregation at Broadmead with a hundred and sixty members. Several other leaders in this church were women.[20]

The English dowager also enjoyed the support of like-minded travelling companions who were looking for freedom. These included James Hubbard, from Langham, County Rutland and his wife Martha; James Grover, his apprenticed servant; George Holmes (Homs); Ralph Cardell and possibly his wife Elizabeth.[21]

Now as Lady Deborah sailed through Long Island Sound the ship's company could make out to port Savanahachee (Long Island) where other exiles from Massachusetts had gone before them while to starboard in an isolated spot at Anne's Hoeck lived the courageous Anne Hutchinson with her six youngest children.

After entering "The Narrows" through what is now Throg's Neck, Hell Gate, and down the East River sails were furled and the

anchor dropped at the southern extremity of Manhattan.   The
non-conformist champion "bringing peace - exalted, and alone"
stepped on shore with the resolution of her Biblical namesake.[22]

---------------------- * * * ----------------------

I Am Deborah, Alone

Yes, I am Deborah, a personage known
For bringing peace - exalted and alone.

For years I have sat beneath my counseling tree
'The Palm of Deborah' between yon Ramah
And Bethel in these hills of Ephraim,
As prophetess and judge of Israel
For years my people have come to me for judgment.
At first, soon after our vows, my Lappidoth,
Would smile with husbandly indulgence when
Our neighbors sought me out to hear their troubles
And arbitrate their personal disputes.
But then I sensed his thinly-cloaked displeasure.

Must woman's self-fulfillment be expense
She pays in loneliness for prominence?

I never left my loom or my cooking crocks
For arbitration; but with wifely chores
Accomplished, I made myself available
Outdoors beneath this palm - away from home,
Away from Lappidoth's resentful frown.

Jehovah spoke through me to our conquered nation,
And I summoned Barak to rally Israel's remnant.
With him I led ten thousand men, defeating
Oppressors of our land. Then Lappidoth
Shut me outside his warm embrace forever.

Must woman's self-fulfillment be expense
She pays in loneliness for prominence?
I am Deborah, a personage known
For bringing peace - exalted, and alone.

- Pauline Durrett Robertson[23]
(used with permission)

---------------------- * * * ----------------------

A NEW HOME ?

It was about June 1643 that Lady Deborah's sailing ship moored in the Dutch colony (near the present South Street). The harbor, one of the best in the world, provided good anchorage and protection from storms. Would Nieuw Amsterdam be a gateway to a new life? There was of course no Statue of Liberty to greet her. The young settlement needed a Lady Liberty - a welcoming hostess to those fleeing from coercion, subjugation and despotism. It was a role the newcomer would fit perfectly.

Manhattan, for which the Huguenot Peter Minuit had paid sixty guilders in 1626, was proving a good investment. Early settlers in Dutch Colonial New York sowed their grain in mid-May and harvested it in mid-August. Proud of its productivity they sent back to Amsterdam samples of wheat, rye, barley, oats, buckwheat, canary seed, small beans, and flax, together with "7246 beaver skins, 178 half-otter skins, 675 otter skins, 48 mink skins, 36 wild-cat skins, 33 mink, 34 rat skins" and "many logs of oak and nut-wood." It was a traders' paradise.[1]

There were houses in Niew Amsterdam for about a hundred families, each having cost from $200 to $1,000; pure water gushed from rock springs and there was a wind-mill. The few streets were crooked and muddy; livestock and wildfowl roamed everywhere. It was Wouter van Twiller, the previous governor, who constructed Fort Amsterdam by employing "negro slaves" [each valued in 1639 at 40 guilders ($16)]. But the four-bastioned citadel was so fragile that it was frequently knocked down by pigs and other livestock!

Lady Deborah found temporary accommodation opposite Blackwell's Island (Welfare Island), now known as 16th Street and York Avenue. There was much to learn about the colony, advertised as enjoying "the best clymate in the whole world...easily fortefied against any enemye and as yett uninhabited...marvelous plenty in all kinds of food, excellent veneson, elkes very great and large...five sorts of grape ^{wch} are very good and grow heere naturally...excellent fat and wholesome fish wch are here in great plenty" and "full liberty to live in ye feare of the Lord." Full liberty - that was the prime attraction![2]

The male population of the region in and about Niew Amsterdam numbered about four hundred. They came from many nations and spoke some eighteen languages. Dutch, English, French and Portuguese were prominent having been attracted by the opening up of the fur trade. Farmers near the fort exported wheat and rye. Artisans, sailors and traders could be seen dealing with colorfully-dressed Indians while young rosy-cheeked housemaids brought over by their mistresses talked with young Dutchmen and soon found themselves a husband. Land had been granted to free immigrants from Africa and to people like Peter Cesar the Italian, Dirck the Norman, and Jan the Swede. There were also Walloons, from the Spanish Netherlands, who settled at the Waelenbogt or Walloon Bay.[3]

The English colonists were mostly Independents or Presbyterians, well educated and of good standing in society. They had a knowledge of laws and business and reputable connections in England. Like Lady Deborah they had left home during the turbulent reign of Charles I when "both civil and religious liberty, were prostrated by the illegal and tyrannical extension of the royal prerogative." Many had suffered from Star Chamber and High Court actions "before the abolition of these arbitrary engines of power." The newcomers looked to the New Netherland colony to provide them with the comfort and relief for which they longed.[4]

Fortunately the religious refugees and dissenters had the instinct to blend. Puritans and non-conformists like Lady Deborah found spiritual accord with French Huguenot settlers (Walloons) who had long suffered persecution for their faith. Indeed hundreds of thousands had died - in spite of the Edict of Nantes - to satisfy the political demands of French royal sovereignty. Unable to enter England they turned to the Dutch, who were glad to send them to America. These Huguenot members of the French bourgeoisie enriched New Netherland with their culture and their descendants became business leaders in New York.[5]

Jews also found an asylum in the Dutch colony. Some became stockholders when the Dutch West India Company was formed in 1620 and began to exert an influence upon the company's fortunes.[6]

The young colony had its limitations. There was no school building in Nieuw Amsterdam. Adam Roelantsen, schoolmaster, charged his scholars two beaver skins annually for the knowledge he imparted and was forced to take in washing to supplement his meager income. But school at an armed camp with frequent skirmishes to interrupt the flow of knowledge was far from ideal.[7]

There was one church for the Dutch Reformed congregation which espoused Calvinist doctrines. For several years services had been conducted by Dominie Jonas Michaelius in a hay loft above a mill at what is now 32 South William Street. New Netherland's first minister recognized that "political and religious persons can greatly assist each other, nevertheless the matters and offices belonging together must not be mixed but kept separate, in order to prevent all confusion and disorder."[8]

Before Lady Deborah's arrival a decision had been taken to erect a new church - a tiny octagonal building with a roof like a pyramid, topped off with a belfry and weather vane. The small windows and opaque glass made the building very dark and there was no heat "but all the women carried foot stoves [containing hickory coals from the fireplace] and some of the men carried muffs." Worship began when the clerk, or *voorleser*, standing in the baptistery below the pulpit read from the Bible and lead the singing of a psalm. Then the *dominie* read his text and gave his sermon. During this time the deacons, holding their cloth or velvet collection bags each suspended from a pole, stood facing the pulpit. When the offering was taken if the deacon thought the donor too miserly a bell hung at the bottom of each bag rang out while the *dominie* talked of the needs of the poor and invoked blessings on the liberal. Requests for prayers were collected by the *voorsinger* and were handed up to the *dominie* in the cleft of a long stick. When these had been read aloud, a psalm was sung and the congregation filed out in orderly fashion.[9]

A majority of the population around the fort was not strongly religious. One-fourth part of the settlement consisted of "grog-shops or of houses where nothing is to be got but tobacco and beer...they all drink here from the moment they are able to lick a spoon," wrote Nicasius de Sille, financial advisor to the Governor and New Utrecht's first historian. The caroling of drunken sailors disturbed the townspeople who asked for restrictions on the sale of beer and a curfew for mariners. It was also considered necessary to prohibit the sale of liquor to the natives, but regulations were not easily enforced.

In spite of his honorable intentions, Willem Kieft, the Governor, unaided by a town council, was unable to cope with the problems. His administration of the colony was weakened by considerable incompetence and injustice. Ensconced in his large stone residence (50 by 100 by 24 feet high) within the fort, the Dutch sea-captain expected to be treated like the officer-in-command of a ship. Refusing any suggestion of a representative government, he considered that his crew, the colonists, were there to obey. The settlers complained of Kieft's exercise of "princely power and authority" and were outraged that the Company to whom the Governor was responsible had given him more arbitrary power over their lives and properties than a king would exert. When in 1639 the Dutch colonists did not pay regular taxes Kieft tried to exact money from them and take their lands without their consent. He distrusted them and they had misgivings about him. When in 1641 there was a serious danger of war with the natives, Kieft called a council of twelve men to advise him. They seized the opportunity to demand democratic government for the colony, but the Governor dismissed them and ignored their request.[10]

Kieft's problems with the Indians grew worse because of the attitude of some of the first colonizer-traders and because the natives had long memories and were loyal to their kin. Many years before, three of Governor Peter Minuit's farm servants had attacked an Indian who came to town with his nephew to sell furs. They robbed him of his furs and killed him. The boy escaped and nursed his outraged sense of justice for twenty years before avenging his uncle's death. Then during Kieft's governorship, pretending to be trading beaver skins for blankets, he set out one afternoon to visit the home of Claes Swits, a harmless old wheel-wright. While the old man was bending over his box, the Indian struck him down with his machete and killed him.[11]

This single act led to a shocking war which started just before Lady Deborah arrived. Men, women and children were murdered, houses burned and farms laid waste. Especially horrible was the night of 25 February 1643 when native American fugitives who had been sheltering in Nieuw Amsterdam were suddenly attacked and brutally cut to pieces on the orders of the enraged Governor. His men went out to carry out his command while Kieft remained in an upstairs room of his well-fortified house. The soldiers came back next morning having murdered men, women and children. They tore infants from their mothers' breasts and hacked them to bits in the presence of their parents, the pieces thrown into the fire and the water. "Dutch and English were slain" wrote Roger Williams who had come to Nieuw Amsterdam en route to England. "Mine eyes saw their flames at their town and the flights and hurries of men, women and children."

The brutal, autocratic character of Kieft was also evident in the cruel treatment of seven Indians who had been arrested by Governor Fordham at Heemstede. They were accused of having killed two or three pigs, a deed actually performed by an Englishman as was later discovered. Kieft sent a group of soldiers led by Captain John Underhill. They killed five of the Indians and made sport of the other two, frightfully mutilating them. Then one died. Strips of flesh were cut from the still living native while the uncivilized treatment continued. Finally the soldiers cut off his head. All this happened in front of the Governor and his aid who stood by laughing heartily.[12]

Kieft's advisers sent a desperate request over his head to the States-General in Holland for a new governor:

> Our fields lie fallow and waste. Our dwellings and other buildings are burnt; not a handful can either be planted or sown this autumn on the deserted places, the crops which God permitted to come forth during the past summer remain in the fields standing and rotting....we have no means to supply necessaries for wives and children...all through the foolish hankering for war. For all right thinking men know here that these Indians have lived as lambs among us until a few years ago; injuring no man; affording every assistance to our nation; and in Director Van Twiller's time when supplies were not sent out for several months) furnishing provisions to the Company's servants until they received supplies. These hath the Director [Kieft] by various uncalled for proceedings from time to time, so enraged from us and so embittered against the Netherlands nation, that we do not believe that anything will bring them and peace back, unless the Lord who bends all men's hearts to His will propitiate these people.[13]

"The High Mightinesses" in Holland made no immediate decision about a change of Governor.

It was clear to Lady Deborah that Nieuw Amsterdam could offer her no refuge and her major need at the age of fifty-seven was to find a new home. Settlers in the colony were considered servants of the Dutch West India Company, and as such were required to render absolute obedience to the Governor. They were also expected to be members of the Dutch Reformed Church. The Governor and Council prohibited public and private gatherings (except those of the Reformed Church). But Lady Deborah may have known of the Company's proviso that these ordinances "do not hereby intend to force the consciences of any ...or to forbid the preaching of God's Holy Word, the use of Family Prayers, and divine services in the family." Lady Deborah needed the Dutch West India Company's assurance of "a religious toleration that reflected the broad tolerance of the mother country." All she wanted for herself and her followers was space and opportunity to practice the right of religious self-determination.[14]

In addition to those who had come with her, other families from New England had arrived in the colony. Lynn and Ipswich men had arrived to view the neighboring Long Island in 1641 and found "a very commodious place for plantations." Another reported "Black wild Vines...a great store of deere...Buffaloes...Turkeys... Chesnuts...Mulberries...Ponds of fresh Water...Fowle and egs of all sorts and sea and shell fish in abundance." The Dutch governor offered them fair terms - no taxes for ten years and then one tenth of their corn, with the same liberties, civil and ecclesiastical, which they enjoyed in Massachusetts and also liberty of appeal to the Dutch authorities. Several families from Lynn had arrived on Long Island but at least two settlements had been broken up: Southold, (named after the English town of Southwold in Suffolk), created in 1638 by congregationalist separatists from the Church of England and Southampton, started in 1640 by a group of Presbyterians.[15]

Lady Deborah found other non-conformists in the fort and in Long Island who were looking for a settlement. "Goodman Thorne and Michael Meler, William Thors (but his name was John)" had left Lynn for Long Island after they were presented before John Endecott in the court in Lynn (28 February 1643) for refusing to join the military watch. Thorne had been convicted of "counsealing, hideing, and suppliing" friends of Anne Hutchinson and Roger Williams, presumably on their flight from jail to Mr. Maverick's protection. Also from Lynn were Edward Browne, Richard Stout, John Ruckman and William Bowne.[16]

Lady Deborah's supporters were augmented by Nicholas Stillwell, George Holmes, Thomas Hall and others whose small English camp at Hopton on Deutal (Turtle) Bay, (a cove on what is now 45th to 48th St.) had been attacked by native Americans. Lieutenant Stillwell, an English soldier driven from his native Surrey by religious persecution, had come to Nieuw Amsterdam in 1638 and started a tobacco plantation on Manhattan Island in 1639. The war with the Indians caused Stillwell and his group to seek shelter at Fort Amsterdam where he purchased a house and lot on the present Beaver Street.   He assisted Lady Deborah in her search.[17]

As all ready-made settlements had proved disappointing, Lady Deborah favored creating her own new town with power vested not in a monarch, a court or a church but in the people. Assuming the leadership in planning she went to see Governor Kieft and found his office secretary, Lieutenant George Baxter was a friendly Englishman with a knowledge of law and eager to help a fellow exile. Amidst a dearth of prospective immigrants Kieft listened to the request for land on which to build, and considered the Grand Dame would be a valuable addition to his colony. He accorded the first woman to make such a request the right to an unappropriated tract of land on Long Island. Conditions under which her town would be regulated were agreed; he would issue a charter and the town would be called Gravesend. Gravesend, the gateway to and from London at the mouth of the River Thames was the port of departure for thousands of emigrants. It was to give its name to the gateway to the New World. Kieft may have chosen the name; he was born at s'Gravensande (the Count's beach) a village on the river Maas, Holland where Counts held their Court before its removal to the Hague. But Lady Deborah's settlement would be known by its English name.[18]

Stillwell is believed to have escorted her across the river. Cornelis Dircksen's ferry left from the site of the present Navy Yard and Park to Long Island, "the crown of the Province." They examined a seven-thousand acre parcel of land which enjoyed access to some excellent bays and harbors. Triangular in shape it was bound on the east by what New Yorkers today know as Flatlands, on the West by New Utrecht and on the south by the Atlantic Ocean. "There is little doubt from the frequent references to such a document, that an informal patent was given to Lady Deborah on her arrival in June 1643." She and her followers made plans and began to build a "city by the sea" but before Lady Deborah could settle in her home, she had to confront a new deterrent.[19]

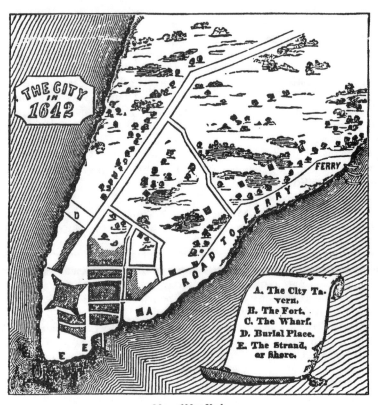

Map of New York

AN ASSAULT BY NIGHT

The English on Long Island generally respected the native Americans and land was taken over only after it had been fairly procured from the chiefs of the tribe who claimed it. The land for the Gravesend settlement was purchased from the Canarsie Indians ('Canarsie' is a corruption of canarde, [duck] used by early French explorers to describe the native tribes).[1]

But the Indians considered the land belonged to everybody and often failed to understand that payment by the newcomers was intended by them to take away their age-old native rights. Soon after Lady Deborah began her new township the Mohican Indians posed a threat to the invaders of their territory. They visited Anne Hutchinson in September 1643 appearing to be friendly as formerly, and then brutally set upon and killed her and five of her six children. They also murdered her son-in-law, Mr Collins. Susannah Hutchinson, aged ten, was carried away captive (and later ransomed by the Dutch). Then the Indians attacked a settlement set up by anabaptist minister, John Throgmorton and theirty-five like-minded families who had arrived from Salem and had settled at what is now Throg's Neck in the East Bronx. The Mohicans killed sixteen persons of the Throgmorton and Cornhill families, drove their cattle into their homes and burnt them. Then they crossed over to Long Island and attacked the new community set up by Francis Doughty, an English clergyman, at Newtown (Mespat). Some were massacred. Their houses and a plantation were burned.[2]

Gravesend was next on the Mohicans list. But such were the citizens' good relations with the neighboring Canarsie Indians that one trusty brave risked his life to warn them. Nicholas Stillwell gathered the inhabitants together in Lady Deborah's house and offered them the chance to retreat to Nieuw Amsterdam. All the men chose to stay. They cleared the surrounding ground of all undergrowth and Stillwell divided them into two companies. As evening drew on they waited for their attackers in deathly silence. In the dead of night they saw a shadowy figure moving stealthily against the background of the dark woods. Satisfied that all the people in the log house were sound asleep, he returned to give the all-clear to his companions. A large body of Mohican Indians furtively approached the house with their tomahawks ready to strike and when they were only a few yards away Stillwell ordered his men to fire their muskets. A volley of shots rang out and many of the braves were killed. The second company took the places of the first who went to the back of the house to re-load their pieces. When this group fired more natives fell, and by the time the first company were in action again the Indian retreat turned into a rout.

Thus Lady Deborah's followers preserved her settlement. Stillwell had delivered Long Island from further Indian retribution, and in the opinion of some, prevented an immediate attack on Nieuw Amsterdam which was ill prepared to defend itself at this time.[3]

Because of the danger to the fort Stillwell and his men were recalled to Nieuw Amsterdam and in this lonely situation Lady Deborah showed as much cool courage as any male. Marauding Indians again attacked Lady Deborah and her followers but they stood their ground. Her substantial house was used as a citadel "and three several times, did the spirited lady and her friends repulse them." Lady Deborah's group found temporary refuge some miles north in Nieuw Amersfoordt.[4]

Other settlements on Long Island were devastated or burnt and the English murdered. Upon the main as far as Stamford the Indians killed all the English. Long Island was reported destitute of inhabitants and stock. Only the homes of Lady Deborah and her supporters remained.[5]

Attacks from Indians were not the only obstacle. Nieuw Amsterdam residents resented the admission to the colony of so many settlers who were not members of the Dutch Church. The welcome Lady Deborah's party received on arrival was now offset by taunts about their faith. Lady Deborah became so exasperated that she wrote a letter to her acquaintance, John Winthrop, Governor of Massachusetts, suggesting as one of her options that she might return to New England. But when Deputy-Governor John Endecott heard of this possibility from the Rev. Edward Norris, he wrote a strong letter to Winthrop urging him to forbid her return:

> vnless shee will acknowledge her evill in opposing the Churches, and leave her opinions behinde her, ffor shee is a dangerous woeman....shee questions her owne baptisme it is verei doubtefull whither shee will be reclaymed, shee is so farre ingaged. The Lord rebuke Satan, the Aduersarie of our Soules![6]

Lady Deborah - Satan! There was no living under a jurisdiction which classified her with the devil. While this must have been one of the most daunting and discouraging periods of her life Lady Deborah's yearning for liberty supported her through disappointment, adverse comments, financial loss and Indian ravages.

There was also a more cheerful side to life! One of Lady Deborah's followers Richard Stout from Nottinghamshire, England, who was employed by Governor Kieft in the February 1643 uprising became enamored with a young Dutch girl, Penelope van Prince. The legend of their romance has come down the centuries to thousands of their descendants.

About the time of the Indian war, a Dutch vessel from Amsterdam was shipwrecked on Sandy Hook, but the passengers succeeded in getting to shore. Among them was a young Dutchman, who had been sick during most of the voyage. Unable to travel he was left behind by the other passengers who, fearing the native Americans, made their way to New Amsterdam with the promise they would send help for him. However Penelope, his newly-married wife, refused to leave him.

It was not long before the pair were discovered by a party of Indians who quickly killed the man, terribly mangled Penelope, slit her stomach and left her for dead. Holding in her protruding bowels she crawled to a hollow log where she lay several days, eating what she could pick and warmed by a fire the Indians had left on the beach. After a week she saw a deer with some arrows sticking in it, followed by two Indians, an old and a young man. She was glad to see them, and hoped they would put her out of her misery.

The young fellow lunged towards her to knock her on the head but the elderly man prevented him. After a considerable argument the old man, who insisted on keeping her alive, picked her up, tossed her over his shoulder and carried her to his wigwam at Middletown where he dressed her wounds. She was soon well and when news of her reached some New Amsterdam settlers, they came to her rescue. The old Indian gave Penelope the choice of staying or going. She preferred to be in Niew Amsterdam among her countrymen. It was there at the age of twenty-one she met the Englishman Richard Stout, reputed to be in his fortieth year.[7]

Stout who had formerly fallen out with his father over a girl he wished to marry, had spent seven lonely years on a man-of-war schooner and was discharged in Nieuw Amsterdam. Now he married Penelope van Prince and plans were made for them to live in Gravesend.[8]

The new colonists held a town meeting on 27 September 1644 and voted that all who were allotted boweries (farms) should also have fifty morgen (about 100 acres) of upland, with meadow sufficient for their stock. Each man would be required to maintain his section of stockade fence (20 poles). Any who failed to build a habitable house by 31 May 1645 was to pay a fine and forfeit his land to the town. Fines would go to the poor.[9]

But building was delayed because the native Americans were growing bolder. An Indian army of about fifteen hundred men from seven allied tribes, well supplied with arms and ammunition, turned eventually against the people of Nieuw Amsterdam. To defend it there were only fifty or sixty soldiers supplemented by 200 armed freemen. One settler, De Vries, told the Governor before fleeing back to England that he expected vengeance for all the innocent Indian blood they had shed would be visited on his head.

The Indian attacks left the Dutch destitute and desperate. "Those who fled for security to Monhaton, lived there and ate up their cattle." The eight advisers wrote a heartbreaking plea to their overlords in the West India Company "for such assistance as your High Mightinesses will deem most proper:

> Almost every place is abandoned. We, wretched people, must skulk, with wives and little ones that still survive, in poverty together, in and around the Fort at the Manhattas where we are not safe even for an hour, whilst the Indians daily threaten to overwhelm us....Very little can be planted this autumn and much less in Spring; so that it will come to pass that all of us who will yet save our lives, must of necessity perish next year of hunger and sorrow, with our wives and children...."[10]

But no help came from Holland. In desperation Lieutenant Baxter led sixty-five men to the Wecquaesgeek forts north of Manhatten, found three of them empty and burnt two.   La Montagne and Captain Underhill led a group against Sachem Penhawitz of the Canarsie, marched to Heemstede and killed over 120 Canarsie for the loss of one man.   The victims they dragged back to Nieuw Amsterdam were cruelly treated.   Then during a snowstorm Underhill and Ensign Hendrick van Dyck sailed with 130 men from the colony in three yachts for Greenwich. They killed 180 warriors and set the village on fire resulting in a cruel massacre of over five-hundred Wecquaesgeeks. Finally on 30 August 1645 Governor Kieft and six Indian sachems sat down outside the Manhatten stockade and "in the presence of the sun and the ocean" signed a peace treaty, concluding five years of sporadic warfare disastrous to both sides.[11]

At last Lady Deborah could renew her town building operations. But where was her charter?

Gravesend 1643

A UNIQUE CHARTER

In the tradition of the Wiltshire farmer Lady Deborah kept pigs and let her livestock roam on Coney (rabbit) Island or Narrioch as the natives called it.

The crew of the English privateer, *SEVEN STARS*, came ashore on 12 October 1643 about noon on property belonging to Anthony Johnson. When they helped themselves to more than two-hundred pumpkins three settlers, Ritschert Aesten, Ambrosius Lonen and Ritschert [Richard] Stout asked them what they were doing there. They said they were looking for hogs to take away with them. But when they heard that the hogs running loose on Coney Island belonged to Lady Moody they responded: "we shall not go there then." Lady Moody was highly esteemed.[1]

After the war with the native Americans Lady Deborah negotiated with Kieft for a new patent for Gravesend. The Governor appears to have "confiscated" the charter forcing Lady Deborah to appeal for her rights. Kieft's admiration for her bravery and the gallant defense made by her followers favored her request.[2]

On 19 December 1645 Governor Willem Kieft granted a town patent for Gravesend to Lady Deborah Moody and her associates. Her name, "ye Honoured Lady Deborah Moody," the first mentioned patentee, was written in gold lettering on the document. Other names were in black ink: Sir Henery Moody, Baronett, Ensign George Baxter: and Serieant James Hubbard. The inclusion of Lady Deborah's son's name need not be taken to indicate his presence at that time. As we have seen there is good reason to believe he was still in England in 1645.

The patent, written in English, (probably by Kieft's English secretary, George Baxter) defined the limits of the "parcell of land." The settlement covered what is known today as Coney Island, Bensonhurst, Unionville, South Greenfield, Brighton Beach, Manhattan Beach and the Sheepshead Bay sections of Brooklyn.[3]

And then came a portion of the patent important to a liberty lover like Lady Deborah:

> To haue and inioyre the ffree libertie of Conscience according to the Custom & manner of Holland, without molestatio[n] or disturbance from any magistrate or magistrates, or any other ecclesiasticall minister that may pretend jurisdictio ouer them, with libertie likewise...to erect a boddy pollitique & Ciuill Combination amongst themselues as ffree men of this prouince & of the towne of GRAUESAND & to make such Ciuill ordinances as the maior part of the inhabit[ts] ffree of the s[d] towne shall think fitting for theyre quiet and peaceable sub[sisting]...[4]

No right to worship publicly - but liberty of conscience! An official charter! It is a noteworthy document. A hundred and thirty years before the American fathers considered the issue, the right to individual conscience was incorporated in a town franchise and issued to a woman.   Almost a century and a half before the American Bill of Rights Lady Deborah Moody obtained an charter from the Dutch Governor assuring Gravesend inhabitants of a basic right.

They were also to enjoy municipal powers, right of assembly and right of nominating officers, subject only to the Governor's confirmation. They had right to hold town meetings and to choose three magistrates (schepens) without fear of disqualification on grounds of anabaptism. Lady Deborah's new town would be as democratic as could be arranged.

Like her Israelitish namesake, Lady Deborah had struck an historic blow for freedom. She would now have room to breathe, a space on earth that was not already invaded by kings, prelates or over-bearing churchmen who imagined they had divine, human or inhuman right to rule and to persecute. The rights of Gravesend's settlers were clear. No clerical elders would have jurisdiction over them. No one would have license to regulate their consciences.

It must have brought great relief. Not only did the charter provide for an English town with self-rule in the middle of a Dutch colony, it was arranged by an Englishwoman - and possibly partly written by her - in English rather than Dutch as generally used in documents for the other towns in the colony. Alone in a strange land, Lady Deborah could create for herself and her followers a secure refuge. Was she favored on account of her rank? Certainly she found her gender was no handicap to leadership ability. The charter was considered "remarkable as being probably the only one of its kind where a woman heads the list of patentees." Later a male-dominated society did not know what to make of it: "the circumstances of this patent being granted to a female and her being also first-named, is a matter of some curiosity; and...exhibits the Lady Moody in a conspicuous light."[5]

"Liberty of conscience" - they were musical words in the ears of exiles who lived by their principles. Now people of variant religions and of no religion could dwell side-by-side and plan their future without fear of reprisal. This valuable right of "liberty of conscience" is retained and cherished in the core of the Gravesend motto: *in libertatem conscientiae credimus*.

Gravesend is the earliest settlement to have been granted this freedom fortified by the assurance that no external civil or ecclesiastical power would have jurisdiction over its citizens. The three and a half centuries old patent (preserved in the New York City Department of Records and Information Services) is the earliest land document to grant such toleration to a group of New World immigrants. It was issued twelve years before the Flushing Remonstrance of 1657 which called for religious toleration in Dutch America and nineteen years before Nieuw Amsterdam became New York.[6]

Lady Deborah and her followers had initial hopes of founding a large commercial city, but when the harbor proved inadequate for anchorage of large ships they necessarily turned to agriculture. Busy as a bee ("Deborah" means *bee*) the New World's first city planner adopted a novel blueprint for Gravesend. It is not clear whether the unique plan was prepared by Lady Deborah or one of her associates but it depicted a square of sixteen acres surrounded by a "Hye-waye." This was intersected by two cross-streets making four smaller squares each of four acres. Each square was divided into ten lots, on which the owners built homes around a common yard for cattle.

Settlers erected a wooden palisade, 15-20 feet high around the perimeter of the town to protect themselves from natives and wild animals. Every man was required to own a twenty-foot ladder, a gun, a pound of gunpowder and two pounds of lead to be used in maintenance of the walls and protection of the inhabitants.

Outside the housing area they provided for forty "planter's lots" (or farms) triangular in shape radiating out like the spokes of a wheel and bordering the street surrounding the town. At a cost of fifty guilders each they were allocated to applicants who included a number of persons mentioned in Lynn records prior to 1644 - William Thorne, Edward Browne, Lady Deborah Moody, James Hubbard, John Ruckman and William Bowne. A lot was granted to William Bowne (originally from Yorkshire) 12 November 1646 and one to his son John Bowne on 20 September 1647. William, John and James Bowne had left Massachusetts on account of ecclesiastical challenges to their personal convictions and opposition to their belief in infant baptism.[7]

George Baxter may have been given a lot in return for help in securing the patent. Plantation tracts were also granted in November 1646 to Richard Gibbons, Cornelius Swellinant, John Morrice, John Ellis, John Tilton, William Wilkins, Richard Uzell, Thomas Cornish, Thomas Spicer, Ambrose London and (two names illegible). In December 1646 lots were allocated to: James Grover, Ralph Cardell, Rodger Scott, Robert Pennoyer, James Ellice, Thomas Greedy and Richard Stout. Each was accommodated with a quantity of land and required to erect and maintain twenty poles of fence around his property. By 1646 twenty-six persons had settled with Lady Deborah in her new city. Later arrivals would make up the full quota of forty.[8]

The center of Lady Deborah's town was at the site now marked by the junction of Gravesend Neck Road and McDonald Avenue. The First Lady was allocated two lots numbered nine and ten with "the Lovinge consent and agreement of the whole Towne thereunto shee injoyed." No other settler occupied two lots. Built by a creek "commonly called by ye Ancient inhabitants the Little pond" Lady Deborah's house is belived to have been located at what is now 27 Gravesend Neck Road.[9]

Mrs Isabelle Platt who purchased the property on this site at the beginning of the twentieth century, described the dwelling she regarded as once occupied by Lady Moody:

> The house which faces south, measures forty-two feet front by thirty-one feet deep, with a kitchen wing fourteen by fourteen. In the front there is a general living room, extending the full width of the building. At either end of this room are two great fireplaces, with large hearths measuring seventeen feet wide by eight feet deep of red Holland tiles eight by nine inches. The

ceiling is beamed - these beams, the largest I have ever seen, still show the marks of the broadaxe, and are twelve by fourteen inches.[10]

It was probably similar to the Gravesend house portrayed in an ancient agreement as having "2 chimneys in ye middle and 2 doors and two windows, and to be clabbord [clapboard] only ye roof and dobe [wattle and daub] the rest parte." at a cost of 110 guilders (about $44) or "one Dutch cow".[11]

In addition to the house lots "Lady Deborah Moodie" was granted "one Bowerie with y^e p^rvelidges thereunto"- the only woman so honored. The bowery, adjoining that of Robert Pennoyer, contained sixty acres of upland with meadow land sufficient for pasturage.[12]

Thus the landed lady of Gravesend became, as Judge Benson said, "the Dido leading the colony." There was a striking likeness between the fair legendary princess who founded Carthage, "built a Towne, reveng'd my husbands death, liv'd with renowne" and the dignified English gentlewoman who founded Gravesend (where she is remembered by a monument in Lady Moody Square, Village Road North).[13]

All inhabitants were required to attend town meetings or pay a fine of five guilders, which underlined the importance of the duties of citizenship. On 7 September 1646 the first election of Gravesend Town officers took place. John Tilton who had been granted lot number eighteen was elected Town Clerk, a position he held until 1662. Each inhabitant was to pay him a guilder annually. James Hubbard was chosen as schout (constable) and Lieutenant George Baxter, Edward Brown(s)e and William Wilkins as civil judges. John Ruckman was appointed collector for the poor. Citizens of the new town confirmed acceptance of the charter on 18 November 1646.[14]

James Hubbard, elected magistrate of Gravesend in 1650, '51,'53 and '60, was the youngest of eleven sons and daughters of Henry and Margaret Hubbard of Langham, Rutland. He had left New England with Lady Deborah Moody and settled in Gravesend where he was known as Sergeant Hubbard. He professed unusual knowledge about his family tree, believing that he and his brothers were the 123rd generation of Hubbards and requested this to be recorded in the Gravesend Town Register. Some have inferred that the Hubbard ancestors were Jews - the only race who make any pretence of tracing their ancestors so far back in history.[15]

While Lady Deborah settled in her new Gravesend home storms hit her flat-roofed property in Salem. John Winthrop in his Journal records the night of 4 November 1646 as "a most dreadful tempest at northeast, with wind and rain in which the lady Moodye her house at Salem...had the roof taken off in two parts (with the top of the chimney) and carried six or seven rods off." The Governor confirmed in a letter dated 16 November to his son John of Connecticut that "the tempest (than which I never observed a greater)" blew off the roof and "ten persons lay under it and knew not of it till they woke in the morning."[16]

There were no plans for a minister or church building in Lady Deborah's jurisdiction - the charter did not permit it. Seekers, of whom there appear to have been a number in Gravesend, did not consider ministers necessary, holding that God revealed his will to individuals. When they met in a house for worship one would read to the rest and it was reported that this happened in Gravesend.   Other   towns   on   Long   Island   had   similar arrangements. Those wishing to attend service could travel to Nieuw Amsterdam but Gravesend settlers like Lady Deborah did not attend the Dutch Reformed Church where baptismal water from the doop-becken or dipping bowl was dropped on babies' heads.   Occasionally   the   Dominie   (minister)   travelled   to   Long Island towns and held services in private houses.[17]

The Mennonite-types among the Gravesend population rejected the Sunday-Sabbath even though disrespect for the day in the colony was punishable.   Seekers   generally   questioned   all   religious ordinances.   Some anabaptists repudiated the Sunday-Sabbath as unscriptural   and   were   among   the   spiritual   forbears   of Saturday-keeping Christians who in Newport, Rhode Island formed their own assembly and organized (1671) under Stephen Mumford the first sabbatarian Baptist church in America.[18]

In Nieuw Amsterdam Sunday-keeping was slack. Governor Kieft had not been to church for over three years and because Dominie Everardus Bogardus castigated him in his sermons both he and his officers encouraged noisy amusements such as nine-pins, bowling, dancing and singing near the church during sermon time. Some inhabitants quarrelled, fought and hit each other, "even on the Lord's day of rest" in contravention of law, to the annoyance of their neighbors and "in contempt of God's ordinances."   Their protests led to a law passed on 31 May 1647 under a new governor by which all brewers, tapsters and innkeepers were required "upon the Lord's day of rest, by us called Sunday, not to entertain people, tap or draw wine, beer or strong waters of any kind and under any pretext before 2 of the clock (or before 4 when there was preaching)."[19]

But citizens of Gravesend believed they were not subject to religious laws passed in Niew Amsterdam or anywhere else. Their charter exempted them!

The love of religious liberty is a stronger sentiment, when fully excited, than an attachment to civil freedom. Conscience, in the cause of religion, prepares the mind to act and to suffer, beyond almost all other causes. It sometimes gives an impulse so irresistible, that no fetters of power or of opinion can withstand it. History instructs us, that this love of religious liberty, made up of the clearest sense of right and the highest conviction of duty, is able to look the sternest despotism in the face, and, with means apparently inadequate, to shake principalities and powers. - Daniel Webster[20]

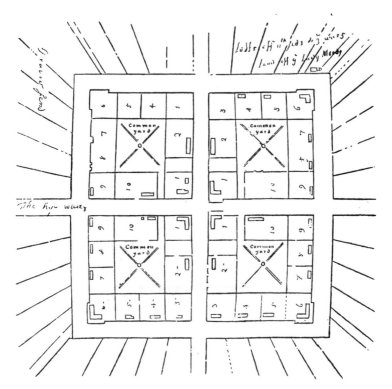

Ye Ancient Plot / Gravesend

A NEW GOVERNOR

The States-General recalled Kieft to Holland in 1647. He and the Reverend Everardus Bogardus with whom he had quarrelled both left on the *Princess Amelia*. The vessel was blown off course in a storm and wrecked on the coast of Wales; Kieft who had taken 400,000 guilders with him was drowned.

The colonists did not have to wait long to discover the temper of the new Governor. Pieter Stuyvesant, arrived on 11 May 1647 at Nieuw Amsterdam on *The Princess* with his wife Judith and sister Anna (Stuyvesant-Bayard) Varleth and her four children, Catherine, Peter, Balthazar and Nicholas. Stuyvesant made a memorable debut as he stamped up the slope to the fort "peacocklike, with great state and pomposity." His long straight hair fell over a broad white collar. His wooden peg-leg was decorated with silver, his right limb having been shattered by a cannon-ball. Although he was not an alcoholic he raged and stormed and pulled faces, probably suffering from the after-effects of his wounds. "I shall be as a father over his children" he told the burghers of Nieuw Amsterdam at their first meeting and left them with heads uncovered for an hour while he kept his own hat on! Imperiously "Old Silver Nails," as he became known, insisted on being addressed as "My Lord General."[1]

Sitting on his "stoep" at number one State Street Stuyvesant "smoked his pipe in lordly silence" and devised new plans for the colony. A God-fearing, honest, hard-working and abstemious man with considerable diplomatic ability, he attempted to improve the previous administration's policies. He forbad the sale of alcoholic beverages to native Americans and demanded that fair compensation be given them for their lands, but added "I value the blood of one Christian more than that of a hundred Indians." In the public interest he had fences erected to reduce property damage from roaming livestock, cracked down on smuggling and built Manhattan's first pier on the East River. But, like Kieft, he was a hot-tempered military man, quick to punish by branding, public whipping, piercing ears or tongue with a hot iron and hanging by the waist from the gallows.[2]

Vice-Director-General of New Netherland, Lubbertus van Dincklagen, depicted the autocratic new-comer: "Our great Muscovy Duke goes on as usual, with something of the wolf; the older he gets, the more inclined is he to bite." To accomplish his will the unscrupulous Governor stacked the votes of extraordinary councilors against those of his regular council members, using "as much discretion as a wolf for the lamb, which it devours be he right or not." Another wolf? Was Lady Deborah about to be "devoured?"[3]

The first patentee of Gravesend could only have been alarmed to discover that Stuyvesant considered himself head of the church. He imprisoned parents who refused to have their children baptized in the Dutch Reformed faith. He directed the building of churches, the installing of ministers, and even ordered them where and when to preach. As if that were not enough he went so far as to direct the placement of pews and seats in church and he expected to be obeyed.

He made regulations requiring seamens' attendance aboard the Company's ships at morning and evening prayers when conducted by a minister. Comment was not tolerated. "No man shall raise or bring forward any question or argument on the subject of religion, on pain of being placed on bread and water three days in the ship's galley."[4]

Stuyvesant showed little toleration for the views of those who were not members of the Dutch Reformed Church such as Quakers, Jews, Catholics and members of any faith which did not follow Calvin's doctrines. The Huguenots fortunately met with his approval as their beliefs were based on the teachings of the Master of Geneva. And in his favor he did provide protection for Jesuit missionaries, Father Jogues and Father Bressani, rescuing them from the Indians and giving them a free passage to Holland.

Lady Deborah was too wise to discuss her beliefs with "stubborn Peter." She knew she was under surveillance - and not solely because of her religious views. Stuyvesant sent his spies to Gravesend because he suspected that the English settlement might one day want an English governor. It would take all of a good woman's art to create mutual understanding between herself and the new Governor.[5]

Gravesend's matriarch waited her opportunity. Periodically Stuyvesant visited the various settlements in his domain and at last the day arrived when he decided to make a personal visit to the only woman of rank in his colony. Along with his wife, Judith, the dour Governor left the fort in a chaise driven by his matching pair of horses about which he was very fastidious. They crossed the river by ferry to Breuklyn and rode along the narrow native trail to the English settlement. From the house on Lot No. 9 Lady Deborah walked out to meet her visitors. A stern, humorless face greeted her as its short-tempered owner stepped down.[6]

In sharp contrast was his picture-book wife, Judith, a minister's daughter, doubtless adorned in the French haute couture of the time. Fashion indicated a jaunty silk or velvet jacket with leg-of-mutton sleeves and wide turned-up white cuffs worn over a colored skirt. Dutch ladies completed their ensemble with a chain around the neck and another of gold or silver as a girdle. On weekdays an ornament dangled from the chain and when attending church a costly bound Bible or Prayer Book. Judith Stuyvesant's jewelry would include a brooch and rings for her fingers. Her hair was worn high under a pretty bonnet.

By comparison Lady Deborah would be plainly dressed but her manners and bearing were those of a cultivated society lady. The two women exchanged greetings and were soon sitting in the large parlor. In addition to Dutch Judith Stuyvesant spoke some English and French, languages in which Lady Deborah could make good conversation. After airing their traditions and interests and sharing their thoughts and feelings the irritable Governor began to thaw. Judith's pleasing singing voice which had been trained by some of the best teachers helped enhance her gentle but strong character. And the cultured Lady Deborah could accompany Judith on her harp and so relax her visitors. Mutual understanding grew quickly.[7]

The Stuyvesants stayed several days and expressed their pleasure in the company of their hostess. Her home, furnished with comparative elegance and good taste, was said to contain the largest collection of books in the colony. The Moody library, doubtless reflecting her interests, contained seventeen books on divinity (titles unknown) but Lady Deborah was too prudent to engage a member of the Dutch Reformed Church in theological argument and too wise to bait a man whose support she needed. Lady Deborah's entertainment of the couple obviously subdued "the wolf" and the rapport between Lady Deborah and Judith brought all-round satisfaction.

Wolves of the four-legged variety were a serious threat in Gravesend. Indeed the danger to cattle was so great in August 1648 that settlers were awarded three guilders for each wolf killed in town and two guilders for a fox.

Farming brought other problems to an aging settler. After a dispute with her tenant Lady Deborah made a contract on 22 November 1648 agreeing to hire out her bowery for three years to Thomas Cornewell who was to use "all her broken up [cleared] ground excepting one peece yt she reserves for her owne pticuler use yt did bare Indian corn this yeare; and for 4 oxen and for 3 cowes both oxen and cowes he to take his choise out of ye rest."

Cornewell was to improve the land and cattle paying ten "skipfulls" of wheat and ten of rye annually, twenty-five pounds of butter per cow and sixty guilders for the oxen. If through negligence the animals were to miscarry Cornewell was to make good the loss. The plow and chain were also to be maintained in good order. When Lady Deborah and Cornewell disagreed about clearing a piece of land, arbitrators decided that her tenant should be allowed to crop the land the next year, and that she should pay him 15 guilders on the surrender of the same.[8]

More of Lady Deborah's frustration is revealed in a letter she wrote to her friend of long standing, John Winthrop jnr., in 1649:

> To ye worshipfull and much honored frend Mr John Wintrop at his house at Pequid:
>
> Worthi sur, - My respective love to you remem-[bered] acknowliging myselfe for your many kindness[es] & respecte to me much obliged to you. I have written divers times to you, but I dout you have not receved it; at present, being in hast, I can not inlarg myselfe, only my request is yt you will be pleased, either by this note, if in your wisdom you see not a convenienter opertunitie to send to me those things yt Mr. Throgmortone brought for me, and I understand are with you, for I am in great need of ym, together with Marke Lucars chest and other things. So with my respective love to you and youre wife, with Mrs Lacke remembered, hoping you and they with youre children, are in helth, I rest, committing you to ye protection of ye Allmighti. Pray remember my nesesiti in this thing.
>
> Deborah Moody
> Indorsed : "Lady Moody"[9]

Lady Deborah had not only known John Winthrop, Jnr. before she left England and held the dowry of his wife and cousin, Elizabeth, but also knew her widowed sister, Mrs Lake.

Lady Deborah also had acquaintance with Mark Lukar, a separatist and later an anabaptist. He had been imprisoned with Pastor John Lothrop (Lathorp) and some forty dissenters who had gathered at the house of Humphrey Barnet, a brewer's clerk in Blackfriars, London. Lady Deborah may have known of this group. It included Elizabeth Denne (relative(?) of the author of the book on Baptism which Lady Deborah had obtained) These members had been summoned from prison to appear before the Court of High Commission on 3 May 1632 and in spite of being threatened by the Archbishop of York all refused to take the oath. Sir Henry Martin told them: "The Law is that those y^t are taken in these Conventicles & remaine obstinate, that they shall be made to abiure ye Kingdome, and if they returne, or obey not, it is felony" - a crime punishable by death. Lukar emigrated to Newport, Rhode Island in 1648 and the church there began to practice immersion soon after his arrival. It thus became the first Baptist Church in America.[10]

There is no record of Lady Deborah's receipt of her belongings. Nor did she ever see John's father's veiled appreciation of her in his diary: "With the exception of her troubling the church with her religious opinions, she appears to have been a lady of great worth."[11]

The "lady of great worth" could not accept Winthrop's view that democracy was "a manifest breach of the Fifth Commandment." But the full cost of her belief she was yet to discover.[12]

Pieter Stuyvesant

A BLOOMING REPUBLIC?

Lady Deborah had a vexing problem. She was unable to complete the sale of her property in Massachusetts. Attempts to obtain a settlement of her real estate while she was living two-hundred miles distant in a Dutch colony were constantly foiled. The shrewd Daniell King, merchant and draper, had taken advantage of her hurried exit from Swampscott and of her acquaintance with his wife. Elizabeth had shared in Lady Deborah's convictions and religious persecution. The fact that King was already in possession of the property encouraged him to defer payments for five or six years. He also had a long-standing debt of £1,000 to his father in Watford, Hertfordshire, who ended his will: "I well knowing how unwilling my sonne Daniell is to part with his money which he once getts into his hands, until it be forced from him." Daniell King grew bolder by the year.[1]

Lady Deborah employed Dexter Fuller and Edward Browse as her agents. Browse went by ship to Massachusetts to obtain settlement for the farm and stock, but while King professed great friendship with Lady Deborah and sent his greetings he failed to produce any money. Because of a general shortage of cash, reflecting conditions in England, many were resorting to barter to settle debts. So a desperate Lady Deborah attempted to secure some payment in goods. Attached to Browse's letter of January 1649 to the draper was a long list of the merchandise Lady Deborah needed:

> [You] may seend mee 2 yards of Black Tuffety; ...commodyty; as follooth of canvise, 40 yeards such you sent [la]st; ...broade dowlesse, 40 yeards; ...of holland 40 yeards at 4s. per yard; of

Broade Cloth of the same finies you sent me last and of the same Culler, 20 yeards, or if not of the same to get of the best mingled cloth you can; of whit fussten, 10 yards; of browne fussten, 10 yeards; owne good greene Rugg, owne paire of blankets, of narrow Teek for boulsters and pylows, 20 yards; on peice of cullered stuff, 1 of shagg bayes, 20 yeards; 8 seyets for mowing, I pray let them be very good; of plow chaines 3, 2 peauter pots, 1 of a quart, on of a pynt, own bason of 3 pynts with brims, own thewart saw of the larger sort; 2 hand sawes, 4 augars, own half inch, own 3 quarters inch, own inch or inch and halfe; 4 cheizells, 3 inch wri bits; own halfe dozzen sheares of the 12"; 2 payre of axes; 2 payre of 6...on Cart Roape, own yeard of Taffety of a freen culler, 1 skilet of bell mettale, own of 3 quarts or therabouts. I pray you what is coming more unto the lady from your selfe besids what is Recd, 4000 of hob nailes, shee would intreat you to send it in lining or wollen cloth according as you in your wisdom see best for her and with all if be so much for to send her a hundered Iron; as Touching the farmers Rent I doe not know whither you haue reciued any more then the £20 that wase Ready when I wase with you which £20 I pray keep in your hand tell you heeare farther from us I pray faile not to doe your best to get the best as you pmised and thet all Remayne in your hand untell you haue farther order from us.[2]

The Wiltshire widow, who never remarried, requested black and green taffeta. Many women of fashion used to heighten their charms by sticking small pieces of black taffeta on their faces, foreheads or chins in the shape of stars, circles and even representations of a coach and four. But Lady Deborah probably only needed dress material. Like other colonists she was not permitted to make or weave any woolen, linen or cotton cloth under threat of banishment. The Dutch West India Company had a strangle-hold on the clothes trade. But it seems unlikely that Lady Deborah ever received the materials she requested.[3]

At this time the frustrated home owner welcomed her son's arrival from England. Sir Henry Moody, 2nd Bart. and the devoted royalist, Francis Lovelace of Hurley, Berkshire [who eventually became the first Governor of New York] had obtained from the Council of State in London a license to go to Long Island dated 6 May 1650. On their arrival, perhaps June/July the same year there was much for Sir Henry to tell about his adventurous life with King Charles I.[4]

Sir Henry brought with him documents which if ever discovered would throw considerable light on his activities. Charles had left London after failing in his attempt to arrest five members of

Parliament, and found himself in a civil war with his own people. He set up the royal court 29 October 1642 in Oxford where Sir Henry joined him on climaxing his studies with a doctoral degree in Civil Law from Magdalen College the following 20 December.

After many battles between Parliamentary and Royalist forces the Scots joined with the Parliamentarians or Roundheads to defeat the king at the Battle of Marston Moor in 1644. Charles and his forces grew weaker as did his courtiers in many a hall and manor. They, like the University of Oxford, melted their gold plate to support the king.[5]

Life in Oxford as the King's Gentleman Usher Extraordinary was not pleasant for Sir Henry. Oxford was a sorry spectacle of war, blighted by sickness, plague and poor food. He had accommodation in All Saints Parish, where on the 10 April 1644 he paid ten shillings for a month's lodging to "Henry roe, collector."[6]

In 1645 the king's forces were defeated again at the Battle of Naseby and the following year on 27 April Charles quietly left Oxford with a minimum of attendants. It is likely that Sir Henry was among them.[7]

It was Sir Henry's unenviable job to tickle the king's ear with his versifying. One of Sir Henry's poems has survived - a panegyric in which he sarcastically regales the proceedings of Parliament at Westminster "since their first sessions to this present 1647." But Sir Henry was singing in the dark. Later that year the Scots sold Charles to the English for £400,000 and the English Roundheads held their king prisoner.[8]

The struggle between absolute and constitutional monarchy finally brought Charles to trial in Westminster Hall before the High Court of Justice. The clerk read the charge, describing the king as "a tyrant, traitor, murderer, and public enemy to the good people of this nation." First the Army, then Parliament condemned him. He was executed on 30 January 1649 at Whitehall - the only English monarch to be beheaded by his people. He died bravely, as a king.

Sir Henry's loyalty to his sovereign cost him more than his position. Like so many of the king's servants he had deep financial problems. Charles extricated money from all his courtiers, harvests had been bad, the price of wheat more than doubled, rents were not paid and property was reduced in value. Parliament passed a sequestration ordinance, 27 March 1643, declaring that all who had assisted the King were to be reckoned as delinquents and their property taken over by the Committee of the county in which it was situated. This law eventually brought Sir Henry to court. At the trial before the Committee for Compounding at Goldsmiths' Hall, London on 28 November 1646 he took the Covenant and the Negative Oath, and pledged never again to bear arms against Parliament.   He was compelled to declare the full value of his estate and order was made "on his petition discharging him from sequestration, he having...deposed that he is not worth £200."[9]

After recounting his adventures Sir Henry turned his professional skills to helping his mother with her estate and went up to New England. He acted as attorney in a civil action "the Honrd. Lady Deborah Moody v. Mr Danyell Kinge, for detaining a farm to the value of £500." It was heard at the Ipswich court on 17 September 1651, but a satisfying outcome eluded Sir Henry. Daniel Kinge was to pay to Lady Moody within one week £20 in cash, within one month a further £30 cash, and at the end of the third month a mare and merchantable goods or cattle, to the value of £100 together with £5 costs. It was a pittance compared with the $1100 Lady Deborah had paid for the property.

In Gravesend houses were much less costly and were frequently being improved by the settlers. Every lot owner was required to pay one guilder toward the common charges of the town and to "fence the end of his lot upon the town square, with a sufficiency of palisades, by the middle of April next [1651]." The fortification enclosed a ten-acre town-plot inside which both the inhabitants and their cattle were secured at night.[10]

The householders of Gravesend agreed at a town meting to perform joint community service and to "be ready to go by the blowing of ye [the] horn on Thursday next to clear ye common ways." But town records indicate that during communal activities or social visiting it was dangerous to pass derogatory comments. In the settlement's first slander case Ambrose London accused the wife of Thomas Applegate of milking his wife's cow. He said he heard Peneloppe Prince who was at Thomas Greedy's house saying that she and Applegate's daughter had milked Applegate's cow. When Peneloppe was questioned she acknowledged her fault, said she was sorry for her words and gave satisfaction on both sides.[11]

More serious was the case of Thomas Applegate, defendant in a case of slander against Stuyvesant in January 1651. It was alleged that Applegate had said that for the wrong the Governor done him, "hee would deale with him well enoughe." Applegate denied the accusation but the Court adjudged that he deserved "to have his tongue bored through with a redd hott yron and to make a publicke acknowledgment of his greate transgression." When the sentence was read Applegate publicly admitted that he had slandered the Governor; he "tooke ye blame and shame uppon himselfe did humblie request forgiveness of ye s^d Governor and that ye Courte and towne would interceed for him." The outcome went unrecorded. But the reckless Applegate was soon involved in another slander action accused of saying that "Seriaunt [Sergeant] Hubbert had but halfe a wife." Fortunately for him he asked the woman's forgiveness, and it was granted.[12]

And what of religion in Gravesend and other towns on Long Island? Dutch Reformed minister Samuel Drisius reported there were Mennonists at Gravesend, Presbyterians at Flushing and a variety of worshippers in the other English towns of Middleburg and Heemstede. Flushing had a preacher but when the Presbyterians stayed away from church and refused to pay him he fled to Virginia. When William Wickendon, "a cobbler" (a term of contempt) from Providence, Rhode Island, preached at Flushing and baptized his converts in the river, he was banished from the Province. No religious disturbance was reported at Gravesend.[13]

Relationships between natives and newcomers in Gravesend appeared good. A deed of 1650 records the purchase of more land known as Masseebackhun from the Canarsie Indians: It cost the town:

> 2 gunnes, 15 els of Cloath, 3 fatham of wampum, one kittle, twoe hatchetts, two howes, three knives, one longe cloath coate, one pair of sissers, two combes, one sword, thirtie Alle blades all readie paied and delivered unto us by the Governor Peeter Stivesant.[14]

But in 1651 Gravesend was again attacked by Indians. Their neighbors in Heemstede complained to the West India Company that the uncontrolled public sale of powder and lead to the Indians was making life intolerable:

> it is probable that those Indians will, in a short time, be the destruction both of the Dutch and English, as such practice renders them powerful and merciless; so that unless a supernatural power keep them under, neither nation will be able to resist them...they have killed our cattle, carried them off to their own plantations to feast on them...driven our surviving cattle through our standing corn....'Tis a matter of small moment in their eyes to kill a good ox merely for the horns to carry

powder in; sometimes they slay a man, sometimes a woman; plunder the houses; purloin our guns; pry into our affairs; endeavor to drown the people; strip the children in the fields and woods; prowl abroad with masks or visors, slaughter our hogs, and when we demand satisfaction, challenge us to fight, boasting of their great number of men and guns.

On 14 September 1651 the Gravesend magistrates sent a letter written by Lady Deborah's right hand man, George Baxter, to the Directors of the West India Company Chamber at Amsterdam. They asked for help to prevent the pillaging of Gravesend and protested that the company's policy of importing muskets, powder and lead to be sold to the Indians had resulted in their becoming "obstinate and daring enemies, highly dangerous to our lives and properties, and difficult to tolerate." Unless the situation was remedied, the letter said, the whole Province faced ruin. The closing paragraph was prophetic:

Gentlemen. 'Tis not with us as in our Fatherland, or as in Kingdoms and Republics which are established and settled by long and well experienced laws and fundamentals, best agreeing with the condition of the people. But in our little body, made up of divers members, namely folks of different nations, many things occur in the laying of a foundation for which there are no rules nor examples, and, therefore, must be fixed at the discretion of a well experienced Governor; for we are as a young tree or little sprout now, for the first time, shooting forth to the world, which, if watered and nursed by your Honors' liberality and attention, may, hereafter, grow up a blooming Republic.

(Signed)	Geo. Baxter,	Richard Gibbons, Schout
	Wil. Wilkins,	James Hubbard,
	Nicholas Stilwil,	Will. Browne, Assistants
	John Tilton, Clerk or Secretary	

[a schout in the Dutch colonies was a bailiff or municipal officer][15]

George Baxter could not have imagined the eventual size and influence of the City and State of New York or of the United States of America. But he solicited support for Lady Deborah's vision of democratic government and freedom for all. Gravesend's First Lady was nursing such young and tender plants as "respect for the individual" and "religious toleration." Her green fingers tilled the soil, watered the seed, tended the "little sprout" and protected it from the frosty intolerance which blighted so many other plants and transplants. It was one of the first seeds, rooted in the soil of a freedom of conscience charter, to germinate in what is now the State of New York. Lady Deborah watched over the delicate shoot, sheltered the young sapling and cultivated a fragile democracy that was spreading and would eventually blossom into nationhood - the flourishing republic of the United States of America!

"THE WATER IS UP TO OUR LIPS"

In 1652 war broke out between the English and the Dutch. English people in Gravesend immediately became suspect and the authorities in Nieuw Amsterdam required all letters addressed to them to be opened and examined before delivery. Gravesend had always given written assurances of loyalty. Baxter and his fellow magistrates had signed a document every year since 1649 showing Gravesend's support for Stuyvesant, even when the Council of Nine opposed him. The English townspeople wished to avoid losing their freedom if the Governor was recalled and did their best to prevent it. Stuyvesant had sent their signed documents to Holland by Cornelius Van Tienhoven, his Dutch secretary so that the company was in no doubt of Gravesend's fealty.

But when war started support for Gravesend evaporated. In a naval battle in the Dover Roads the Dutch sailor Van Tromp defeated the English Admiral Robert Blake and after a series of bloody fights Blake obtained a decisive victory in July 1653 off Cape LaHogue. Now there was more reason for Dutch suspicion of the English on Long Island. English allegiance in the colony was eroded not solely by the outcome of the war but by Stuyvesant's arbitrary edicts and his increase of taxes. Settlers were irritated by an autocrat who "used torture to extract confessions and mismanaged almost everything, especially Indian relations."[1]

On 11 December 1653 representatives from the Long Island towns of Gravesend, Brooklyn, Flushing, Newtown, Hempstead, Flatlands and Flatbush expressed their discontent in a multi-signature remonstrance against the Governor titled: "Apprehension of the establishment of an Arbitrary Government among us." They feared that a new Indian war would break out and leave them exposed with no government plan to protect their lives and property. George Baxter, an ensign (commissioned infantry officer and standard-bearer) who is thought to have drafted the remonstrance, and James Hubbard, a sergeant in the British service, signed on behalf of Gravesend. They could not countenance the Governor's tyranny. Stuyvesant blamed Baxter, his outspoken, one-time secretary for the document and nursed his suspicions of Gravesend.

On December 13 the deputies signed a further protest and said that if they could not obtain redress from the Governor they would appeal to their superiors in the Netherlands. This irked Stuyvesant who ordered them to disperse. On behalf of the English residents the magistrates of Gravesend wrote 27 December 1953 to the "Honorable, right good Lords and Patroons" of the West India Company at Amsterdam to assure them of their allegiance. It was a moderate document:

> ...we hope and trust that your Honors and all honorable people will keep us free from all aspersion that may be flung at us, of our intending to revolt from that due obedience which we owe your Honors, as our Patroons, from whatever quarter it may proceed. [Whatever] ill treatment we have received, we shall do no injury nor wrong, although, perhaps, they think so. Our town or place, one of the oldest planted on Long Island...hath been loyal to you on all occasions, and...hath ever been good friends of our present Governor, as he himself hath frequently acknowledged...
>
> Therefore, do we now,...make our application or address to your Honors,...who, we not only hope but doubt not, will afford us such proper satisfaction as God shall direct you according to right equity and our due liberty, &c.
>
> Obedient and loyal, in all becoming respects, your Honor's servants and farmers of Gravesend.

(Signed)   Georg Baxter,   N. Hubbart,
              William Wilkings,   John Moris, Schout.[2]

The next year the inhabitants of Gravesend again elected Baxter and Hubbard as magistrates confirming their decision in a letter to the Governor, signed by the clerk, John Tilton, Wednesday March 25, 1654. Stuyvesant considered these men traitors and refused to confirm the appointment, even though they were original patentees of Gravesend, had previously been elected to office and enjoyed the confidence of the inhabitants. The Governor was angry that his predecessor had granted a charter giving Gravesend power to elect their own magistrates and to be independent regarding religious belief. He sent a letter to the magistrates saying they must provide their patent or an authenticated copy of it to prove their right to elect their own magistrates.

The Gravesenders were annoyed that their democratic election process was unacceptable. They held that every householder had the right and duty to vote and a majority vote carried. They continued to do municipal business as usual. One o'clock meetings were called by the noon drum on the last Saturday of each month at James Hubbard's house.[3]

Stuyvesant and his Council became more uncertain of English support and passed a resolution:

> As to the English villages, it has been sufficiently proved by their utterances and actions that, although under oath of allegiance to us, they would fight against rather than for us, and therefore the Director-General and Council have unanimously concluded to pass them in silence and not to call upon them either for the repairs or for the defense, that we may not ourselves drag the Trojan horse within our walls.[4]

Then it came to the ears of Council members in Nieuw Amsterdam that about fifty Englishmen in Gravesend had held secret meetings in June with the intention of capturing the ship *Coninck Salomon*, which was loaded with goods and official papers, and sailing her to Virginia. Council officers also heard that Gravesend magistrates were spreading rumors that the Dutch were hiring Frenchmen and savages to plunder English towns and kill English residents. So the magistrates of Gravesend and Middleburgh were called to Nieuw Amsterdam. But because of pressure from Holland the authorities decided not to press charges and decided to "communicate the matter to them as a current rumor."

Baxter and Hubbard whose election as Gravesend's magistrates was not approved by the Governor were imprisoned and then banished to New England. There they told representatives of the East India Company of the Dutch Governor's arbitrary rule and expressed their fears that he was inciting the Indians to another war. They discussed the possibility of joining forces to oust "Wooden Leg," as Stuyvesant was nicknamed, and overthrow the Dutch.[5]

Back in Gravesend residents made repeated complaints that no order was kept in the town and fences and palisades were neglected because the Governor and Council had removed from office their former magistrates George Baxter and Sergeant

Hubbard.   Stuyvesant finally sent a letter to Lady Moody at
Gravesend regarding the need to define boundaries :

> My Lady.
>
> Agreeably to your Ladyship's request and our promise we
> have commissioned Messrs. *Nicasius de Sille, Jan de la Montagne*,
> members of our High Council and *Paulus Leendertsen van der Grift*
> and *Olaff Stevensen Coortlandt*, Schepens of this City, to settle the
> boundaries between the lands of the village of *Gravesend*, of
> *Anthony Jansen* on *Coney Island* and the land formerly owned by
> *Robert Penoyer*, according to the letters-patent and deeds.   Our
> aforesaid commissioners will, if it so pleases God, report to-
> morrow morning and these lines are to request and admonish
> your Ladyship to send some persons there, who may take care of
> your Ladyship's rights.   ´
>
> Recommending your Ladyship with cordial greetings to
> God's protection, we remain, my Lady,
>
> New Amsterdam,   Your Ladyship's
> Septbr 3, 1654.   affectionate friend
> To My Lady *Deborah Moody*   P. STUYVESANT.
> at *Gravesend*.[6]

Stuyvesant obviously admired Lady Deborah, trusted her and
recognized that he needed her help.

The Governor, knew that the Gravesend populace was enraged
and ready to give him a rough ride, but believed he could
manipulate them to his advantage.   In November Stuyvesant
decided to visit Gravesend and invited the members of the Council
to accompany him, arranging to assemble one morning at Breuklyn
after they had ferried across the East River.

(See Appendix III for a segment of H.L.Bartlett's sketch (made 1875)
of the Honorable Director-General's visit to Lady Moody in "the
English town."   While he claimed it was compiled from "authentic
records, family traditions and ancient legends" he admitted also
calling upon "the Weird Sisters to assist him in spinning history
from the web of fancy.")

Historical records confirm that Stuyvesant held a meeting "at the
house of Milady Moedy, 23 November 1654." taking with him two
Council members, The Honorable Mr. Nicasius de Sille and Mr Jan
LaMontagne and was forced to enlist the services of Lady Deborah
to negotiate with the citizenry.   During the visit Stuyvesant
permitted Lady Deborah's nomination of magistrates to stand and
such was her popularity that the people accepted her guidance and
mediation.   The whole community came to the meeting to decide

whether to nominate new magistrates or retain the present incumbents, viz William Willckens, Commissary; Jan Mourits, Schout; and John Tilton, Secretary. The group unanimously answered that they were satisfied with the current officers until time for a new election. The Governor accepted their decision, admonished them "to fear God, honor their magistrates and obey both" and hoping that sedition had been quelled returned to his fort.[7]

News of this remarkable accomplishment reached New England. John Winthrop wrote of her in his *Journal*: "She acquired influence in the parts to which she emigrated and rendered help to Peter Stuyvesant."[8]

At this time Gravesend settlers were having trouble with the Indians and the government offered no assistance. Guttaquoha, a friendly native, declared to be the owner of Coney Island, (called Narriockh) formally put his mark on a deed dated 7 May 1654 conveying the island to the people of Gravesend. It cost "fifteene fathom of sewan [sea shells used for money], two gunns and three pounds of powder." (Value: about $15)[9]

Other tribes were not so amicable. "Sixty-seven white settlers in Staten Island were killed when the Indians crossed Gravesend Bay headed for Gravesend." Lady Deborah's house was besieged and the settlers were unable to beat them off. But they held their ground until soldiers from Nieuw Amsterdam relieved them. The position was becoming very serious.[10]

A Gravesend inhabitant wrote to the Dutch Director-General :

> we hear strange reports from Heemsted, Newtown and elsewhere, that the Indians intend to pitch out the Dutch from among the English in order to destroy them....The water is already up to our lips, and if we once leave here Long Island is no longer inhabitable by Dutch people.[11]

A CAT IN THE YARN

During the winter of 1655 Dominie Johannes Polhemus from Brazil preached on Sundays in Gravesend and the surrounding towns, administering the sacraments "to the satisfaction of all."

But the population became increasing discontent with the Dutch West India Company. Settlers believed that the Company was striving "through motives of selfishness, to scrape all the fat into one or two pots." The Dutch on the other hand considered the English were quick to use them "as a cloak in time of need, but again when this is past, they regard them not and make fools of them."[1]

In January George Baxter came back from New England, crossed the frozen East River at White Stone and returned to his home in Lady Deborah's town. He spread a report that Oliver Cromwell, the English Protector, had ordered the governors of the New England colonies to take the whole of Long Island from the Dutch by force if necessary. Within a couple of months a group of Englishmen, eager to throw off Dutch shackles, pulled down the Dutch colors in Gravesend and ran up the English flag in its place. Baxter and Hubbard wrote a defiant letter on behalf of the aggrieved English inhabitants :

> We, individuals of the English nation here present, do for divers reasons and motives, as free born British subjects, claim and assume unto ourselves the laws of our nation and Republic of England over this place, as to our persons and property, in love and harmony, according to the general peace preserve the

Republic of England and his Highness, the Lord Protector, and the continuance of peace between the two countries. Amen.

> Publicly proclaimed in this village now named Gravesend, situate on the west of Long Island this 9th March 1655. And this being published 3 times it was openly₂ proclaimed whereof all and every may take notice.
>
> The rebellious dispatch was written in the presence of two commissioners, Fiscal Tienhoven and Burgomaster Allard Anthony who had arrived at Gravesend from Nieuw Amsterdam just as Baxter, Hubbard and Grover were hoisting the English flag. Baxter and Hubbard were arrested and kept in "close and stringent confinement."

The Director General reacted with great anger. He accused Baxter and Hubbard of choosing "to throw a cat into the yarn." proposing "a union with some malignant opponents", suggesting a new form of Government and "at this precarious time" intending to "join in a plot with a nation, which they and everybody else suspect and which only a short time ago they called untrustworthy." The mutinous action confirmed Stuyvesant in his strong objection to the magistrates being chosen by the people. If free elections were permitted, he said, "then everyone would want for Magistrate a man of his own stamp, for instance a thief would chose for Magistrate a thief and a dishonest man, a drunkard, a smuggler" and added "we derive our authority from God and the Company, not from a few ignorant subjects."

Stuyvesant sent a copy of the treasonous letter to the States-General in Holland along with his report:

> ...on the 9th of March 1655 when the difficulties between England and Netherland had long been adjusted,...some seditious Englishmen, among whom were George Baxter and James Hubbard, inhabitants of this State and under the Company, did in the town of Gravesend on Long Island publicly and before all the world, declare themselves subjects of the Government or Republic of England to that end setting up its arms there....
>
> Notwithstanding these mutinous subjects knew for a certainty that the State or Government of England had not a shadow of a claim in the world to this village of Gravesend which was lying, with Heemstede, Amersfort, Breuckelen, Flushing and some others, on Long Island, as can be clearly enough seen by the supplicatory and humble letters which the aforesaid English and Magistrates of the villages aforesaid and particularly Gravesand and Heemsted, have from time to time addressed to the Directors

of the West Indies Company, Chamber at Amsterdam, as their Lords and Patrons.

The English do not only enjoy the right of nominating their own Magistrates, but some of them also usurp the election and appointment of such Magistrates as they please without regard to their religion. Some, especially the people of *Gravesend*, elect libertines and Anabaptists, which is decidedly against the laws of the *Netherlands*.[3]

But the selection of magistrates by the inhabitants was in harmony with the Gravesend charter. Their High-Mightinesses, the Lords Directors in Holland "the absolute masters and owners of this Province", conveniently chose to forget Kieft's charter when they rounded on the Gravesend remonstrants:

> they pretend and usurp...the right of appointing their own Sheriffs, Secretaries, Clerks and Delegates.

Concerning the mutiny the Dutch overlords wrote to Stuyvesant:

> You can well believe that the treacherous action of George Baxter and his accomplices has startled us very much; the papers and documents sent over have been translated and we are busy examining them to form an opinion, but we are expecting the remaining papers which you promised to send by the *Groote Christoffel*; upon receipt of them we shall inform you of our opinion and wishes in this matter. Meanwhile you are strictly charged to keep the aforesaid men in close and stringent confinement, as it is required in so important a case; we further recommend that henceforth you dispense in the government of the respective places with such foreigners who have no domicile in this country, for little or no confidence can be placed upon them...

This letter did not arrive in the colony until August 13. Meanwhile, Governor Stuyvesant had taken matters into his own hands doubtless with the tactful prompting of Lady Deborah. Englishwoman she was, but she knew which country had granted the Gravesend patent guaranteeing freedom of conscience without interference. She could never forget the harsh treatment she and other Gravesend citizens had received in an English colony, and reminded her people of the liberty they now enjoyed. She gently urged them to maintain their loyalty to the Dutch Council as she was convinced that a return to English rule would mean a reversion to religious servility.[4]

Gravesend's First Lady negotiated both with the inhabitants of her town and with the Governor to prevent their High Mightinesses in

Holland from making any unfavorable decisions. Her skills were valued at Nieuw Amsterdam where a resolution was passed Friday, 18 June 1655:

> *Whereas* for good and various reasons no Magistrates for the present year have as yet been elected in the village of Gravesand on Long Island and whereas at present it has been deemed necessary for the service of the country and the administration of justice that it be done as soon as possible,
>
> *Therefore* it is resolved to write to the Schout of the said village and to the Lady Deborah Moody as the oldest and first patentee, that she and the inhabitants of Gravesand proceed immediately to nominate Magistrates in pursuance of their patent and send the nomination to the Council for the Confirmation and swearing in of the nominated magistrates, after which a committee shall be sent there to restore order.
>
> Done at Amsterdam in N.N.   Date as above.[5]

An election was held in the village on July 8 1655 by twelve persons chosen by the former magistrates. Not all agreed with the outcome. Nine Dutch inhabitants who thought their interests had been ignored wrote a disapproving letter next day to the High Council of New Netherland. Lady Deborah's townspeople were still deeply divided and to combat the danger she spent several days trying to bring about mutual understanding. She diplomatically listened first to one side and then the other and used her gift of reconciliation, softening and synthesizing conflicting viewpoints and "bynding up that which is broken." Then on 19 July she wrote to Director-General Peter Stuyvesant:

> Honoured Sr
>
> We have according to the tenur of our pattent (although thus long deferred:) made choice of William Browne, William Wilkins and Edward Brower (Browse) for our Magistrates and John Morris for Schout all which have formerlie borne office amongst us and hope will prove faithful and peaceable indeavoring to bynde up that which is Broken amongst us whome wee present unto your Honour with desire of their Confermation and Establishment and Remaine yours the inhabitants Gravesand in our Loyalltie and fidelitie.
>
> subscribed: Deborah Moody
John   Tilton,   Clerk   in
behalf of the Rest[6]

John Bowne, the Schout, and two other inhabitants carried the letter to Nieuw Amsterdam. Bowne promised the Council that henceforth they would not act in the election of Magistrates otherwise than in pursuance of the patent and by a majority vote of all the inhabitants of Gravesend. Stuyvesant accepted the nominations and with them the English closed-corporation municipal system.

Once again Lady Deborah had saved the day. She appears to have been the first woman in North America to vote as a householder and to exercise influence with the Governor in a state-sanctioned election. It was an unusual accomplishment and a tribute to her gifts, for women had no such powers in England or its colonies. Mrs Margaret Brent of Virginia who had sought the right to vote in the assembly in 1647 had been evicted. Women's rights were curtailed as an English writer explained : "All of them are understood either married or to be married and their desires are subject to their husband."[7]

Lady Deborah's vote in a town election took place over two centuries before Susan Anthony (the first woman who registered to vote in 1872), and more than a century before the widow of Joseph Taft of Uxbridge, Massachusetts voted her approval of levying a town tax - long before the suffragette movement.

Lady Moody's house, Gravesend

THE QUAKERS COME

Governor Stuyvesant and the burgomasters in Nieuw Amsterdam had always ruled with a rod of iron. Now they began to turn the screw on religious practice by stiffening previously-enacted ordinances. The company directors liberal policies towards those who held other than the approved Reformed doctrine was reversed. Dominie Megapolensis and his fellow clergy had support from the Classis of Amsterdam in 1656 for their policy: "Let us then - we here in this country and you there - employ all diligence to frustrate all such plans, that the wolves may be warded off from the tender lambs of Christ." Megapolensis became vigilant for the repression of dissenters.[1]

Fines for Sabbath-breaking were enforced in 1656. The Governor decreed that "on the Lord's day, by us called Sunday" there was to be no work and he specified: no plowing, sowing, mowing, building, woodcutting, hunting, fishing or working in iron or tin. Also banned were games, card playing, backgammon, tennis, ball playing, bowling, rolling nine pins, racing with boats or wagons. Taverns were to be closed and if colonists infringed the law before, after or between services the penalty was doubled.[2]

The laws applied to all, although the ministers, Johannes Megapolensis and Samuel Drisius, were well aware of the religious differences among the colonists whom they described as: "Papists, Mennonites and Lutherans" and "many Puritans or Independents and many Atheists, and various other servants of Baal among the English under this Government, who conceal themselves under the name of Christians." The ministers had told the authorities in

Holland that "it would create a still greater confusion if the obstinate and immovable Jews came to settle here."[3]

When twenty-three penniless Jews, refugees from Brazil, arrived at the Dutch colony, Stuyvesant offered no welcome and called them a "deceitful race,...blasphemers of the name of Christ." He attempted to ban Jews from New Netherlands but his Directors in Holland told him that to fulfil his wishes would be unreasonable and unfair "because of the large amount of capital which they [Jews] still have invested in the shares of this company." And they generously added: "the conscience of men ought to be free and unshackled." So the Directors recommended that Jews be segregated in their own community and permitted to worship in private but not allowed to build a synagogue. As a result they enjoyed more freedom in Nieuw Amsterdam than in any other North American colony.[4]

On occasions respect was shown for the Jewish faith. When licenses were issued to Assa Levi and Moses Licena as sworn butchers they were permitted to take "the oath of the Jews" and make the reservation that they should not be bound to kill any hogs. On 3 June 1658 the Court of Burgomasters in Nieuw Amsterdam, apparently on its own initiative, declined to permit judgment in civil actions against Jacob Barginson, a Jew, holding that "although defendant is absent, yet no default is entered against him, as he was summoned on his Sabbath." This instance of religious toleration and just dealing foreshadowed a New York statute which two centuries later made it a misdemeanor maliciously to serve any one with process of law on his Sabbath or with process returnable on that day.[5]

Official reaction to other religious groups was mixed. Stuyvesant denied the Lutheran request for a Pastor from Holland, imprisoned several Lutherans in 1656 and two years later banished a Lutheran clergyman.[6]

Lady Deborah's town was still independent. "At Gravesend there never has been a minister" reported Johannes Megapolensis and Samuel Drisius on 5 August 1657: "it is therefore to be feared that errorists and fanatics may find opportunity to gain strength." The tolerance offered by Lady Deborah and the civic leaders of Gravesend had become widely known much to the annoyance of the ministers in Nieuw Amsterdam who complained they were Mennonites and anabaptists in sentiment and practice. Their ministerial report to the Classis of Amsterdam said of the Gravesend townspeople: "they, for the most part, reject infant baptism, the Sabbath, the office of preacher, and the teachers of

God's word; saying that through these have come all sorts of contention into the world. Whenever they meet together, the one or the other reads something for them."[7]

So officials knew that religious meetings were held in Gravesend though they had no church and no minister. Their lack of confidence in religious teachers suggests the presence of Seekers who believed that no true Church had existed since the spirit of Antichrist became uppermost in the Church, and that God would in His own time ordain apostles or prophets to found a new Church. Lady Deborah had evident sympathy with or belonged to this group who questioned the need for ministers as interceding priests.[8]

One Seeker who called for "more praying, and less preaching" considered that "much preaching breeds faction". She suggested that controversial subjects should be written in Latin, that disputations should be confined to schools, and "that every clergyman should be kind and loving to his parishioners, not proud and quarrelsome."[9]

"More praying and less preaching" was the accepted religious style for anabaptists like Lady Deborah. It was a trend which gave rise to Ranters, Quakers, and Muggletonians and is said to have contributed to the rapid peopling of North America by the English. Attracted by the town's tolerant religious policy Gravesend became home for all - pioneers, rebels, cranks, martyrs, saints and heroes.

The people of Gravesend and other Long Island towns were stunned by the severe strictures against Richard Smith of Southampton, Long Island. After a visit to England in 1654 where he was influenced by William Dewsbury he returned a convinced Quaker - the first in the American colonies. Smith was peremptorily given a week to leave and called "an emissary of Sathan, a Quaker."[10]

Ghastly Quaker stories emanated from Boston. Two women had arrived by ship via Barbados on the first of July 1656, Anne Austin of London, a mother of five children "stricken in years" and Mary Fisher, aged twenty-two, a former servant who had suffered two imprisonments at York and a public flogging at Cambridge. The women's boxes were searched and a hundred of their books seized and burned. They were taken ashore, put in a dark prison and nobody was allowed to speak to them. The deputy governor whose own sister-in-law had been burned as a witch a few months previously gave the order to strip and examine them for marks of witchcraft. After five weeks the master of the ship who had brought them was compelled to take them back to Barbados. Two days after they left nine more Quakers came - four men and four women from England and a man from Long Island. Their boxes were searched for "erroneous and hellish pamphlets" and after eleven weeks they were sent back.

Massachusetts enacted legislation against Quakers in 1656 and two years later the first Quakers were hung for violating the law. Men and women were flogged, fined and imprisoned under the Cart and Whip Act (one man was flogged nine times for allowing a meeting to be held in his house).[11]

But in Gravesend there was still freedom of conscience. The magistrates Thomas Spicer and William Bowne elected on 20 March 1657 at a general assembly were charged with keeping the peace of Gravesend and dispensing justice "according to evidenc and ye light of your conscienc without parciallity favor or afecttion hatred or malles."[12]

Then in August 1657, the first Quakers came to the Dutch colony aboard the *Woodhouse*. The ship flew no flag, fired no salute and when Captain Fowler came ashore at Nieuw Amsterdam he stood in front of the Director-General "with his hat firm on his head as if a goat(!)" He refused to offer the usual greeting - for to say "Good morning" or "Good evening" would have implied that God also gave bad days which Quakers did not accept.[13]

On this occasion Stuyvesant reacted moderately. Some of the party went on to Rhode Island, but Robert Hodgson, Richard Doudney, Sarah Gibbons, Mary Weatherhead and Dorothy Waugh stayed in New Netherland. As soon as the ship left Mary Weatherhead and Dorothy Waugh started to preach, went into a frenzy, and wailed in the middle of the street that people should repent for the day of judgment was at hand. Townspeople did not know what to make of this and ran around, one calling "fire" and another something else. Then an officer seized both young women by the head and led them to prison.[14]

After eight days in a "noisome filthy dungeon" they were released and sent with their hands tied behind their backs to join their companions at that "sewer of heretics," Rhode Island. "The devil is the same everywhere" wrote the Dutch clergy in their report on the Quakers and expressed the hope that "our God will baffle the designs of the devil and preserve us in the truth." The authorities rigidly refused to permit public worship of God except in a Dutch Reformed Church, allowing freedom of religion only as long as worshippers kept their opinions within their own houses. When colonists held meetings in the open and tried to make converts to other than Dutch Reformed Church beliefs, they were fiercely opposed and frequently imprisoned or punished as were those who gave them food and lodging.[15]

In September-October the other three Quakers, Hodgson, Doudney and Gibbons visited Gravesend, Jamaica and Hempstead and found many anabaptists of the Mennonite type. Lady Deborah invited Hodgson and his associates for a meeting in her house. Some have supposed that Lady Deborah herself became a Quaker while others think they may have misinterpreted her toleration towards them:

> The first Quaker meeting in America was held at her [Lady Deborah Moody's] house in 1657 by Richard [Robert?] Hodgson and two associates, ones of that party of eleven propagandists who had then crossed the ocean. From their welcome here, Gravesend was called the 'Mecca of Quakerism.'[16]

A contemporary Quaker historian wrote of Lady Deborah:

> And there was a Noble Lady the Countess of Mordee; who was a Puritan turn'd Quaker, and resided chiefly at this place, gave the remaining people of this Society the liberty of Meeting in her house; but managed it with that prudence and observance of time and place, as gave no offence to any stranger or person of another Religion than her own and so she and her people remained free from all Molestation and Disturbance.[17]

After this the new Quaker arrivals chose to disregard local laws. In the village of Hempstead, inhabited mostly by English Brownists (Puritan separatists, inclining to congregationalism), Robert Hodgson was "at such a pitch of boldness" that he induced some of his own sect to meet on a certain "first day" in an open garden. His enemies finding him with a Bible in his hand and a dagger in his cloak, violently seized and confined him. The officer apprehended his prisoner but left him in order to attend the morning service. When he returned he found Hodgson preaching out of the window to a group of people. He moved him to the magistrate's house and his congregation followed "to hear truth." The officer despatched a messenger to Governor Stuyvesant in Nieuw Amsterdam who sent a sheriff, a jailor and 12 musketeers to bring back the harmless captive.

Meanwhile search was made for the people who had entertained Hodgson. Two women were arrested one of whom had two small children including a babe at the breast. They were put in a cart to the tail of which Hodgson was tethered with his hands tied behind his back. He was forced to walk by night through rough terrain for some twenty miles to the Brooklyn ferry before crossing the East River to Nieuw Amsterdam.

Stuyvesant freed the women but taking Hodgson for a disturber of the peace, threw him into a dark, filthy place. He charged him with sedition and "in order to suppress the evil in the beginning" pronounced sentence in Dutch (which somebody translated for Hodgson): Pay a fine of 600 florins, be clothed in sackcloth, be chained and tied to a "Barbarous slave" and work for two years on the city walls.

Hodgson declined to pay the fine, as Quakers always did. He was chained to a wheelbarrow and ordered to work. Believing himself innocent of any legal violation Hodgson refused to work and a black slave laid on him fifty lashes with a cat-o'-nine-tails, a tarred rope about four inches thick. At the end of the treatment Hodgson was still standing up so the punishment was repeated, the slave redoubling his blows until the innocent victim fell to the ground. Then the Governor ordered the prisoner stripped to the waist and hung up by the hands with a log of wood tied to his feet. He was beaten severely with whips and left in a prison "too bad for swine." Disabled and unconscious, the poor man was almost dead. There was little hope he would recover but an unnamed English woman, moved with grief and pity bathed his wounds, gave him medicines and restored him to life again. Her husband offered the officer-in-charge one of his fat oxen if he would release the man. Others proposed to pay the fine. But Hodgson declined to accept considering himself blameless.

At last Madam Anna Bayard, the Governor's sister, of Huguenot stock and with a fair share of the imperious temper which characterized her brother, persistently pleaded his cause with "hard-headed Peter." With imposing presence this "woman of very enlightened views" implored him to release the poor man and she was so determined that Stuyvesant eventually gave in and Hodgson was sent to Rhode Island.[18]

Apart from his sister, none could dilute the Governor's wrath. The Directors in Holland tried to moderate Stuyvesant's actions reminding him that his Province would benefit if he practiced restraint. They told him he should shut his eyes and "not force people's consciences but allow everyone to have his own belief, as long as he behaves quietly and legally, and gives no offence to his neighbors and does not oppose the government."[19]

The tyrannical Governor ignored the counsel. And the haughty ministers, Johannes Megapolensis and Samuel Drisius, supported

Stuyvesant. Dominie Megapolensis wrote that "the scum of all New England is drifting into Nieuw Nederlandt." The ministers insisted, in the fall of 1657, that Stuyvesant issue a proclamation subjecting any ship bringing Quakers to New Netherland to seizure. Any colonist receiving Quakers into his home or attending a Quaker meeting was to be fined fifty Flemish pounds with half the sum going to the informer.[20]

And so persecution continued. But Quakerism spread. Long Island's travelling preacher, Samuel Bownes, spent almost a year in a Jamaica jail. And Gravesend's John Tilton was arrested on the tenth of January 1658 for providing lodging for a Quaker woman, the fine for which was £50. After reporting that she came to his house with other neighbors while he was away he was sentenced to payment of £12 and costs for harboring some of "the abominable sect of Quakers."[21]

Meanwhile Gravesend's neighbors in Flushing protested against the Governor's persecution of Quakers. Urged on by Sheriff Tobias Feake, the Town Clerk, Edward Hart, drew up a statement signed by thirty-one townspeople. The Flushing Remonstrance, as it came to be known, written on 27 December 1657, moderately and fairly stated the expectations of religious toleration which they believed ought to be allowed by reasonable people. They desired "not to judge lest wee be judged, neither to Condem least wee bee Condemed, but rather let everyman stand and fall to his own...our desire is not to offend one of his little ones in whatsoever forme, name or title hee appears in, whether Presbyterian, Independent, Baptist or Quaker; but shall be glad to see anything of God in any of them."[22]

The Council was unmoved and inflexible. It called the document a "seditious, mutinous and detestable letter of defiance." The sheriff and town clerk were both arrested and charged with violation of Stuyvesant's orders. For refusal to admit error and ask for pardon Feake was sentenced to be removed from office and banished from the colony forever. At the last he recanted and got off with a two-hundred guilders fine. Stuyvesant spent the next four years in hunting down Quakers.[23].

And the Quakers kept coming to Long Island. Thornton and Josiah Cole visited Gravesend and found "some friends in the truth, by whom they were much refreshed" who may have included the Tiltons, Townsends, Farringtons, Thornes and Feakes. Some Quakers found refuge with Nathaniel Sylvester on Shelter Island. Two other Quakers, John Taylor and Mary Dyer made a tour of the island, terminating their trip with a visit to Gravesend. Both were later hanged in Boston.[24]

Many inhabitants of New Netherlands were suffering "hot fevers, heavy Rheums, Dizziness of the head and many more diseases." The continuing inhuman treatment of her present and former neighbors sapped Lady Deborah's strength. Stuyvesant's cruel despotic punishment of Quakers was a bitter disappointment. By no stretch of the imagination could he now be called her "affectionate friend." True, he had been kind to her. She could practice her religion in her own home. But Stuyvesant was now showing a demonic streak. No ecclesiastical bigot could have worked harder to thwart Lady Deborah's simple desire for religious freedom.[25]

Like an expectant mother she had waited long to hug her new child. But complete religious liberty had been as elusive as a much-wanted child to a barren woman. Wherever Lady Deborah and her friends settled in hope of seeing the arrival of full toleration, all they witnessed was a still birth. In Old England, in New England and New Netherland there had always been some tyrant, some "wicked King Herod" hovering around the midwives circuit to ensure that any longed-for religious-freedom-babe that drew breath was quickly smothered in infancy.

The unjust and unnecessarily harsh treatment of the Quakers must have torn at the heart of Gravesend's First Lady. By her seventy-third year her bruised spirit and weary body could take no more. Lady Deborah Moody died sometime between November 1658 and 11 May 1659.[26]

It is believed that Lady Deborah was buried in the old Gravesend cemetery or an adjoining lot devised by John Tilton for burying his "successors and all friends in ye Everlasting Truthe of ye Gospell." The two-acre lot originally owned by the Town of Gravesend is situated between Gravesend Avenue, Lake Street and the Village. Lady Deborah's grave has never been identified, although a 1917 newspaper refers to it as unmarked except by a broken headstone with undecipherable inscription.[27]

The quintessence of Lady Deborah Moody lives on in those under persecution and tyranny who have courage to dissent. It persists in those who search patiently for relief from autocracy on their road to freedom. The spirit of New York's first Lady Liberty survives in those who recognize the fragility of our democratic and religious liberty heritage, and employ their energies to preserve and extend it.

The achievements of Lady Deborah Moody shine against the back-drop of history. After being denied freedom of conscience in Massachusetts she established in Gravesend a community where religious and civil liberties were respected 46 years before the British Parliament passed the Bill of Rights (1689), and 146 years before the Bill of Rights passed as amendments to the Constitution of the United States (by 1789).

Gravesend's matriarch appears to have been the first woman colonist to participate in an election in North America and the first woman to establish an operational self-governing township with freedom of conscience for all inhabitants. The first Lady Liberty was the only woman granted a colonial enterprise in which the people's right to freedom of conscience was secured by a charter.[28]

The Grand Dame of Gravesend lived in the town she created till the day of her death, and gave her settlement "the benign influence of a refined and accomplished woman of more than ordinary power of mind."[29]

Five years after her decease the English, under Colonel Richard Nicolls, conquered Nieuw Amsterdam and changed its name to New York. Lady Deborah's English town along with five Dutch settlements: Flatlands; t'Vlade Bos (Flatbush, the wooded plain); Boswijk (Bushwick, the town of woods); Nieuw Utrecht and Breukelen (both named after Dutch towns) later became the City of Brooklyn (King's County).

In 1898 Brooklyn and King's County were united in the Greater City of New York. Residents of the City and State may be proud of Gravesend with its motto: IN LIBERTATEM CONSCIENTIAE CREDIMUS (We believe in liberty of conscience).

United States citizens can justly honor their early civil and religious freedom champion from England - the "dangerous woman" from Massachusetts - New York's First Lady Liberty - Lady Deborah Moody.

> Long may our land be bright
> With freedom's holy light;
> Protect us by Thy might,
>   Great God, our King.[30]

A Woman of Valor

Deborah Moody haunts me
a figure veiled by time.
A lone widow who sailed the rough Atlantic.

She joined a Puritan church.
Her rebel ideas labeled dangerous,
She feared for her soul.

Excommunicated, but free in conscience,
She sailed with friends
to New Amsterdam.
Persuaded the careful Dutch
to grant her land.
Soon, Indians attacked Gravesend.
She fled, feared, despaired.

Later she could rebuild,
guided friends to try;
dared to light a lamp
against tyranny
in her free colony.

- Lucille Koppelman
(used with permission)

Memorial Plaque

The Curator of Collections, Brooklyn Historical Society preserves a plaque which was first placed in the lobby where the present ticket booth is located. It was later removed. It reads:

LADY DEBORAH MOODY
Leader of First English Colony
which Settled Gravesend 1643

Granted First Patent to the Town December 19,
1645
By Governor Kieft of Nieuw Amsterdam in Recognition
of Her Distinguished Administrative Ability in the
Civic Affairs of the Early Settlers

Erected by New York State Education Department
and
New York Chapter
Daughters of the American Colonists
1939[1]

POSTSCRIPT

SIR HENRY MOODY, 2nd Bart.

Sir Henry Moody sold lots nine and ten "by vertue of his dew & true righte of inherritance from his Dyceased Mother Deborah Modye Pattentee" to Jan Jansen Verryn "for the use of his sonn Abraham." Sir Henry later took Jansen to court for slandering and abusing him. His witness, Annetje Wall, who had been scouring pewter said she heard Jansen call Sir Henry a dog, a rogue and a "skellumme" [*scallywag*]. The Court awarded Sir Henry 10 guilders to be paid as a fine by Jansen.[1]

When Jansen (or Johnson) failed to pay for his purchase of land, house, plate and cattle Sir Henry brought further action against him. He was able to produce a bill of sale amounting to thirteen ankers of brandy. Jansen had no defence. The Court awarded the full amount to be paid within fourteen days and costs. In another action Sir Henry took him to court over a matter of detaining corn, a case which he also won.

Sir Henry raised a foot company to assist the Dutch in defending a fort which for weeks had been "beleaguered by some thousands of Indians, their corn burnt and many slain." It was eighty miles north of Manhattan. When Sir Henry entered the fort in September 1659 he set up the English flag (which the Dutch retained) and this English interference produced a cessation of hostilities by the native Americans.[2]

By 1660 Sir Henry was in Virginia. He was chosen as an ambassador to represent the state in ratifying a treaty with the Dutch authorities. The terms had already been discussed at Jamestown. The pact was for mutual fellowship, commerce and protection against "the savage and barbarous nations, the enemies of both."[3]

Sir Henry made the journey to Nieuw Amsterdam and appeared before the Director and the Council on 21 June 1660. He carried courteous letters from Sir William Berkeley, Governor, and Theodore Bland, Speaker of the Assembly of Virginia, authorizing him to receive their signatures to the proposed treaty and to honor his draft for 4,000 pounds weight of tobacco. Tobacco was at that time an item of currency, one pound of tobacco being equal to three shillings according to a Virginia law. Sir Henry was graciously received, treated with great respect by Governor Stuyvesant and on leaving two members of the Council and two halberdiers escorted him.

He disposed of Lady Deborah's "tract and plantation" at Gravesend to John Bowne, 6 September 1660. Bowne was one of a group which on 12 April 1660 had sent a letter to the Director complaining of the licentious mode of living in Gravesend and asking for a minister.[4]

While in Nieuw Amsterdam Sir Henry stayed with Sergeant Daniel Litschoe, an innkeeper whose popular tavern was situated by the Water-poort (water gate), near the present junction of Wall and Pearl Streets. Before departing for Virginia Sir Henry left his books (doubtless many originally belonged to Lady Deborah) accompanied by a partial inventory with Litschoe, a retired soldier who had been an ensign in the Dutch army. He signed his name "Henry Mody."

Sir Henry did not return. He died at the house of Colonel Morrison in Virginia on an unknown date, and like his mother rests in an unknown grave. Daniel Litschoe also died and in April 1662, his widow, Anna Claas Croezens, asked the court's permission to sell some books "belonging to Sir Herry Moedy, as according to obligation she has a claim on him for a considerable sum." The petition was granted.[5]

But who bought the books? In May 1880, James W. Gerard, delivered a discourse entitled "Lady Deborah Moody" before the New York Historical Society. At that meeting he held up "a book in quarto - Bartas' Six Days' Work of the Lord" - believed to be a translation by the poet Sylvester of "La Semaine" - and said that the book published in 1605 was from the Moody library and "cut down by a ruthless modern binder to its present size." Gerard said the title page was missing but that he found on one page the name: Cornelius Island, 1662. He probably purchased it at the sale held that year. Gerard indicated that other Moody books were doubtless in the city of New York. Where are they now?

And where are Sir Henry's sword and belt? Miller Hageman claimed in an 1890 edition of the Brooklyn Daily Eagle that the sword and belt were in the possession of Judge Stilwell of Gravesend. Do his heirs have them today?[6]

I

PURITANS and NONCONFORMISTS

The words *Puritan* and *Nonconformist* as applied to political and religious parties have changed their meanings through the centuries. *Puritan* was used after 1564, in reference to those members of the established Church of England who desired a further purification of the Church from forms of worship that were superstitious, idolatrous, anti-Scriptural and Roman Catholic. They attempted to carry the Reformation further than established by Queen Elzabeth but repudiated the idea of separation from the Church. As the puritan party nourished the non-episcopal denominations: Presbyterians, Independents and Baptists, the name *Puritan* continued to be utilized in reference to those who left the Church of England and was less used about those who stayed in it. These groups all rejected the Papal doctrine of salvation which centered in the Mass and the priesthood; they attacked church ornaments, vestments, surplices, rochets, organs, the sign of the cross and ecclesiastical courts. The word *Puritan* (as a party name) began to be superseded by *Roundhead* about 1640. It is of course used today in reference to persons considered extremely strict regarding morals and religion.

The term *Protestant* was first used of the reforming members at the Diet of Speyer (1529) who were against the decisions of the Catholic majority. In the seventeenth century the word *Protestant* was sometimes used of members of the Established Church to distinguish them from *Presbyterians* and other dissenters, and in this sense it continued to be known in Ireland after the usage had died out in England. The Independents who broke away from the Established Church were at first called *Brownists* (a section of the *Barrowists*); they and other detached persons were called *Separatists*, the equivalent of *Nonconformist* or *Dissenter* as these words are now used.

Nonconformist at first had a meaning similar to that of *Puritan* - one who, in the main, adhered to the doctrine of the Church of England, but refused to conform to certain points of discipline and ceremonial. Later the word acquired its present-day meaning - one who stands outside the Established Church. Toward the middle of the seventeenth century the word *Dissenter* also came to have this meaning; it was never used of members of the Established Church, and neither it nor *Non-conformist* was used of Roman Catholics.[1]

II

THE MOODY LIBRARY

The books left by Sir Henry as listed in the Notorial Register of Solomon LaChaire, N.P. of Nieuw Amsterdam, Anno 1661 :

"A latyn Byble in folio

"A written book in folio Contining priavet matters of the King. seventeen severall bookx of deviniti matters

"A dictionarius Latin and english

sixteen severall latin and Italian books of divers maters

"A book in folio contining the voage of ferdinand mendoz, &c.

"A book in folio kalleth Sylva Sylvarum

"A book in quarto calleth bartas, six dayes work of the lord, and translat in English by Joseph Sylvester

"A Book in quarto Kalleth the summe and substan of the Conference Which it pleased His Excellent Magst to have with the lords, bishops &c. at Hampton Court contracteth by William barlow

"A book in quarto Kalleth Ecclesiastic Interpretatio, or the Expositions upon the difficult and Doubtful passage of the seven Epistles callet Catholique and the Revalation collecteth by John Mayes

"Elleven several bookx moore of divers substants.

"the verification of his father's Knights ordre given by King James"[2]

III

THE GOVERNOR'S VISIT
from a "Sketch of Long Island"
by H.L.Bartlett,M.D. (1875):

The mansion of the Moodys was a large double stone house with small, deep-set, diamond-shaped windows. and low projecting roof, and was enclosed on three sides with a rustic verandah, overgrown with creeping vines. It stood within the palisades, though a little apart from the rest of the village, near the north eastern corner of the enclosure. Opening into the great hall was a ponderous double door, in the center of the upper half of which were two immense glass 'bull's eyes' for giving light. On either side of the house were hung antlers of elks and deer, stuffed birds and animals killed in the chase, and numerous guns, pistils and swords, and relics procured from the Indians; while in the corner stood a high old-fashioned clock which not only told the time of day, but the day of the month and year, the phases of the moon &.

As you entered on the right was the parlor, or room of state, only used on great occasions like the present, in which blazed huge oaken logs in the wide-mouthed chimney. This room was richly ornamented with heavy English oak furniture, curiously carved, and faded silk hangings, both the relics of other days and other lands; while on the left was the family room, used both as a sitting and dining-room, furnished with stiff, high-backed and easy arm chairs, and an oaken table in the center, standing on a tripod deeply carved in the fashion of a lion's claw, while against the wall stood a dresser filled with rows of pewter dishes and one of Delft china, used on great occasions. Between the windows was a bookcase well-filled with historical and religious books, and on the hearth blazed a glowing fire, shedding warmth and happiness upon all around, and flashing brightly on the dresser and its contents.

Here the Governor, together with the Fiscal, Minister, and Historian, were received by Lady Moody and her son, Sir Henry, with high-bred courtesy and entertained with noble hospitality.

On the tri-legged table was a damask cloth made by Lady Moody herself, while the china plates, adorned with marine views, were the same she had used in old England, as was also the service of silver.

The hospitable board fairly groaned beneath the weight of its profusion of goodly pabulum. Oysters and fishes, prepared in various and alluring styles, captivated the eye, while the mouth watered at the sight of roast duck and goose and turkey, flanked by venison and beef; while a lavish display of foreign wines and stoups of home-brewed ale inspired rosy visions, and arranged in tasteful order on a side-table were dishes of native plums, apples, cherries and other fruits forming the fascinating dessert.

The party gathered on this festive occasion presented a brilliant and animating spectacle, and furnished a picture in glowing colors of the aristocracy of the period.

At the head of the table sat Lady Moody, clad in attire which strikingly contrasted with the general glitter of the assemblage. Her wealth of hair was gathered under a lace cap, a snowy neckerchief encircled her throat and was folded over her breast, while the plain fashion and hue of her robe gave her the appearance of a Lady Abbess. Opposite sat the Governor, with powdered hair and queue, scarlet vest and yellow breeches, fastened at the knee with silver buckles, his wooden leg strapped with silver bands, his sword lying by his side.

On the right of the hostess was seated Nicasius de Sille, Lord Councillor and Fiscal of the Province, clothed in velvet and gold lace; and by his side sat Sir Henry Moody, the scion of a noble house, robed in courtly costume; opposite Sir Henry sat Herr Van Der Donk and Dominie Megapolensis, the former in satin vest and scarlet coat, loosely embracing his rotund figure, powdered hair and queue, the minister in full canonicals.

After the dinner had received ample justice the company returned to the room of state where the hostess cautiously and with womanly tact, adverted to the object of the Governor's visit; and though at first he was disposed to bluster, and roundly swore he would never give in; still the fair Lady brought such persuasive arguments to bear upon the doughty warrior, that he was perforce obliged to do as the good St. Anthony did, as many a lesser saint since has done - capitulate - and finally surrendered unconditionally; and, strange to say, instead of breathing out destruction and death, as he had fully intended, he then and there agreed to mind his own business, and allow Lady Moody herself to nominate the magistrates in future![3]

CHAPTER 1

[1] Silas Wood, *A Sketch of the First Settlement of the Towns On Long Island...*(1824) p.18; Alexander Young, *Chronicles of the First Planters of the Colony of Massachusetts Bay from 1623 to 1636*, (Williamstown, Mass.: Corner House Publishers, 1978) pp.438-42.

[2] A.B.Hart, *Commonwealth History of Massachusetts*, (New York: Russell and Russell, 1966) 1:389; Alonzo Lewis and James Newhall, *History of Lynn*, (Boston: Essex County, Mass., 1865) p.134; Sydney E. Ahlstrom, *A Religious History of the American People*, (New Haven: Yale University Press, 1972) pp.142-3.

[3] *A Tablet for Gentlewomen*, (London, 1574) sigs. F2-F5, cited in Helen C. White, *English Devotional Literature*, University of Wisconsin Studies in Language and literature, No.29 (Madison, 1931).

[4] Philip F Gura, *A Glimpse of Sion's Glory - Radicalism in New England 1620-1660*, (Middletown, Conn.: Wesleyan University Press, 1984) p.108; Richard C. Simmons, "Richard Sadler's Account of the Massachusetts Churches," *The New England Quarterly*, (September 1969) pp.416,417,424; Richard D.Pierce, ed., *The First Church in Salem Records 1629-1736*, (Salem, Mass.: Essex Inst., 1974) p.9; Charles Lloyd Cohen: *God's Caress: The Psychology of Puritan Religious Experience* (New York: Oxford University Press, 1986) pp.137-161.

> Sadler returned to England in 1646, became a reader and preacher at Ludlow and was later rejected at the Restoration. His manuscript is in the National Library of Wales.

[5] John Winthrop, *Winthrop's Journal*, "History of New England" 1630-49 ed. James Hosmer (New York: 1908) 1:297; 2:39,53; Joseph Felt, *The Annals of Salem*, (Salem: W. & S.B.Ives, 1827) p.529.

[6] McLaughlin and Davidson, eds., "Baptist Debate of 1668" pp.101-3.

[7] Alonzo Lewis, *History of Lynn*, (Boston: 1844) 1642: p.118.

> This European interpretation of Scripture had come to England from Zurich, Switzerland, where the city's reformer, Ulrich Zwingli, had said "it would be much better that children should have their...baptism when they reach an appropriate age."

[8]
> Simons, a pacifist, is linked with the movement's repudiation of violence. Although he was not the founder most descendants of the Anabaptists are today called Mennonites.

William Spicer, *Youthful Witnesses*, Review and Herald Publishing Association, 1921. pp. 82,83.

[9] *Winthrop's Journal*, 1:251; 2:123-4.

[10] Joseph Felt, *The Annals of Salem*, p.160.

[11] George Francis Dow, ed., *Records and Files of the Quarterly Courts of Essex County, Mass., 1636-1656*, (Salem, 1911) 1:48; Sidney Perley *History of Salem, Mass. 1638-1670* (Salem, Mass.: 1926) 2:142; Felt, *Annals of Salem*, p.160; Francis Theodore Tilton, *History of the Tilton Family in America*, Vol.1. No.1 p.11.

[12] Felt, *Annals of Salem*, p.160; *Heritage of Freedom*, (Tring, Eng.: A Lion Book, 1984) p.51.

[13] James D. Hart, *The Oxford Companion to American Literature*, (Oxford University Press, 1983) p.839; Frances Diane Robotti, *Chronicles of Old Salem* (Salem, Mass: 1948) p.23.
Winthrop wrote in his Journal under date of June 1643:

> The Ladye Moodye, a wise and anciently religious woman, being taken with the error of denying baptism to infants, was dealt with by many of the elders and others and admonished by the church of Salem (whereof she was a member)... Winthrop, *Journal*, ed. Hosmer, 2:126.

[14] Felt, *Annals of Salem*, p.160.

[15] John Endecott, Salem to John Winthrop, Boston, 22 April 1644, *The Winthrop Papers,* *Massachusetts Historical Society Collections*, Vol. 6, Fourth Series (Boston: 1683) p.146-148.

CHAPTER 2

[1] See I.G.I. and transcript by Charles Langley and Martyn Burwell of "Christenings in the Church of St Giles Cripplegate" for "Aprill 1586" London: Guildhall.

[2] Charles Lethbridge Kingsford, ed., *A Survey of London by John Stowe,* (Reprint of the Text of 1603), (Oxford: Clarendon Press, 1908) 2:80; W.Page, ed. *Victoria History of the County of Middlesex,* (1911) 2:128-132 cited in Valerie Pearl, *London and the Puritan Revolution,* (Oxford University Press. 1961) p.16; Ms.3710 Guildhall.

> The church, which still stands, was dedicated to Giles, a seventh century Greek monk considered patron of cripples and beggars. The fabric escaped the Fire of London but was damaged by bombs in World War II and the decorated font where Deborah was christened was subsequently vandalized.
> The many famous people connected with the Church of St Giles, Cripplegate, make it "forever a place of pilgrimage for the English-speaking race."

[3] The Service of Baptism in the Book of Common Prayer (1549); Francis J.Bremer, *The Puritan Experiment: New England Society from Bradford to Edwards,* (London: St. James Press, 1976) p.17.

[4] Mark Noble, *Memoirs of the Protectoral House of Cromwell,* (Birmingham, Eng.): Pearson and Rollason. 1784) 2:189-203; P.W.Hasler, *The History of Parliament: The House of Commons, 1558-1603.* (London: H.M.Stationery Office, 1981) 2:388,389;

> Wood (*Athenae Oxiensis*, 2:786) says Pilkington's wife's name was Alice of the Knightly family of Kingsmills in Hampshire.

[5] Erasmus Middleton, *Biographia Evangelica,* (London. 1780) 2:112; *Dictionary of National Biography* "Pilkington, James."

> Pilkington's dispute with Dr William Glynn at Cambridge, June 24, 1549 is described by John Foxe in his *Acts and Monuments*. London merchants, Richard Springham, John Abel, and Thomas Eton supported Pilkington.

[6] C.N.Elvin, *Elvin's Handbook of Mottoes,* (London: Heraldry Today, Hollen Street Press, 1971)

> The Pilkington motto: "Pylkington Polledowne" means Pilkington polls(*mows*) downe(*meadow*). His crest bore the picture of a mower and refers to the ancestor of this family who when flying from the battle of Hastings in 1066 changed clothes with a mower in order to escape the Normans.

[7]

> Edmund Grindal, who spent time in Frankfurt with Pilkington, was Bishop of London and later Archbishop of Canterbury. He had similar views, was a competent and efficient churchman, a committed Protestant and a figure of international renown. He dared to express forthright sentiments. When the queen interfered in religious affairs and ordered him to suppress 'prophesyings' (informal gatherings of preachers for study and discussion of the Bible), Grindal refused to obey, offered his resignation and spoke his mind:
>
>> "I am forced, with all humility, and yet plainly, to profess, that I cannot with safe conscience, and without the offence of the majesty of God, give my assent....Bear with me, I beseech you, Madam, if I choose rather to offend your earthly majesty than to offend against the heavenly majesty of God. And although ye are a mighty prince, yet remember that He which dwelleth in Heaven is mightier." - Hans J. Hillerbrand, *The World of the Reformation,* (London: J.M.Dent and Sons Ltd., 1975) p.145.
>
> In requesting the Queen to leave church business to the bishops he went so far as to write: "Remember, Madam, that you are a mortal creature." It was one of the bravest letters in the history of England. - David L.Edwards, *Christian England,* 2:161,2.
>
> Elizabeth was furious, suspended him from his jurisdictional functions in 1577 and kept him in Lambeth Palace under house arrest where he went blind. Broken in spirit and health this brave defender of human rights died in 1583.

[8] David L.Edwards, *Christian England,* (London: Collins, 1983) 2: 160.

[9] Francis J.Bremer, *The Puritan Experiment*, p.26; James Pilkington, *Works*, pp. 361,364.

[10] *Wiltshire Archeological and Natural History Magazine* 60 (December 1913): *The Genealogist* 29:(1913):13; P.W.Hasler, *The History of Parliament: The House of Commons: 1558-1603*, 2:66. *Wiltshire Notes and Queries*, 7 (March 1915) p.215.

[11] William Dunch's will: Shire Hall, County Registry Office, Reading, Berkshire.

[12] Under the 1974 reshaping and renaming of some English counties Little Wittenham was transferred to Oxfordshire.

[13] Wilfrid R. Prest, *The Inns of Court under Elizabeth I and the Early Stuarts: 1590-1640*, (1972) cited in Christopher Hill, *Change and Continuity in Seventeenth Century England*, (London: Weidenfeld and Nicolson, 1974) p.155; Mark Noble, *Memoirs of the Protectoral House of Cromwell*, 2:190,191.

> Gray's Inn is one of four Inns of Court, which enjoy the exclusive privilege of admitting law students to practice as advocates in the courts of England and Wales. Students must pass examinations before they can be *called to the Bar* after which they are entitled to plead for others in a court of law. Barristers remain outside the bar (originally the division in hall between the senior members, called *benchers* and the barristers) until they become King's Counsellors or Queen's Counsellors, when they 'take silk' (*don silk gowns*).

[14] Mark Noble, *Memoirs of the Protectoral House of Cromwell*, pp.190,191; P.W.Hasler, *The History of Parliament: The House of Commons: 1558-1603*, 2:65. Michael Pitts, *Footprints through Avebury*. (Avebury: Michael Pitts, 1989) See: Queen's Signet Office Register: July 1585, Public Record Office.

> In 1988 Ken King paid one million pounds sterling for Avebury Manor, one of the finest examples of an Elizabethan Manor in England. It has since been taken over by the National Trust.

[15] Joseph Stowe, *A Survey of London,*,reprinted from the text of 1603, (Oxford, 1908); Joseph Foster, *Alumni Oxiensis*, (Oxford: Kraus Reprint Ltd. 1968).

> Fox's classic was in more homes than any other book, apart from the Bible. Frightened by St Bartholomew's Day stories of corpses floating down the River Loire, streets running with blood and thousands bravely dying for the Protestant faith, his readers craved the full details, and John Foxe provided them in his book and in his preaching.

[16] Rowland Parker, *Men of Dunwich*, (William Collins and Sons and Co. Ltd. 1978); DNB s.v. "Foxe, John"; *Encyclopaedia Brittannica*, s.v. "John Foxe", "Robert Crowley"; Alan Kreider, "John Foxe" in Tim Dowley, ed.,*The History of Christianity*, (Tring, Herts.: Lion, 1977) p. 19.

> Fox's printer was John Daye, a native of Dunwich who emigrated to London and teamed up with Fox. His epitaph in Little Bradley, Suffolk reveals their joint role:
>
> > Here lies the Daye that darkness could not blynd
> > When popish fogges had overcast the sunne,
> > This Daye the cruell night did leave behynde
> > To view and shew what bloudie Actes weare donne
> > He set a Fox to wright how Martyrs runne
> > By death to lyfe. Fox ventured paynes and health
> > To give them light. Daye spent in print his wealth,
> > But God with gayne retorned his wealth agayne
> > And gave to him as he gave to the poore.....

CHAPTER 3

[1] Paul Johnson, *Elizabeth I*, (London: Weidenfeld and Nicolson, 1988) p.173.

[2] Marchette Chute, *Ben Jonson of Westminster*, (New York Dutton, 1953) p.78.

[3] *State Trials* 1. (1975)p.125 cited in Walter Walsh, *England's Fight with the Papacy* (London: James Nisbet, 1912) pp. 218-228.

[4] P.W.Hasler, *The History of Parliament: The House of Commons 1558-1603*, p.66.

[5] David Howarth, *The Voyage of the Armada*, (London: Collins, 1981) p.17; J.M.D.Meiklejohn, *A New History of England and Great Britain*, (London: Simkin, Marshall, Hamilton, Kent and Co., 1891) p.346.

> A woodcut of the whips found aboard Don Pedro de Valde's ship, which the English alleged the Spaniards meant to use on English men and women, if they had invaded, is illustrated in Maria Perry, *The Word of a Prince*, (Woodbridge, Boydell Press, 1990) p.283.

[6]

> Some believe that ley lines (mysterious currents of magnetic force) pass through this enigmatic site. Attempts have been made to explain the behavior of compasses, electrical and radio equipment near this and other ancient English monuments suggesting the operation of an unidentified force.

[7] A 1620 notation, P.R.O., Trowbridge

[8] G.D.Squibb, ed., *Wiltshire Visitation Pedigrees, 1623*, (London, 1954) p.87,88; Elias Ashmole, Windsor Herald, *Visitation of Berkshire*, 1664-6, (Metcalfe, 1882) pp.28,29; *Wiltshire Notes and Queries*, p.215.

[9]

> The earliest memorial in Little Wittenham Church is to: Walter Dunch Esq., son of William and Mary Dunch, Bencher of Gray's Inn, who died June 4, 1594.

[10] Elias Ashmole, *Visitation of Berkshire 1664-6*, p.28; P.W.Hasler, *The History of Parliament: The House of Commons, 1558-1603*, 2:65.

[11] D.A.Crowley, ed., *Victoria History of the Counties of England: Wiltshire*, (Oxford University Press, William Dawson, 1983) 12:91,92; Cokayne, *The Complete Baronetage*, (Gloucester: Alan Sutton, 1983) 1:197.

[12] P.W.Hasler, *The History of Parliament: The House of Commons, 1558-1603*, 2:66.

[13] B.W.Beckingsale, *Burghley*, (New York: St Martin's Press, 1967) p.194; *The Victoria History of the Counties of England: Wiltshire*, 12:92; Mark Noble, *Memoirs of the Protectoral House of Cromwell*, p.190.

> A brass memorial plate set in a Jacobean stone frame on the north wall of St Peter's Church, Little Wittenham, records the deaths of Deborah Dunch's grandfather and grandmother and depicts them kneeling at a faldstool (a portable stool or desk used in praying), in front of their two sons, Edmund and Walter. The date is blank and two enamelled heraldic shields may still be seen. In closely written cursive script are listed the estates Deborah's grandfather owned in Avebury, Wiltshire; Little Wittenham, Berkshire [the mansion was demolished about 1800]; Wookey Hole, Somerset; and in Hampshire and Oxfordshire. His largest purchase was from William Paulet in 1582 which included the manor of Charney Bassett in Berkshire.

CHAPTER 4

[1] *Oxford Dictionary of English Proverbs*, (Oxford: Clarendon Press, 1970) p.458.

[2]

> The Dunch Manor was on the site of Abingdon Abbey once occupied by Siward, the Bishop of Upsala & co-adjutor-Archbishop of Canterbury c.1048 A.D.

[3] P.W.Hasler, *The History of Parliament: The House of Commons, 1558-1603*, 3:26-7.

[4] Suzanne W. Hull, *Chaste, Silent and Obedient: English Books for Women 1475-1640* (San Marino, Calif.: Huntington Library, 1982); Betty S Travitsky and Adele F. Seeff, *Attending to Women in Early Modern England* (Newark: University of Delaware Press, 1994) pp.36,37.

[5] Marjorie and H.B.Quennell, *A History of Everyday Things in England: 1500-1799*, 2 (London: B.T.Batsford Ltd.1960) :99; Phyllis Woodham Smith, "The Education of Englishwomen in the Seventeenth Century" (unpub. M.A. thesis, University of London, 1921) p.113; Roger Thompson, *Women in Stuart England and America*, (London: Routledge and Kegan Paul, 1974) pp.190,205,213; See: Beatrice Saunders, *The Age of Candlelight*, Centaur Press, London. 1961)

---

[6] James I, King *Works*, (London: 1616) pp.529-31; Richard Lockyer, *The Early Stuarts*, p.127; Elizabeth Longford, *Oxford Book of Royal Anecdotes*, (Oxford University Press, 1989) pp.250,254,256.

[7] James F Larkin and Paul L Hughes, *Stuart Royal Proclamations: James*, (Oxford: Clarendon Press, 1973) pp 87-90.

[8] Antonia Fraser, *King James*, p.105.

[9]
> The family estates are listed in the *Wiltshire Inquisitions Post Mortem returned to Chancery in the reign of Charles I.* 1:151-5. Extent of property is shown on a large map of Garysdon (now known as Garsdon) in the Trowbridge Record Office.

[10] Eileen Spring, *Law, Land and Family* (Chapel Hill and London: University of North Carolina Press, 1993)p.50

[11] City of London Guildhall Library manuscript 8990/1: Joseph Lemuel Chester, ed., *The Parish Register of St Mary Aldermary, London* containing Marriages, Baptisms and Burials from 1558 to 1754. (London: 1880); George Edward Cokayne, *The Complete Baronetage*, p.88. Marriage entry in church records is at the Greater London Public Record Office.

[12] Quennell, *A History of Everyday Things in England*, 2:103,104.

CHAPTER 5

[1] Commission for compounding announcement was on July 17 1603.
See: William. A Shaw, *The Knights of England*, (London: Sherratt and Hughes, 1906) Vol. 1.

[2] The parish registers for Garsdon prior to 1737 perished in a fire at a churchwarden's house. Bishop's transcripts: 1605 onwards, at Public Record Office, Trowbridge, Wiltshire.

[3] "Star Chamber: James", bundle 303, no.6, Public Record Office, London. See: Eric Kerridge,"The Agrarian Development of Wiltshire, 1540-1640" (London Ph.D. thesis, (1951) p.582.

[4] John Richard Green, *History of the English People*, (London: Macmillan and Co. Ltd, 1896) 5:133,134. [No reference given]

[5] F.L.Cross, ed., *Oxford Dictionary of the Christian Church* s.v."Melville, Andrew" (London: OUP, 1958); See: Mark Noble, *Memoirs of the Protectoral House of Cromwell*; T.C.Button, "The Dunch Family," *Berkshire Notes and Queries*, July 1890, ed. George F.Tudor Sherwood, 1:2-6.
> The Dunches were connected to the Buttons, the Bethunes, the Cromwells and Chicheles and through them to the Barringtons, Hampdens, St Johns, Wallers, Whalleys, Goffes, Trevors, Hammonds, Hobarts, Gerrards, Waltons, Pyes, Knightleys, Mashams, Ingoldsbys, Flemings and the Brownes.

[6] Skelton's engraving of Magdalen College from the first quadrangle: Joseph Foster, *Alumni Oxonienses:The Members of the University of Oxford, 1500-1714*, (Oxford: Parker & Co., 1887-92) See opp. p.1075.

[7] Latimer *Works*, 2:222 quoted in Philip Edgcumbe Hughes, *Theology of the English Reformers*, (London: Hodder and Stoughton, 1965) p.239.

[8] Jan Morris, ed., *The Oxford Book of Oxford*, (Oxford University Press, 1984), pp.47-49.
> A small stone cross let into the road in Broad Street marks the site of the execution.

[9] Star Chamber 8/218/5 and Star Chamber 8/184/19 cited in *Victoria History of the Counties of England - Wiltshire*, 5:93.
Antrobus Deed, Museum of the Wiltshire Archaeological and Natural History Society, Devizes.
> On March 1, 1620 Sir Henry was in Malmesbury with Sir George Ivye taking recognisances (obligations or bonds) from alehouse-keepers and butchers.

[10] Thomas Wotton, *The English Baronets*, (London, 1714) I:xviii; John Burke and John Bernard Burke, *A Genealogical and Heraldic History of the Extinct and Dormant Baronetcies of England, Ireland and Scotland*, (London, 1844) p.365.

[11] *The Compact Edition of the Dictionary of National Biography* (O.U.P, 1975) p.277; Ida Gandy, *Round About the Little Steeple: Story of a Wiltshire Parson, 1573-1623*, (Gloucester: Alan Sutton. 1989) p.127; G.D.Squibb, Ed., *Wiltshire Visitation Pedigrees, 1623*, (London: Harleian Society, 1954)

> Sir William Button was knighted in 1605 a few months before Sir Henry and made a baronet a week after Sir Henry in 1622. He was Member of Parliament for Wiltshire County in 1628. A Royalist, Button was twice stripped of his possessions at Tokenham Court: In June 1643 Sir Edmund Hungerford took property worth £767 and in June 1644 a party of horse from Malmesbury garrison took £526. 6s worth of goods. In November 1644 Sir William's estate was confiscated after which he lived at the Manor of Shaw near Overton. On January 2 1646/7 he was fined £2,380 for "delinquency." His wife, Ruth, was buried 16 January 1654/5 in the vault in the north side of the church at Wraxall, Wilts. Sir William died 28 January 1654/5.

[12] Cross, *Oxford Dictionary of the Christian Church*, p. 1068.

[13] *Visitation of Wiltshire*, p.60; *Misc. Genealogica et Heraldica*, New Series. 1:313.

[14] "Notes on Wiltshire Parishes: Avebury," *Wiltshire Notes and Queries*, 7 (Devizes: March 1915) p.220.

[15] Recovery Rolls, 146, no. 12 in *Wiltshire Notes and Queries*: 7 (March 1915) p.220; *Notes and Queries for Readers and Writer, Collector, and Librarians* 180 (Jan. - June 1941) p.81; *Prehistoric Avebury*, (New Haven and London: Aubrey Burl Yale University Press, 1979) p.40; *The Victoria History of Counties of England: Wiltshire* 12:92,93.

> In 1628 the Manor of Avebury Trusloe was also held by Sir William Dunche. He sold it in 1633 to Sir Edward Baynton. By 1639 William was so far in debt he was forced to sell Avebury Farm, the Parsonage Barn and other property to Sir John Stawell of Somerset for £8,550.

[16] An elaborate alabaster monument in his memory is erected in St Peter's Church, Little Wittenham.

[17] William Cobbett ed., *The Parliamentary History of England*, (London: 1809-26) 2:56 (29 March 1626).

[18] Francis J.Bremer, *The Puritan Experiment: New England Society from Bradford to Edwards*, pp.106,107.

[19] A. Searle, ed., *Barrington Family Letters : 1628-40*, Camden Society, 4th series XXVIII,(London: Royal Hist. Soc., 1983) p.39.

[20] John Rushworth, *Historical Collections*, 1680-1701, (London, 1696) 1:670; John Kenyon, *The Stuart Constitution*, (Cambridge University Press: 1966) p.61.

[21] *State Tracts - a Collection of Several Treatises relating to the Government..* III (London: 1693) pp.293-4,309-310; Roger Lockyer, *The Early Stuarts*, (London: Longman, 1989) p.142,143; J.M.D. Meiklejohn, *A New History of England and Great Britain*, pp.388,389; Richard Green, *History of the English People*, 5:273; *Cabinet Cyclopaedia: England*, 5 (London, 1835) p.118.

[22] Norskov Olsen, *John Foxe and the Elizabethan Church*, (Berkeley: University of California Press, 1973) pp.52,53,206 note b.

CHAPTER 6

[1] *Winthrop Papers*, (Massachusetts Historical Society, 1931) 1:143; 2:82.

[2] P.R.O., C 104/91/2, abstract of title; CP 25(2)/509/6 Chas. I Mich. cited in *Victoria County History* 14:142; George Edward Cokayne, *The Complete Baronetage*, s.v. "Henry Mody" p.188;

Abstracts of Wiltshire Inquisitiones Post Mortem: returned to Chancery in the reign of Charles I, George S. Fry and Edward Alexander Fry, eds. (London, 1901) pp.151,155.

[3] *Wiltshire Notes and Queries* 7:5,6.

> Sir Lawrence Washington was a younger son of the Washingtons of Sulgrave, Northamptonshire from whom George Washington descended. His memorial plaque in Garsdon church has the coat of Arms of the Washingtons, the "Mullets and Bars" of which became the famous "Stars and Stripes" of the American flag "Old Glory."

[4] J.P.Kenyon, *The Stuarts,* (London: Severn House Publishers, 1977) p.21; *Letters of Thomas Wood,* p.xxviii in Michael Walzer, *The Revolution of the Saints - A study in the origins of radical politics,* (London: Weidenfeld and Nicolson, 1966) p.123.

[5] F. Johnson, *An Enquirie and Answer of Thomas White his Discoverie of Brownisme* (1606) and Trans. Bapt. Hist. Soc 3:(1912-13)1-4; Baptist Quarterly 12: (1946-8) 252-8; 14:165 cited in Marjorie E Reeves, "Protestant NonConformity" R.B.Pugh and Elizabeth Crittall, eds., *The Victoria History of the Counties of England,* 3:99-101.

[6] William Spicer, *Youthful Witnesses,* (Washington DC: Review and Herald Publishing Association, 1921) pp.80-83.

[7] Edward C.Pike, *The Story of the Anabaptists,* (London: Thomas Law, 1904) pp.116-8.

> Pike cites Dr E.B.Underhill, editor, Hanserd Knollys Society: "Though not the first of the noble band who manfully claimed liberty of private judgment in divine things for himself and for all others, Busher's work remains to us as the *earliest treatise known to be extant* on this great theme"

[8] *Pagitt's Heresiography* (London, 1661) pp 196-210; *C.S.P.D., 1639,* pp.466-7; Patricia Crawford, *Women and Religion in England,* (Routledge, 1994) p.92.

[9] Christopher Hill, *Change and Continuity in Seventeenth century England,* p.160.

[10] Walter Besant, *London in the Time of the Stuarts,* (London: Adam & Charles Black, 1903) p.34.

[11] John Richard Green, *History of the English People,* 5:279, 280,311.

CHAPTER 7

[1] Gerald D.McDonald, *Notable American Women, 1607-1950,* (Cambridge, Mass.: Belknap, Harvard 1971-80)) p.569; Eric J. Ierardi, *Gravesend: The Home of Coney Island,* (New York: Vantage Press, 1975) p.12. Ierardi states, without reference, that Lady Deborah "sailed up the Thames" - though if she went by boat she would go *down* the Thames to London.

[2] Harry B.Wheatley, *London Past and Present* (Detroit: Singing Tree Press) cited in Peter Cunningham, *The Handbook of London,* (London: John Murray, 1891) 3:295; William Harrison, *A Description of England in Shakespeare's Youth,* London, 1877-1908, ed. by F.J.F.Furnivall from *Holinshed's Chronicle,* 6 vols. (New York: AMS Press) 1:35.

[3]
> Gravesend meaning *at the end of the grove* has nothing to do with graves. Eric J.Ierardi in *Gravesend: The Home of Coney Island* , p. 12 reports without reference that "she [Lady Moody] left her estate in Wiltshire and moved to an estate at Gravesend in the County of Kent." Kent County Archivist M. Carter comments: "I can find no apparent family connection between Lady Deborah Moody and any manors in Rochester or Gravesend...Hasted's *History of Kent,* for instance, which is expansive on the provenance and ownership of Kentish manors and families, gives no mention of her name as linked to a manor in Rochester or Gravesend."

[4] Sir Arthur Denton in a letter to Thomas Isham, c. 1601-5, cited in Christopher Simon Sykes, *Private Palaces: life in the great London House,* (London: Chatto and Windus, 1985) p.13; International Genealogical Index; Walter Kendall Watkins, "Some Early New York Settlers from New England" in *New York Settlers from New England,* (Oct. 1901) pp.377,378; John Stow, *Survey of London* ed. C.L.Kingsford, (London: 1988); Saretta G.Hicks, "Documentary History of

Gravesend town and Dame Deborah Moody, 1643-1659" [N.p.] 1964 typescript p.29A (41) at Brooklyn Historical Society.

> Henry Moody (son? nephew?) married Ann Weaver, daughter of William and Ann Weaver, 13 September 1630 at St Giles Church Cripplegate where Dame Deborah had been baptized.

[5] Christopher Hill, *The Century of Revolution, 1603-1714*, p.64; Mark Noble, *Memoirs of the Protectoral House of Cromwell*, pp. 196,197.

> In 1626 clergymen were instructed to preach that refusal of financial support for the king was sinful.

[6] Felicity Heal, *Hospitality in Early Modern England* (Oxford: Clarendon Press, 1990)pp.118-21.

[7] J.T.Cliffe, *The Puritan Gentry*, (London: Routledge and Kegan Paul, 1984) p.160; Eric J.Ierardi, *Gravesend: The Home of Coney Island*, p.12. George Edward Cokayne, *The Complete Baronetage*, p.188; B.R.White, *The English Separatist Tradition: From the Marian Martyrs to the Pilgrim Fathers*, (London: Oxford University Press, 1971) chapter 4.

[8] Edward T.Corwin, ed., *Ecclesiastical Records of the State of New York*, 7 vols., (Albany, 1902-16) 1:411; John Browne's letter (*Cal. sec. parte. reg* i. 59-61) in Vol. B,625-9 of the Morrice MSS. at Dr. William's Library, cited in B.R.White, *The English Separatist Tradition from the Marian Martyrs to the Pilgrim Fathers*, (Oxford University Press, 1971) p.28.

[9] William Haller, *The Rise of Puritanism*, (New York: Harper Torchbooks, 1957) pp.161.170.

[10]
> The Dunchs' early minister, Bishop Foxe, had written to the Queen begging her not to sully her name with the execution of anabaptists "To punish with the flames the bodies of those who err, rather from blindness than obstinacy of will, is cruel, and more suitable to the example of the Romish church, than to the mildness of the gospel". But Queen Elizabeth did not take his advice. - Erasmus Middleton, *Biographica Evangelica*, (London: 1780) 2:246,7.

[11] David Edwards, *Christian England*, 2:269.
> See later references to Denne and Mark Lucar

[12] See appendix; Joseph Sylvester, *The Divine Weeks*, (Waukesha, Wis.: H.M.Youmans, 1908) p.153.

> The author was 34-year old French poet and soldier, Guillaume Saluste du Bartas, who received royal support for his writing while in diplomatic service at the courts of Queen Elizabeth and King James of Scotland. Sylvester, said to be England's second poet after Milton, wrote regarding worship on the "seventh day":
> > God would that men should in a certain place,
> > This day assemble as before His face
> > Lending an humble and attentive ear
> > To learn this great name's dear dread loving fear.

[13] See also: Thomas Gataker, "The Gaine of Godlinesse", in *Sermons* (1637), p.145; Venables, *The Primary Visitation of the Diocese of Lincoln* p.51.

[14] Christopher Hill, *Change and Continuity in Seventeenth Century England*, p.171.

[15] *A Treatise of the Sabbath Day*, (London, 1635) p.110.

[16] Robert Cox, *The Literature of the Sabbath Question*, 2, (Edinburgh: Maclachlan and Stewart, 1865) pp.46-54; John Milton, *Prose Works*, Bohn ed., 2:401-2.

[17] Robert Cox, *Sabbath Laws*, (Edinburgh: Maclachlan & Stewart, 1853) p.333.

[18] W.W.Ireland, *The Life of Sir Henry Vane the Younger*, (London: E.Nash, 1905) p.443.

[19]
> In Dorset, the county adjacent to Dame Deborah's Wiltshire home an undated event described by a Quaker historian. It shows official reaction to people of conscience who were considered difficult or unreasonable:

"At Sherborn in Dorsetshire there were thirty Quakers got together into an House, for to Worship God in an innocent, harmless manner, who, as if they had been a knot of Men come together for to Drink, Revel, Rebel and Conspire against the Government were haled out by the Townsmen, Officers and School-Master of the Place, followed with many Swords and Clubs, and entertained with Curses and Blows, were carried before the Magistrate, who blamed, sentenced and condemned them, as vile Persons bent upon Rioting, and while they were met together did only contrive and rashly machinate Innovations, and this they did without any Proof, Judgment, and Defence; the Quakers at the same time however crying out that there was not one Person that could make any such thing good against them, or that they met upon such an Account, and urging the King's promise in vain, that while they were only met together to Celebrate their Worship to God, that none should suffer any Injury because of his Religion, Some of the Quakers were shut up in Dorchester Gaol from the sight of all men, and even from the common Light, others of them meeting the Danger, make their Appearance at the next Quarter Assizes, where when nothing that had been urged against them could by any means be proved that these Men did now appear before the Court with their Hats on, this was now objected as a Crime unto them, and looked upon as a certain diminution of the King's Majesty, and so they were fined for their Punishment to pay great Sums of Money which when they did not forthwith pay, there were all adjudged by the Court to be shut up in the same prison of Dorchester, upon Condition they should not be released from thence till such time as they had paid the said Sum."

Gerard Croese, *The General History of the Quakers*, Book I, translated from the Latin, 1636, pp. 157,158.

[Quakers refused to take their hats off lest they break the command of Christ - "salute no man in the way" (Luke 10:4)]

[20] Cardwell, *Documentary Annals,* 2:217-220 cited in Christopher Hill, *Society and Puritanism in Pre-revolutionary England*, p.341; Gerald D. McDonald, *Notable American Women: 1607-1950*, pp.569,570.

[21] James Pilkington's Haggai (*Aggeus*, 1560) and Obadiah (*Abdias*) were published with a new edition of (*Aggeus*, 1562) and *Nehemiah*, (1585, edited posthumously by John Fox).

CHAPTER 8

[1] Walter Besant, *London in the Time of the Stuarts*, p.139.

[2] H.R.Trevor-Roper, *Archbishop Laud*, (London: McMillan, 1965) pp.424-5; John Edward Christopher Hill, *God's Englishman*, (London: Weidenfeld and Nicolson, 1970) p.12; Charles Colton, *Charles I*, (London: Routledge and Kegan Paul, 1983) p.140.

[3] Christopher Hill, *The Century of Revolution, 1603-1714*, p.76; J.P.Kenyon, *The Stuarts*, pp.75,76; W.R.Dalzell, *The Shell Guide to the History of London*, (London: Michael Joseph, 1981) p.135.

[4] *A Briefe Relation* (1638) cited in Godfrey Davies, *Oxford History of England: The Early Stuarts, 1603-1660*, (Oxford: Clarendon Press, 1959) p 75; David L.Edwards, *Christian England*, 2:201.

[5] Christopher Hill, *The Century of Revolution: 1603-1714*, p.83; State Papers, Domestic, ccclxii.42; Samuel Rawson Gardiner, ed., *Documents Relating to the Proceedings against William Prynne in 1634 and 1637*, (The Camden Society, 1877) p.87; Letter of Garrard to Wentworth, Strafford's Papers 1:266 cited in Dionysius Larder, *Cabinet Cyclopaedia: England*, (London: 1835) 5:153n.

[6] *Wiltshire Visitation Pedigrees*, 1623. p.135; John Burkes *Extinct Baronetcies of England, Ireland and Scotland* 2nd ed. (London: Russell Smith, 1844) p.365
> Arms: Vert, a fesse engr. arg. surmounted of another gu. between three harpies of the second crined or.

[7] George Macauley Trevelyan, *English Social History*, (London, Longman Group Ltd., 1978) p.158.

[8] William Reed-Lewis, comp., *Some Genealogical Notes Regarding the Moodys of County Suffolk, and America*, (Bedford: F. Hockliffe, 1899)

[9] J.T.Cliffe,*The Puritan Gentry*, p.182.

[10] Dionysius Lardner, ed., *The Cabinet Cyclopaedia*, 5:161.

[11] Green, *History of the English People*, 5:321.

[12] Hill, *God's Englishman*, p.41,42.

[13] *The Journal of Sir Simons D'Ewes* pp.11,12 cited in J.T.Cliffe, *The Puritan Gentry*, p.195.

CHAPTER 9

[1] Anthony Wood, *Fasti Oxonienses*, ed. Bliss 2:43; (L.C. 3/1)= P.R.O., List of his Maties (sic) seruants (sic) in ordinary of the Chamber 1641" in Toynbee and Young, *Strangers in Oxford*, (London: Phillimore, 1973) pp.249,257.

[2] C.V.Wedgwood, *The King's Peace : 1637-1641*, (Harmonsworth: Penguin Books, 1955) p.65; G.E.Aylmer, *The King's Servants: The Civil Service of Charles I*, (London: Routledge and Kegan Paul, 1974) p.206,405.

[3] Asa Briggs, *A Social History of England*, (New York: The Viking Press, 1989) pp.138,9.

[4] Walter Besant, *London in the time of the Stuarts*, p.366.
G.E.Aylmer, *The King's Servants*, Routledge and Kegan, appendix: pp.470-487.

[5] James F. Larkin, ed., *Stuart Royal Proclamations: 2: Royal Proclamations of King Charles I, 1625-46*, (Oxford: Clarendon Press, 1983) pp.350-3.

[6] Felicity Heal, *Hospitality in Early Modern England*, p.120.

[7] N.H.Nicolas, ed., *Memoirs of Lady Fanshawe, wife of ...Sir Richard Fanshawe...* (London: 1835) p.35.

[8] Harvard Law School MS 1128, fos. 71-2; Felicity Heal, "The crown, the gentry and London, the enforcement of proclamation, 1596-1640" in Claire Ross, David Loades and J.J.Scarisbrick, eds, *Law and Government Under the Tudors*, (Cambridge University Press, 1988) p.222. Simon D'Ewes, *Autobiography and Correspondence*, ed. J.O.Halliwell (2 vols. 1845) 2:78.

[9] *Commons Debates 1621*, 2:463; Roger Lockyer, *The Early Stuarts*, (London: Longman, 1989) p.291.

[10] Caroline M. Hibbard, *Charles I and the Popish Plot* (Chapel Hill: North Carolina Press, 1983) p.170.

[11] Roger Lockyer, *The Early Stuarts*, (London: Longman, 1989) p. 297; John Kenyon, *The Popish Plot* (N.Y., St Martins Press, 1972) p.8.

[12] Caroline M. Hibbard, *Charles I and the Popish Plot*, p.37.

[13] Walter Walsh, *England's Fight with the Papacy*, (London: James Nisbet, 1912) p.344-370.

[14] ibid. p.243; Christopher Hibbert, *Charles I*, (London: Corgi, 1972) p.135.

[15] John Mayer,   *Ecclesiastic Interpretatio*, Expositions on the seven catholic epistles and Revelation. (1627)

[16] C.N.Elvin, *Elvin's Handbook of Mottoes*, (London: Heraldry Today, 1971) p.199.

CHAPTER 10

[1] Samuel Rawson Gardiner, *The Constitutional Documents of the Puritan Revolution: 1625-1660*, (Oxford: Clarendon Press, 1889) pp.137-144; See also: Stuart E.Prall, *The Puritan Revolution - A Documentary History*, (New York: Anchor Books, Doubleday. 1968).

[2] Milton, *Lycidas* cited in A. Neave Bradshaw, *The Quakers*, (York: William Sessions Book Trust, The Ebor Press, 1982). p.25.

[3] John Holloway, ed., *The Oxford Book of Local Verses*, (Oxford University Press. 1987) p.5.

[4] Ed. Knowler, *Letters and Dispatches of the Earl of Strafforde*, I:188 in Hill, *God's Englishman*, p.346.

[5] Milton, *Of Reformation in England*, Bohn ed., *Prose Works*, II:402-4; James W.Gerard: *Lady Deborah Moody - A Discourse delivered before New York Historical Society, May 1880*.(New York: Patterson, 1880) p. 20; Eric J. Ierardi, *Gravesend: The Home of Coney Island*, p.12.

> Ierardi refers to an unidentified document with a variant date: "It was on the 21st April, 1639 that the court ordered 'Dame Deborah Mowdie, and the others, should return to their hereditaments in forty days, in the good example necessary to the poorer class.'"

Martha Bockee Flint, *Early Long Island, A Colonial Study*, (New York, NY: G.Putnam and Sons, 1896) p.105.

[6] [Anon.], *Englands Complaint to Jesus Christ against the Bishops Canons* (1640), Bv-B2v cited in Christopher Hill, *Society and Puritanism in Pre-Revolutionary England*, p.288.

[7] An Information in the Star-Chamber against divers Persons of Quality, for residing in Town contrary to the Kings Proclamation:

> To the Kings Most Excellent Majesty:

> the late Sovereign Lord King *James*, Your Majesties Father of Blessed Memory, by several Proclamations published throughout the Realm did command, That Persons of Livelihood and Means should reside in their Countries, and not abide or sojourn in or about the City of *London*, and other Towns, for that hereby the Countries [counties?] remained unserved...

> - John Rushworth, *Historical Collections*, 2:288-293.

> The Public Record Office, Chancery Lane, London, preserves volumes detailing actions of the Pre-rogatory Courts, but the Star Chamber action in ref. to Lady Moody, (along with most case reports during the reign of Charles I) is missing.

[8] Transcript of *Three Registers of Passengers from Great Yarmouth to Holland and New England 1637-39*, by Charles Boardman Jewson, (Baltimore Genealogical Publishing Co. 1964) p.6; James F. Larkin, ed., *Stuart Royal Proclamations 2: Royal Proclamations of King Charles I, 1625-1646*, (London: Clarendon Press,1983) pp.462-4.

[9] Eric J. Ierardi, *Gravesend: The home of Coney Island*, p.12. No documentation given.

[10] Richard Overton, *A Remonstrance of Many Thousand Citizens*, (1646) in Asa Briggs, *A Social History of England*, (London: Book Club Associates, 1983) p.132.

CHAPTER 11

[1] John Demos, *Remarkable Providences 1600-1760*, (New York: George Braziller, 1972) pp.37,38; Walter Besant, *London in the Time of the Stuarts*, p.32,34.

> On 28 July 1635 the minister of St Giles Cripplegate heard the pledges of Thomas Treadwell, passenger with his family on the *Hopewell* of London.

[2] Joseph B. Felt, *Ecclesiastical History of New England* (Boston: Congregational Library Assn., 1855) 1:17. Winthrop *Journal* 1:134,136; Perry Miller, *Orthodoxy in Massachusetts 1630-1650*, (Harper Torchbook 1933) p.120.

[3] Cotton Mather, *Magnalia*, (1702) p.74.

[4] Winthrop, "Introduction," *Journal*, ed. Hosmer, 1:8;
Robert C. Winthrop, ed., *Life and Letters of John Winthrop*, (Boston, 1864) 1:194, 2:130-31; Letter from Emmanuel Downing to his nephew, John Winthrop, Jr., September 9, 1631, in *The Winthrop Papers*, *Massachusetts Historical Society Collections*, Fourth Series, 6:40-40a; Raymond Phineas Stearns, *The Strenuous Puritan: Hugh Peter, 1598-1660*, (University of Illinois, 1954)

p.93; Linda Biemer, "Lady Deborah Moody and the Founding of Gravesend," *The Journal of Long Island History*, 2:28;

> Mrs Henry W.Edwards in "Lady Deborah Moody", *Historical Collections of the Essex Institute*, 31 (Jan-July 1894) :102 note, says "Lady Moody seems to have been a cousin to Sir Henry Vane, the Governor of Massachusetts..."

[5] Emery Battis, *Saints and Sectaries: Anne Hutchinson and the Antinomian Controversy in the Massachusetts Bay Colony*, (Chapel Hill: University of Carolina, 1962) p.93; Raymond Phineas Stearns, *The Strenuous Puritan: Hugh Peter*, p.93.

[6] James Duncan Phillips, *Salem in the Seventeenth Century*, (Boston. 1933) p.131; Richard D.Pierce, ed., *Records of the First Church in Salem, Massachusetts, 1629-1736*, (Salem, Mass.: Essex Institute, 1974) p.9.

[7] New England Genealogical Register 55/377 cited in Charles Edward Banks, *Topographical Dictionary of 2885 English emigrants to New England 1620-1650*, ed. Brownell, (Baltimore Genealogical Publishing Co. 1963). p.178; Walter Kendall Watkins, "Some Early New York Settlers from New England", *New England Historical and Genealogical Register*, (October 1901) 55:377. William P.Filby and Mary K. Meyer, in *Passenger and Immigration Lists Index*, (Detroit, Mich: Gale Research Co., c.1981) refers to: "Moody, Deborah. The vessel: n.a. Lynn, Mass. 1640". See also: John Farmer, *A Genealogical Register of the First Settlers of New England*, (Lancaster, Mass.: Carter, Andrews and Co., 1829) Reprinted with Samuel G.Drake ed., *Additions/Corrections*, (Baltimore Genealogical Publishing Co., 1976) p.198; Margaret Toynbee and Peter Young, *Strangers in Oxford*, p.257.

> A resource of 130 passenger lists has been checked. Many lists were destroyed by fire in 1814.

> Historian, James W. Gerard, *Lady Deborah Moody:*
>> *A Discourse delivered before the New York Historical Society, May, 1880*, (New York: F.B.Patterson, 1880) p.21,23 says without supporting evidence that Lady Moody came over at the same time as the Tilton family - which was sometime after William Tilton's marriage on 18 December 1638 to his second wife, Susanna, at Wolston, Warwickshire, England.

> George Edward Cokayne, *The Complete Baronetage*, p.188 based on "Notes and Queries" 7th S. Vol 5:415 says: "His widow, being a Nonconformist, emigrated in 1636, with her son, to Massachusetts."

[8] See: Charles C.P.Moody, *Biographical Sketches of the Moody Family embracing notices of ten ministers and several laymen, from 1633 to 1842*, (Boston: Samuel G. Drake, 1847)

[9] Thomas Lechford, *Note-Book Kept by Thomas Lechford, Esq., Lawyer in Boston, Massachusetts Bay, From June 27, 1638 to July 29, 1641* in *Transactions and Collections of the American Antiquarian Society*, 7 (Cambridge, Mass., 1885) 67.

[10] Alexander Young, *Chronicles of the First Planters of the Colony of Massachusetts Bay from 1623-1636*, pp.438-442.

CHAPTER 12

[1] Lewis and Newhall, *History of Lynn, Essex County, Massachusetts*, pp.133,134.

[2] Nathaniel Shurtleff, ed., *Records of the Governor and Company of the Massachusetts Bay in New England*, (Boston, 1883) 1:43; Joseph B. Felt, *Annals of Salem*, p.530.

[3] Walter Kendall Watkins, "Some Early New York Settlers from New England", *New England Historical and Genealogical Register*, 55 (October 1901) :377.

[4] Waldo Thompson, *Historical Sketches of Swampscott*, (Lynn: Thomas P.Nichols, 1885) pp.13,14; Swamscott Town Centennial, p.8; Richard B Johnson, *Swampscott in the Seventeenth Century*, Swamscott Historical Society, n.d. pp.252-4.

[5] James Duncan Phillips, *Salem in the Seventeenth Century*, (Boston: Houghton Mifflin, 1933) p.129.

[6] Waldo Thompson, *Historical Sketches of Swampscott*, pp.13,14.

[7] Thomas Lechford, *"Plaine Dealing, or Newes from New England"* Volume 3 Series 3 (Cambridge Mass., 1883) p.97.

[8] Eric Ierardi, *Gravesend: The Home of Coney Island,* p.13 (no ref.); Joseph B.Felt, *Annals of Salem,* (Salem: W. and S.B Ives, 1827) p.239.

[9] Thomas Lechford, *Note-Book,* in *Transactions and Collections of the Antiquarian Society,* 7 (Cambridge:1885) 67; James R. Newhall, *History of Lynn,* pp.187,201; Henry. S. Baldwin, "Swampscott - Past and Present" *Swampscott Historical Society Journal,* (Spring-Summer Issue, 1944) pp.7-13.

[10] Henry S Baldwin, "Swampscott - Past and Present: 1629-1944" Spring-Summer Issue 1944 p.9; Lewis and Newhall, *History of Lynn,* pp.99,198.

Identification of Lady Moody's house : Governor John Winthrop, in a report to his associates in England in 1634-35, included a copy of the Thomas Graves Map of the Bay Colony, drawn in 1633-34, and in his own handwriting in marginalia on a sketch located the 'Ferme House of John Humphrey' at a point near Black Will's Cliff in Swampscott, then included in Saugus. This map is now in the collection of the British Museum.

The price of £1100 appears high compared with the cost of Mr John Whittingham's house on High street, Boston containing kitchen and parlor, and chambers over, sumptuously furnished, as the inventory records in 1648 and valued with the barn, cow house and forty-four acres of land, at £100.

The Swampscott house bought by Lady Moody was removed in 1891 from its original site when the area was developed and is known as the John Humphrey House after its original owner. Situated at 99 Paradise Road, Swampscott it became the home of the Swampscott Historical Society in 1921.

The hand-made bricks visible in some of the rooms are said to have been brought over by John Humphrey from England to make up the walls. The mortar was mixed with seaweed. The beams are boxed in with wood on which there are genuine Indian markings. Much of the oak panelling is original, as are the framing and handrail on the fine staircase, fixed with hand-made nails. The ceiling beams are original white oak with wooden pegs. Intriguing are a secret stairway from the kitchen to the second floor and a secret hideaway behind a cupboard.

CHAPTER 13

[1] Henry S. Baldwin, *History of Salem,* 2:142; Waldo Thompson, *Sketches of Swampscott,* pp.3,4.

Lady Deborah's house was on a site later occupied by the old Salem Post Office.

[2] *Tercentenary of Massachusetts Bay Colony 1630 - 1930 and of the General Court and the One Hundred Fiftieth Anniversary of the Constitution* - Material suggested for Use in the Schools in observance of the Tercentenary, Department of Education 1930. Number 1, Whole Number: 212:177.

[3] Henry S. Baldwin's notes at Swampscott Historical Society; ii *Winthrop,* p.123.

[4] Sidney Perley, *History of Salem, Mass. 1638-70,* 2:63,64.

[5] *History of Essex County, Massachusetts,* (J.W.Lewis and Co. 1888) 1:263; Richard D. Pierce, ed., *Records of the First Church in Salem, Massachusetts, 1629-1736* (Salem: Essex Institute, 1974) pp.5-10.

The list of names of members who joined the Salem church in 1640 [marginal notes were added later]:

Samuell Corning	
his wife	
Jane wife of Phillip Veren	removed
Jonathon Porter	dead
Lady [Deborah] Moody	excommunict. dead
Thomas Ruck	recommended to Boston
his wife	
Charles Glover	removed
Rose Howard	

William Rennolls	
Robert Moullin Junr.	
Esdras Read	
Elizabeth Sanders i.e. Kitchen	excommunict.
Sarah Bowdish	excommunict.
Widow Eastwick	
Elizabeth Corwin	
Alice Barnett	
Elizabeth Woodbery	
Elizabeth Scudder	dead
Richard Bartholomew	dead
Jane wife of Joshua Verin	removed
John Marstone	
the wife of Richard Graves	
Jane Reeves	dead
the wife of John Cooke	removed
Abigaile Good	
Sarah Hopcott	removed
Thomas Marstone	recommended
Frances Lawes	
his wife	dead
Mary Beachum	
Abigail Fermayes	recommended
George Byam	
William Geere	
Goodman Bulfinch	dismist.

[6] It was not until the end of the seventeenth century that women, who for centuries were not allowed to sing, moved into the liberated zone.   Ola Winslow, *Meetinghouse Hill*, (New York: 1952) p.159; Roger Thompson, *Women and the Puritan Churches*,(London: Routledge and Kegan Paul, 1974) p.97.

[7] Lewis and Newhall, *Annals of Lynn*, 1:209.

[8] Sidney Perley, *History of Salem, Mass.:1638-1670*, 2:134.

[9] Massachusetts Bay Colony Records: I (November 1630) cited in William Addison Blakely, *American State Papers on Freedom in Religion*, (Washington DC.: Review and Herald, 1943) p.22.footnote.

[10] See: Everett Emmerson, *Letters from New England*, (University of Massachusetts Press, 1976)

[11] Jerome Burnel, ed., *Chronicles of the World*, (Ecam Publications, 1990) p.628.

[12] Massachusetts Bay Colony Records, (March 1635) 1:22.

[13] D. McConnell, *History of the American Episcopal Church*, (London: Wells, Gardner, Darton and Co., 1897) pp.32,33.

[14] Selmer Williams, *Demeter's Daughters*, (New York: Atheneum, 1976) p.129.

[15] James W. Gerard, *Lady Deborah Moody*, A Discourse delivered before the New York Historical Society, May 1880 (New York: F.B.Patterson, 1880) p.18.

[16] Dow, ed., *Records and Files of the Quarterly Courts of Essex,County Mass.* 1(1636-1656):33; *Encyclopaedia Britannica*, 11th ed., s.v. "Massachusetts".

[17] Masson, *Life of Milton*, 7 (London: Macmillan, 1859-94) 4:391-397,442.
Vane received a sonnet sent July 3, 1652 by the English poet Milton

CHAPTER 14

[1] Joseph B.Felt, *Annals of Salem*, p.71; Alonzo Lewis, *History of Lynn*, p.109.

[2] Frances Winwar, *Puritan City - The Story of Salem*, (New York: Robert McBrien and Co. 1938) p.34.

[3] J.Franklin Jameson, ed., *Early Narratives of Early American History: Johnson's Wonder-Working Providence 1628-1651*, p.243.

[4] *Winthrop's Journal*, pp.244-246.

[5] Emery Battis, *Saints and Sectaries*, p.52.

[6] W.W.Sweet, *Religious Colonial America*, (New York: Scribners, 1943) p.17; *Winthrop's Journal*, ed. Hosmer, p.251.

[7] Emery Battis, *Saints and Sectaries*, pp.246,247.

[8] Stokes and Pfeffer, *Church & State in the United States*, (New York: Harper and Row, 1950) p.10.

[9] William Haller, *Liberty and Reformation in the Puritan Revolution*, pp.153,154; Emery Battis, *Saints and Sectaries*, p.248.

[10] Master Thomas Shephard minister of Cambridge, Massachusetts, cited by Hugh Brogan, *Longman History of the United States of America*, (London: Longman) p.49; H.S.Tapley, *Women of Massachusetts, 1620-89* cited in A.B.Hart, ed., *The Commonwealth History of Massachusetts Transactions* (Boston, 1928-9), p.311; Roger Thompson, *Women in Stuart England and America* , (London: Routledge and Kegan Paul, 1974) p.88.

[11] John Fiske, *The Beginnings of New England*, (Cambridge: Houghton, Mifflin and Co. Riverside Press, 1890) p.146; Travelyan, *English Social History*, (London: Longman, 1978) p.467; John Farmer, *A Genealogical Register of the First Settlers of New England*, (Lancaster, Mass. 1829) 39:42,45; W.W.Sweet, *Religion in Colonial America*, (New York: Scribners, 1943) p.133.

CHAPTER 15

[1] Dow, ed., *Records and files of the Quarterly Courts of Essex County, Mass. 1636-56* (1911) 1:52; John E. Stillwell, *Historical Genealogical Miscellany*, (Baltimore: Genealogical Publishing Co., 1970) 5:134; Richard Brigham Johnson, *Swampscott in the Seventeenth Century*, (Swampscott Historical Society, no date) p.260.

> Two months after the court action seven townspeople were charged with the same offence including William Witter. He was reported "willing to see light" and apologized for his beliefs, though later at the age of 67 and having turned blind he was baptized.

[2] See Shurtleff, ed., *Massachusetts Records* for 1643. The author of New-England's First Fruits, writing from Boston, Sept 26, 1642 cited in Alexander Young, *Chronicles of the First planters of the Colony of Massachusetts bay from 1623 to 1636*, p.185 footnote; Gerard: "Lady Deborah Moody", p.24; Jacqueline Overton, *Long Island's Story*, pp.41-42; Alexander C Flick, "Lady Deborah Moody Grand Dame of Gravesend," *The Long Island Historical Society Quarterly*, Vol. 1 No.3 (July, 1939) :72. State historian, Flick, gave no reference.

[3] *Records of Plymouth Colony, 1633-1689*, (Boston: 1857) p.191; N.Y. *Genealogical and Biographical Record* 92 (N.Y. Biographical Society. Jan. 1961):10; *The Register of Solomon Lachaire, Notary of New Amsterdam*, (Baltimore, Genealogical Publishing, 1978) p.97.

[4] Nathaniel Shurtleff, ed., *Records of the Governor and Company of the Massachusetts Bay in New England* 2:85

[5] Winthrop, *Journal*, ed., Hosmer 2:126

[6] William H Whitmore ed., *The Colonial Laws of Massachusetts, Reprinted From the Edition of 1660, With the Supplements of 1672, Containing Also The Body of Liberties of 1641*. Boston: City Council, 1889) [1646,44]; Gerard, "Lady Deborah Moody", p.16.

[7] Samuel Gorton, *Simplicities Defence against Seven-headed policy OR Innocency Vindicated*, (London: 1646)

> Some anabaptists were punished. In 1644 the authorities tied up and whipped Thomas Painter, a Baptist from Hingham who refused to have his child baptized and stoutly protested that such a ceremony was an anti-Christian ordinance. He was proceeded against without authority of law as an example - "not for his opinion, but for reproaching the Lord's ordinance by expressing his opinion." Winthrop, *History of N.E.* 2:213-14

[8] David W. McCullough, *Brooklyn: How it got that Way*, (Dial Press, NYC; 1983) p.10.

[9] L.E.Froom, *The Prophetic Faith of Our Fathers*, (Washington DC: Review and Herald, 1961) 3:50.

[10] Charles M. Andrews, *The Colonial Period of American History*, (Yale University Press, 1934) 1:471.

[11] Roger Williams to John Winthrop, *Massachusetts Historical Society Collections*, 4th Series, 6:186-7; Oscar and Lilian Handlin, *Liberty in America: 1600 to the Present*, Vol 1. *Liberty and Power*, (New York: Harper and Row, 1986) p.126.

[12] John E. Pomfret, *Founding the American Colonies: 1583-1660*, (New York: Harper and Row, 1970) p.218; William Haller, *Liberty and Reformation in the Puritan Revolution*, p.157.

[13] Re: Davenport on doctrine of baptism see E.Brooks Holifield, *The Covenant Sealed* (New Haven: Yale U.P., 1974) pp.176-179. Champlin Burrage, *Early English Dissenters* 1:316-310; Thomas Crosby ed. *History of English Baptists* (London:1738) 1:272; Henry Denne, *Antichrist Unmasked in Two Treatises* (London? 1645) p.41.

> For Denne baptism signified entrance into the "part of the covenant of grace" that was "Spirituall" hence only believers were to be baptized. In 1644 Denne was apprehended and sent to gaol in Cambridgeshire for preaching against infant baptism and presuming to baptize again those who had not received adult baptism. He later became a member of the Bell Alley Baptist congregation in London.

[14] John Endicott to John Winthrop, *The Winthrop Papers*, (Boston: Massachusetts Historical Society Collection, Vol 6, Fourth series, 1863) 6:146-148; Newman Smith, "Mrs Eaton's Trial (in 1644); as it appears upon the Records of the First Church of New Haven", in *Papers of the New Haven Colony Historical Society*, (New Haven: Printed for the Society, 1894) 5:133-48; Lilian Handlin, "Dissent in a Small community" *The New England Quarterly*, 57:197-201.

[15] Connecticut State Library: New Haven First Church Records, I:17-22, printed as "Mrs Eaton's Trial," in New Haven Colony Historical Society *Papers*, (1894) 5:133-148; Isabel MacBeath Calder, *The New Haven Colony*, (Hamden, Conn.: Archon Books, 1970) p.93.

[16] Lewis and Newhall, *History of Lynn*, p.188; Hoadly, ed., *Records of New Haven Col. 1638-49*, pp.243,246,254.

[17] J.N. Andrews and L.R. Conradi, *History of the Sabbath*, pp.707,8.

[18] William Haller, *Liberty and Reformation in the Puritan Revolution*, p.153; John E. Pomfret, *Founding the American Colonies, 1583-1660* (New York: Harper and Row) pp.256-273; *New York Yearly Meeting Bicentennial Anniversary 1895*, Friends Book and Tract Committee p.10; T Armitage, *History of the Baptists to 1886*, (New York: 1887) p.747.

[19] Genesis 8:9. (A.V.)

> As might be expected most males were not ready for this early women's liberation movement! R. Royston in his dual work (found on the library table at Avebury Manor, Wilts.) decried the freedom allowed to women and the new sects:
> "...To make the Cry louder they permitted all Sects and Heresies a Licence of publick profession, (which hitherto Discipline, the Care of the Common Peace and Religion had confined to secret corners) and permitted the Office of Teaching to every bold and ignorant undertaker: so that at last the dreggs of the People usurped that Dignity, and Women who had parted with the natural modesty of their Sex, would not onely speak, but also rule in the Church."

- *The Workes of King Charles the Martyr with a Collection of Declarations, Treaties, and other papers concerning the Differences betwixt His said Majesty and His Two Houses of Parliament* and: *The Workes of King Charles I, Defender of the Faith with the History of his life as also of his tryall and martyrdome,* (printed by James Flesher for R.Royston, Bookseller to his Most Sacred Majesty, 1662) pp.28,29.

[20] *Records of First Church,* Boston, p.46; *Winthrop,* I:285,6; Thompson, *Women in Stuart England and America,* (London: Routledge and Kegan Paul, 1974) p.88; Keith Thomas, *Women and the Civil War Sects'* cited in Trevor Aston, ed., *Crisis in Europe, 1560-1660* (London: Routledge, Kegan Paul, 1965), pp.317-40; Patricia Higgins, "Women in the Civil War" (unpublished M.A. thesis, Manchester University, 1965); *Records of a Church of Christ in Bristol,* p.85; Claire Cross, '"He-Goats before the Flocks": a note on the part played by some women in the founding of some Civil War churches', SCH 8, 1972, pp.195-202.

[21] Teunis Bergen, *Early Settlers of Kings County, Long Island,* (CottonPort: Polyanthos, 1973) pp.58,144,148,303; *History of the Reformed Protestant Dutch Church of Gravesend, King's County,* N.Y. printed for the Consistory, Gravesend. N.Y. 1892. p.9.

[22] L.G.Pine, *Dictionary of Mottoes,* (Boston: Routledge, Kegan Paul, 1983)

[23] Pauline Durrett Robertson, Ed., *Eve's Version: 150 Women of the Bible Speak Through Modern Poets,* (ISBN 0-942376-04-9. Paramount Publishing Company, 1983), p.54.

CHAPTER 16

[1] Original in General Government Archives, The Hague, Holland cited in *The Columbia Historical Portrait,* p.29.

[2] Edmund O'Callaghan, ed., *Documents Relative to the Colonial History of the State of New York.*(Albany, 1856) 3:38,39.

[3] Max Savelle, *A History of Colonial America,* (Hinsdale, Ill.: Dryden Press, 1973) p.206; *History of New York,* p.224.

[4] Silas Wood, *A Sketch of the First Settlement of the Towns on Long Island,* (1824) pp.17,18.

[5] Michael Tepper, ed., *New World Immigrants: A Consolidation of Ship Passenger Lists and Associate Data from Periodical Literature,* (Genealogical Publishing Co. Inc. 1979) 1:198; Parker, *Europe in Crisis,* pp.118-119; *France under Richlieu and Mazarin,* chap. 16, Caroline M. Hibbard, *Charles I and the Popish Plot,* p.237.

[6] *The Jewish Encyclopedia,* s.v, "New York," 9: 259.

[7] Max Savelle, *A History of Colonial America,* p.210.

[8] *Ecclesiastical Records N.Y.* 1:55

[9] Maud Wilder Goodwin, *Dutch and English on the Hudson,* pp.90,91; Alice Morse Earl, *Home Life in Colonial Days,* p.386; Jacqueline Overton, *Long Island's Story,* (New York: Doubleday Doran and Co. 1929) p.23. Alice P. Kenney, *Stubborn for Liberty,* (Syracuse, NY: Syracuse University Press, 1975) p.127.

[10] Max Savelle, *A History of Colonial America,* pp. 207,210; David W. McCullough, *Brooklyn,* (New York: The Dial Press, 1983) p.129; Edmund B.O'Callaghan ed. *Documents Relative to the Colonial History of the State of New York,* I (Albany, 1855-1883): 211,213.

[11] Albert Ulmann, *A Landmark History of New York,* (New York: D. Appleton and Co. 1901) p.34.

[12] Underhill had been excommunicated and charged with adultery for having looked "lustfully" at Sister Miriam Wilbore in Boston during a lecture. Sister Wilbore had already been punished for "coming to the lecture with a pair of wanton open-worked gloves, slit at the thumbs and fingers for the purpose of taking snuff." - Rodman Gilder, *The Battery,* Boston: Houghton Mifflin Company, 1936) pp.10,11.

[13] Max Savelle, *A History of Colonial America*, p.207; Jacqueline Overton, *Long Island Story*, (Garden City: Doubleday, Doran and Co., 1929) p.8.

[14] Max Savelle, *A History of Colonial America*, p.206.

[15] Jacqueline Overton, *Long Island's Story*, (Ira J Friedman: Port Washington, L.I., N.Y. 1961) pp 29,30.

[16]
>On the committee were: Deputy Governor Mr William Hathorne, Mr Simon Broadstreet, Esq. and Mr Edward Hollick.
>- Henry B. Hoff, *Genealogies of Long Island Families*, from the N.Y. Genealogical and Biographical Record. (Genealogical Publishing Co. Inc., 1987) 2:156-9.

[17] Cleveland Rodgers, *Brooklyn's First City Planner: Lady Deborah Moody's Idealistic Community at Gravesend*, presented to The Long Island Historical Society by William Jerome Cosgrove, (Brooklyn, New York: Kings County Trust Co. 1956) p.3; Maud Wilder Goodwin, *Dutch and English on the Hudson*, (Yale University Press, 1919) p.167 n.1.
>The lot was at Nos. 23 and 25 on the north side of Beaver Street, midway between Broadway and Broad Street.

[18] Joyce D. Goodfriend, *Before the Melting Pot : Society and Culture in Colonial New York City, 1664-1730*, (Princeton: Princeton University Press, 1992) p.10; David W. McCullough, *Brooklyn...and how it got that way*, p.5.
>"Named from the English town of this name, or from the deep sounds on the shore" - Benjamin F. Thompson, *History of Long Island*, 2 (New York: Gould Banks Co., 1843) :169.

[19] Martha Bockee Flint, *Early Long Island*, (N.Y. Putnam and Sons, 1896) p.109.

CHAPTER 17

[1] Edward Robb Ellis, *The Epic of New York City*, (New York N.Y.: Coward-McCann, Inc., 1966) p.53.
>There appears to have been more than one payment for Gravesend: "In 1684, when all the trouble was at an end, they secured another deed...for all the lands in Gravesend, in exchange for 'one blanket, one gun, one kettle'." Peter Ross, *History of Long Island* (New York: Lewis Publishing, 1905) 1:361.

[2] "Early History of the Thorne Family of Long Island', *New York Genealogical and Biographical Record*, 92 (January 1961) p.6.

[3] Martha Bockee Flint, *Early Long Island: A Colonial Study*, p.110. Chapter 6 "Lady Moody's Plantation" contains a copy of the first map of Long Island.

[4] James Grant Wilson, ed., *The Memorial History of the City of New-York, From Its First Settlement to the Year 1892* (New York, 1892), 1:238.

[5] Edmund B.O'Callaghan, *History of New Netherland*, (New York: 1845) 1:289-290; Henry B. Hoff, *Genealogies of Long Island Families*, (Genealogical Publishing Co. Inc., 1987) 2:158.

[6] John Endecott to John Winthrop, 22 April 1644, *The Winthrop Papers*, ed. Allyn B. Forbes, 4 vols. (Boston: Massachusetts Historical Society, 1929-47) 4:456.
>Lady Moody's letter has not been found!

[7] Teunis G.Bergen, *Early Settlers of King's County, Long Island, N.Y.*, (Polyanthos, 1973) pp.286,7; John O.Raum, *The History of New Jersey*, (Philadelphia: John E. Potter and Co., 1877) 1:76,77; John Edwin Stilwell, *Historical and Genealogical Miscellany: Early Settlers of New Jersey and their Descendants*, (Baltimore Genealogical Publishing Company, 1970) 4:296-301.

[8]
>Deborah Crawford, *Four Women in a Violent Time*, says Penelope married Kent van Princes in 1642, then stayed with Lady Deborah. Crawford gives January 1 1644 as date of the marriage to Stout at the church within the Amsterdam fort. According to

Raum (p.78) Penelope was born c.1602. Clemens in *American Marriages: Records before 1699* reports the marriage of Richard Stout to Penelope Kent or Lent (widow of Von Printzen) at Gravesend, 1634-5 [typo? - this was before Gravesend existed!]

See also: Miller K. Reading, *William Bowne of Yorkshire England and his descendants*, (Flemington N.J.: H.E.Deats 1903) p.8.

Gravesend records state that Richard Stout was assigned Gravesend plantation lot No. 18 in 1646. Penelope and her husband later moved to Middletown, Monmouth County, New Jersey where the old Indian who saved her life frequently visited her. On one occasion by informing her of a plot to massacre the whites, the settlement was put on guard and saved from destruction. The Stouts had seven sons and three daughters. Richard is said to have lived until the age of 88 and Penelope to the age of 110 and at the time of her death her posterity numbered 502.

[9] Peter Ross, *A History of Long Island*, (New York: Lewis Publishing Co., 1905) 1:441.

[10] *Winthrop's Journal*, 2:137-8.

[11] *Genealogies of Long Island Families*, Vol II. selected by Henry B. Hoff, (Genealogical Publishing Co. Inc., 1987) p.158.

CHAPTER 18

[1] Arnold J.F.Laer, (translator) *New York Historical Documents: Dutch: 1642-7* (Baltimore Genealogical Publishing Co. Inc., 1973) 2:165,166.

[2] O'Callaghan, *New York Colonial Documents*, Holland Documents 4:285.

[3]

"lyeing & being uppon and aboute the Weastermost part of Long Island, and beginning att the mouth of a Creeke adiacent to Coneyne Island, & being bounded on the weastward parte thereof with the land appertaining to Anthony Johnson & Robert Pennoyre, and soe to runne as farre as the westernmost part of a Certaine pond in an ould Indian field on the North side of the plantation of the s[d] Ro: Pennoyre, & from thence to run direct East as far as a valley, beginning att the head of a fflye or marsh somtimes belonging to the land of Hugh Garretson; & being bounded on the south side with the Maine Ocean...& perpetuallie to inioy and possesse as theyre owne ffree land of inheritance, and it to improue & manure according to theire owne discreations, with libertie likewise... to put what Cattle they shall thinke fitting to feed or grase upon the afores[d] Conyne Island...wee do giue and graunt...full power and authoritie...to build a town, or townes, with such necessar[ie] fortifications as to them shall seem expedient..."

[4] Gravesend Town Records, I:5-7; Edmund B. O'Callaghan, ed., *The Documentary History of the State of New York* 1:629; *Colonial Charters* No XXX Town of Gravesend pp.494-8;See also: Thompson, *History of Long Island*, pp.438,9.

[5] *Who's Who in American History: Who Was Who in America: Historical Volume 1607-1896*, (Wilmette Il.: Marquis Who's Who, Inc. 1967); Nathaniel S. Prime, *A History of Long Island, From its first settlement by Europeans to the year 1845, with special reference to its ecclesiastical concerns*, (New York: 1845), p.439; J.T.Bailey, *An Historical Sketch of The City of Brooklyn*, (Brooklyn: Bailey, 1840) p.45.

Elizabeth Pole is said to have bought from the Indians the plot of land on which Taunton, Mass. was founded in 1639. The city bears the motto: "Dux Femina Facti" meaning *A Woman was Leader of that which was done*

[6] Silas Wood, *A Sketch of the First Settlement of the Several Towns on Long Island with their Political Condition to the End of the Revolution.* (Brooklyn: Alden Spooner, 1828)

It may be noted that the Flushing patent of 10 October 1645 also included the right to "have and enjoy liberty of conscience according to the custom and manner of Holland." The Gravesend settlement was begun earlier in 1643 and their charter of 1645 appeared to provide greater liberty, though neither settlement was entitled to absolute freedom of religion.

[7] Martha Bockee Flint, *Early Long Island*, p.110; *New York Genealogical and Biographical Record*, January 1961. (New York Genealogical and Biographical Society) 92:7.

[8] Teunis Bergen, *Early Settlers of King's County*, p.208; Stilwell, *Historical and Genealogical Miscellany*, 4:301.

[9] Gravesend Town Records I: May 11 1659.

[10] Isabelle Platt, "An Old Colonial Homestead Born Again" *Country Life in America*, 16(No.2) June 1909 cited by Eric J.Ierardi, *Gravesend: The Home of Coney Island*, p.18.

[11] Cleveland Rodgers, *Brooklyn's First City Planner*, (Brooklyn New York: Kings County Trust Co., 1956) p.6.

[12] The Rev. A.P.Stockwell, *N.Y. Genealogical and Biographical Record* cited in Mrs Henry W. Edwards, "Lady Deborah Moody", *Historical Collections of the Essex Institute*, (Jan/July 1894, Nos 1-6) 31:101,102; Teunis Bergen, *Early Settlers of King's County, Long Island*, p.207.

[13] Martha Bockee Flint, *Early Long Island : Colonial Study*, (New York; G.P.Putnam and Son, 1896) p.107.

> Dido was the legendary daughter of Belus, king of Tyre. On the murder of her husband Sychaeus by her brother Pygmalion, she fled to north Africa and founded there the city of Carthage. Devoted to the memory of her dead spouse she committed suicide rather than submit to a forced marriage with Iarbas, a neighboring monarch.

> I am that Dido which thou here do'st see,
> Cunningly framed in beauteous Imagrie
> .....
> I did with weapon chast, to save my fame,
> Make way for death untimely, ere it came.
> This was my end; but first I built a Towne,
> Reveng'd my husbands death, liv'd with renowne.
> (Ausonius, Epigr. cxviii)

Sir Walter Ralegh, *Metrical Translations* from *The History of the World*; Robert Nye, *A Choice of Sir Walter Ralegh's Verse*, (London: Faber and Faber, 1972) p.67.

[14] Gravesend Town Records, 18 November 1646:

> Att a Generall assemblye held at the towne of Gravesan(d) within this (Province) by the inhabit:(s)

> Whereas it pleased the righte (honourable) Governour Generall of this pr(ovince to graunt and) confirme a Certaine quan(tity of land uppon) this Iland called Longe Iland (within the s^d) iurisdiction unto the Lady Debora(h Moody her) pattentees and associates for the(m) to (injoye and to) manure with Certain p^{r}ivelidges (and appurtinances to) the said pattentees and their associa(tes as by ye s^d) patent - more att large doth and may (appea)re it is) therefore this day Generallie agreed (and determined) uppon by the s^d inhabitants that these su( ) orders shall be reestablished and confirm(ed).

[15] G. Bergen, *The Bergen Family*, (Albany. N.Y. 1876) p.35; Teunis Bergen, *The Early Settlers of King's County, Long Island*, p.45.

> Tacy Hubbard became the first known Saturday Sabbath keeper in North America on Sabbath, March 11, 1665 after the arrival in Rhode Island of Stephen Mumford sent over by the London Seventh-day Baptists in 1664. - Andrews and Conradi, *History of the Sabbath*, p.735.

[16] J.Franklin Jameson, ed., *Original Narratives of Early American History: Winthrop's Journal I (1630-1649)*, 2:289; Charles W. Upham, *Salem Witchcraft*, (Upham, 1867) p.183.

> Upham appears not to know of Lady Moody's more substantial house and farm at Swampscott or her house in Gravesend, fortified against storms and Indians.

[17] Maud Wilder Goodwin, *Dutch and the English on the Hudson*, (New Haven: Yale University Press, 1919) p.85; W.H.Stillwell, *History of Reformed Protestant Dutch Church of Gravesend, Kings County*. cited in Goodwin, p.167:1.

[18] Megapolensis and Drisius to Classis of Amsterdam, August 5, 1657. Eccl. Recs. N.Y. 1:396-7; Andrews and Conradi, *History of the Sabbath*, pp.734-6.

The presence in the colony of "Anabaptists, here called Mnistes [Mennonites]" was confirmed in 1643 by Isaac Jogues, "Novum Belgium" - J. Frankin Jameson, ed., *Narratives of New Netherland* (1909 repr. N.Y.: Barnes and Noble, 1967) p.260.

[19] Esther Singleton, *Dutch New York*, (New York: Benjamin Blom, 1968) pp.1,188; Berthold Fernow, ed., *Ordinances of New Amsterdam: Records of New Amsterdam*, (New York, N.Y.: Knickerbocker Press, 1897) p.1.

[20] *The Dictionary of Thoughts*, comp. Tyron Edwards, C N Catrevas, Jonathon Edwards, (London: Universal Text Books n.d.)p.339.

CHAPTER 19

[1] Jacqueline Overton, *Long Island Story*, p.40.

[2] Henry H.Kessler and Eugene Rachlis, *Stuyvesant and His New York*, (New York: Random House, 1959) p.148; Frederick J. Zwierlein, *Religion in New Netherland, 1623-1664*, (Rochester New York: John P.Smith, 1910) p.55; Samuel Eliot Morison & Henry Steele Commager, *The Growth of the American Republic*, (Oxford University Press, 1950) 1:62; Rodman Gilder, *The Battery*, (Boston: Houghton Mifflin Co., 1936) p.13.

A 1651 portrayal of Nieuw Amsterdam features the wind-driven sawmill, flagstaff, church, prison and a law-breaker hanging from the gallows.

[3] Henry H Kessler and Eugene Rachlis, *Peter Stuyvesant and His New York*, p.110 (cited without reference), pp.113,114.

[4] Maud Wilder Goodwin, *Dutch and the English on the Hudson*, p.85.

[5] Esther Singleton, *Dutch New York*, pp.186,187; Eric J. Ierardi, *Gravesend: The Home of Coney Island*, p.25.

[6] Early this century Mrs Platt found documents in the attic of her home which stated how Lady Deborah entertained Governor Kieft and later Governor Stuyvesant. - Eric Ierardi, *Gravesend: The Home of Coney Island*, p.18.

[7] Peter Ross, *A History of Long Island*, 1:357; Miller Hageman, "Lady Deborah Moody," Brooklyn Daily Eagle, 23 November 1890.

[8] Gravesend Town Records, I. p.26; Teunis Bergen, *Early Settlers of King's County, Long Island*, p.207.

[9] Mrs Henry W. Edwards "Lady Deborah Moody," *Essex Institute Historical Collections*, (Aug/Dec 1894) 31:96-101.

[10] Lewis and Newhall, *History of Lynn*, p.187; Champlin Burrage, *Early English Dissenters: 1550-1641*, (Cambridge University Press, 1912) 1:321,322,326,366; 2:296-304.

[11] Lewis and Newhall, *History of Lynn*, p.187.

[12] Edmund Sear Morgan, *The Puritan Family*, (Boston: Trustees of the Public Library, 1944) p.115, and R.C.Winthrop, *Life and Letters of John Winthrop* (Boston: Ticknor and Fields, 1867) p.430.

CHAPTER 20

[1] Richard Brigham Johnson, *Swampscott in the Seventeenth Century*, Swampscott Historical Committee, n.d. p.267.

[2] Town Records of Salem; *Swampscott in the Seventeenth Century*, p.258.

[3] Charter of Freedoms and Exemptions to Patroons - June 7, 1629: E.B.O'Callaghan, ed. *Documents Relative to the Colonial History of the State of New York*, Vol. II, p.553ff.; Walter Besant, *London in the time of the Stuarts*, p.302.

[4] *Dictionary of National Biography*, s.v. "Francis Lovelace."

[5] Sir Winston Churchill, *History of the English Speaking Peoples*, (London: Cassell, 1969) 5:1526.

[6] Margaret Toynbee and Peter Young, *Strangers in Oxford*, p.257.

[7] Patrick Morrah, *A Royal Family : Charles I and his family*, (London: Constable, 1982) p.85.

[8] Oxford: Tanner, 466 fol 60.

[9] Mary Anne Everett Green, ed., *Calendar of the Proceedings of the Committee for Compounding*, (London: 1890) 5:1577.

[10] Benjamin Thompson, *History of Long Island*. pp.441,442.

[11] *Gravesend Town Records*, vol. I. Town Meetings, etc. 1646-1653 incl. transcribed by Frank L. van Cleef, 1909 s.v. September 12 1648.

[12] *Gravesend Town Records*: January 8 1651

[13] Esther Singleton, *Dutch New York*, p.188.

[14] *Gravesend Town Records*, 1 November 1650

[15] O'Callaghan,ed., *Documents Relative to the Colonial History of the State of New York*, 2:154-6.

CHAPTER 21

[1] Samuel Eliot Morison & Henry Steele Commager, *The Growth of the American Republic*, 1:62.
[2] *New-York Colonial Manuscripts: Holland Documents*, 9:158,159.

[3] Gravesend Town Records, 1:122; A.P.Stockwell, "Gravesend, L.I. Old and New" *New York Genealogical and Biographical record*, 16:104.
> "They fled from tyranny and oppression and were urgently devoted to the cause of civil liberty, and zealous for the purity and simplicity of the Protestant religion; they were resolute of their rights and resolute in their defence."
> - Silas Wood, *A Sketch of the First Settlement of the Several Towns on Long Island with their Political Condition to the End of the Revolution*, (Brooklyn: Alden Spooner, 1828) p.18.

[4] Court Minutes of New Amsterdam, s.v.2 June 1654

[5] E.B.O'Callaghan, ed., *Documents Relative to the Colonial History of the State of New York*, 1:550-555.

[6] B. Fernow, *Documents*, (Albany, 1833) 14:290.

[7] B.Fernow, *Documents*, 14:299,300.

[8] Lewis and Newhall, *History of Lynn*, p.183; *Winthrop's Journal*: 1630-1649. 2:126footnote.

[9] The Coney Island deed is at: The City of New York, Department of Records and Information Services; Eric J.Ierardi, *Gravesend: The Home of Coney Island*, p.43; Edo McCullough, *Good Old Coney Island*, (N.Y.: Charles Scribner's Sons, 1957) pp.18,19.

[10] Ierardi, p.43; Gerard, "Lady Deborah Moody" p.31.

[11] N.Y.Colonial Documents, 13:40.

CHAPTER 22

[1] O'Callaghan, ed., *Documents Relative to the Colonial History of New York*, 4:285.

[2] Edmund B. O'Callaghan, ed, *Documents Relative to the Colonial History of the State of New York*, 1:597. John R Brodhead, *History of the State of New York*, (New York: 1853) 1:596-7. Letter E : 6 March 1655.

[3] B. Fernow, *Documents*, (Albany: 1883) 14:235,236.

> A libertine was a member of a pantheistic sect of the sixteenth century in Holland, who maintained that nothing is sinful but to those who think it sinful, and that perfect innocence is to live without doubt.

[4] William Elliott Griffis, *The Story of New Netherland*, (Cambridge: Riverside Press, 1909) p.237; Henry Kessler, *Peter Stuyvesant and His New York*,(N.Y.: Random House, 1959) p.226.

> The problem was never resolved because of outside English pressures on the Dutch province. In 1657 Grover, Baxter and Hubbard returned from England with a letter from Oliver Cromwell affirming "the English rights to the northern part of America" and mentioning John Cabot's voyage, Sir Walter Ralegh's colony and the patents issued to New England and Virginia. Later King Charles II sent "secret instructions" to his five commissioners in and about New England. They were ordered not only to take possession of Dutch-held territory but to withdraw the charters from colonists or adjust them so that municipal officers and even church officials would be under royal appointment.

[5] "Resolution of Council to Notify Lady Moody and the Inhabitants of Gravesend to Send In a Nomination for Magistrats," June 18, 1655 in Fernow, ed., *Documents Relating to the Colonial History of the State of New York*, 14:327-8.

[6] "To the Noble Worshipful, their Honors of the High Council of New Netherland," July 19, 1655, in Fernow, *Ibid*, 14:329-30.

[7] T.E., *The Lawes Resolutions of Women's Rights* (1632) p.6 quoted in Sarah Heller Mendelson, *The Mental World of Stuart Women: Three Studies*, (Hemel Heamstead: Harvester Press, 1987) p.2.

> "The only woman voter that Albert E. McKinley was able to discover in the seventeenth century was Lady Deborah Moodey, late of Massachusetts, who in the summer of 1655 voted in a New Netherlands election. She was, of course, a woman of very high social standing, and was furthermore the oldest patentee of Gravesend, Long Island, and its civic leader."
>
> > - Albert E. McKinley, *The Suffrage Franchise in the American Colonies*, (Philadelphia: Ginn and Co., 1905) pp.192-3 in Roger Thompson, *Women in Stuart England and America*, (London: Routledge and Kegan Paul 1974) p.222.

CHAPTER 23

[1] Michael Kammen, *Colonial New York: A History*, (New York: Charles Scribner's Sons, 1975)p.61.

[2] Fernow, ed., *Records of New Amsterdam*, 2:204,205.

[3] *Colonial Documents* s.v.letter of Rev. John Megapolensis to the Classis of Amsterdam dated 16 March 1655

[4] Oliver A. Rink, *Holland on the Hudson*, (Cornell University Press, 1986) p.234; David W. McCullough, *Brooklyn and how it got that Way*, p.6.

[5] New York Penal Code No. 271. *The Jewish Encyclopedia*, s.v. "New York", 9:259.

[6] Harry J.Kreider, *The Beginnings of Lutheranism in New York* (N.Y. 1949) pp.25-30,38-42.

> Stuyvesant's Directors reacted against this persecution and wrote (1656): "We would have been better pleased if you had not published the placat against the Lutherans, a copy of which you sent us, and committed them to prison for it has always been

our intention to treat them quietly and leniently. Hereafter you will therefore not publish such or similar placats without our knowledge, but you must pass it over quietly and let them have free religious exercises in their houses." Esther Singelton, *Dutch New York* p.190.

[7] Megapolensis and Drisius to Classis of Amsterdam, *Ecclesdiastical Records, N.Y.* 1:396-7; Wilson, ed., *The Memorial History of the City of New York*, 1:238; James A Holden, *Ecclesiastical Records of the State of New York*, 1:411; Peter Ross, *History of Long Island* (New York: Lewis Publishing, 1905) p.362.

[8] *Encyclopaedia Britannica, Micropaedia* 6 s.v. "Bartholomew Legate" by T.Fuller.

Seekers' opinions stemmed from English preacher Bartholomew Legate who with his brother Thomas was imprisoned for unorthodox views in 1611. Thomas died in Newgate Prison, London. King James argued with Bartholomew Legate and on several occasions had him brought before the Consistory Court of London, which eventually found him guilty of heresy and he was burned to death at Smithfield, 18 March 1612. Legate was the last person to be burned in London for his religious convictions.

[9] Margaret, Duchess of Newcastle, *The Life of the Duke of Newcastle*, (Everyman edn. 1915) pp.153,154.

[10] *Ecclesiastical Records of New York*, 1:393-9; Rufus M.Jones, *Quakers in American Colonies*, (London: McMillan and Co. Ltd., 1911) pp.218,219; Francis Ellington's Tract, *A True Discovery*, (London, 1655)

[11] A. Neave Brayshaw, *The Quakers: Their Story and Message*, (York: Ebor Press for William Sessions Book Trust, 1982) p.89.

[12] Gravesend Town Records - s.v. 20 March 1657

[13] *Ecclesiastical Records, State of New York*, 1:399.

[14] Gerard Croese, *The General History of the Quakers; containing The Lives, Tenents, Sufferings, Tryals, Speeches and Letters of all the most Eminent Quaker, both Men and Women; from the first rise of that Sect, down to this present Time*, (London, 1696) 2:157; Frederick J. Zweierlein, *Religion in New Netherland*, (Rochester, NY: 1910) p.219.

[15] Rufus M Jones, *Quakers in the American Colonies*, 2:219,220.

[16] Martha Bockee Flint, *Early Long Island, A Colonial Study*, p.113.

Quaker was a nickname first given by Justice Bennet in 1650 to th group's founder, George Fox, because he bade the Justice tremble at the Word of the Lord. Early Quakers also explained it by the spiritual trembling sometimes experienced at their religious meetings. Later they were called the Society of Friends (i.e. Friends of the Truth)

Hempstead's inhabitants had been ready to receive Richard Denton, a pious, godly and learned preacher but when he began to baptize children "many persons rushed out of the church."

[17] Gerard Croese, *The General History of the Quakers*, 2:156,157.

[18] Mrs John Van Rensselaer, *The Goede Vrouw of Mana-ha-ta*, (Arno Press. 1972) p.110; Gerard Croese, *General History of the Quakers*, 2:157; *Ecclesiastical Records, State of New York*, (Albany: State of New York, 1901-1916) 1:410; Rufus M.Jones, *Quakers in American Colonies*, pp.210-213.

[19] "Extract From A Letter of the Directors to Stuyvesant..." 16 April 1663, in Fernow, ed., *Documents Relating to the Colonial History of the State of New York*, 14:526.

[20] Edmund B. O'Callaghan, ed, *Documents Relative to the Colonial History of the State of New York*, 14:402-3; Martha Bockee Flint, *Early Long Island*, p.112.

[21] Stiles, *History of Kings County*, 1:178.

Some years later on October 5, 1662 John and Mary(Goody) Tilton were charged
with having entertained Quakers and attending their conventicles. They were both
arrested, imprisoned and ordered to leave the Province before November 20, 1662
upon pain of corporal punishment.   They went to Oyster Bay, outside of
Stuyvesant's despotic jurisdiction and returned home in 1667 when Tilton was again
elected Town Clerk of Gravesend. See: Henry Whitemore address p.33; Stilwell,
Historical and Genealogical Miscellany, 5:133.

[22] Smith, *Religion and Trade*, pp.224,5.
[23] Gerard Croese, pp.155,156; Gerard, "Lady Deborah Moody" p.17.

In New England, merely for remarking that two Quakers were unjustly hung,
Edward Wharton of Salem was fined and whipped. In Newhaven Quakers were
branded with the letter 'H' if they came a second time into the colony, and for a
fourth visit both males and females were to have their tongues bored through with a
hot iron. In 1658 three Quakers each had a right ear cut off for visiting Boston a
second time without permission. Three Quakers were hung on October 1658 for
violating the Massachusetts law of 1656.

[24] Robert Wilson reported on Quaker persecution in New England:

22 have been Banished upon pain of death
3 have ben martyred
3 have had their Right Ears cut
1 hath been burned in the hand with the letter H
31 Persons have received 650 stripes
1 was beat while his Body was like a jelly.
Several were beat with pitched ropes
Five Appeals made to England were denied by the Rulers of Boston
One thousand forty-four pounds worth of goods hath been taken from them, (being
poor men) for meeting together in the fear of the Lord and for Keeping the
Commands of Christ
One now lyeth in Iron-fetters, condemned to dye.
- Hugh Barbour and Arthur O. Roberts, eds., *Early Quaker Writings: 1650-
1700*, (Grand Rapids MI.: William Eerdmans Publ. Co., c.1973) p.137.
Rufus M Jones, *Quakers in American Colonies*, 2:223.

[25] Fernow, *The Records of New Amsterdam: 1653-1674*, 3:148.

[26] E.I.H.C., 31:96-102, quoted in James D. Phillips, *Salem in the Seventeenth Century*, p.131.

[27] *King's County Records*, 1:108; Peter Ross, *A History of Long Island*, 1:364

[28] David McCullough, *Brooklyn: How It Got That Way*, p.10; Barber and Watson, *The Struggle for Democracy*, p 33,34.

It is noteworthy that the Iroquois Confederacy, an alliance of Indian nations was
democratic in terms of law, society and equal rights.

[29] quoted without reference in Jacqueline Overton, *Long Island's Story*, p.42.

[30] Samuel Francis Smith: "America"

MEMORIAL PLAQUE
[1] Plaque held by Curator, Brooklyn Historical Society.

POSTSCRIPT
[1] Gravesend Town Records, re: May 11, 1659. 2:38.

[2] *The Clarendon Papers*: Collections of the New-York Historical Society for the year 1869, (1870) p.14.

[3] Gerard, "Lady Deborah Moody" A Discourse delivered before the New York Historical Society, May 1880 (Patterson: New York: 1880 p.36.

[4] John Edwin Stilwell, *Historical and Genealogical Miscellany*, (Genealogical Publishing Co. 1970) 3:32.

> The company directors sent a letter to Stuyvesant in 1663: "Your last letter informed us that you had banished from the Province and sent hither by ship a certain Quaker, John Bowne by name, although we heartily desire, that these and other sectarians remained away from there, yet as they do not, we doubt very much, whether we can proceed against them rigorously without diminishing the population and stoppinng immigration, which must be favored at a so tender stage of the country's existence. You may therefore shut your eyes, at least not force people's consciences, but allow every one to have his own belief, as long as he behaves quietly and legally, gives no offence to his neighbors and does not oppose the government." - Hugh Hastings, comp., *Ecclesiastical Records: State of New York*, I (Albany, 1901) p.530.

[5] See Appendix II; Berthold Frenow, ed., *Records of New Amsterdam*, [1662], 4:64.

[6] James W Gerard, "Lady Deborah Moody" p.39.

APPENDICES

[1] See also: "The Established Church" (chapter 4) in J.P.Kenyon, *The Stuart Constitution - Documents and Commentary*, pp.125-146.

[2] *New York Historical Manuscripts: Dutch: The Register of Solomon LaChaire, Notary of New Amsterdam 1661-1662 translated from the original Dutch Manuscript in the office of the Clerk of the Common Council of New York by E.B.O'Callaghan*, (Genealogical PUblishing Co. Inc. Baltimore: 1978)p.2.

[3] Based on Homer L Bartlett, M.D. "Sketches of Long Island" - No.8 of 28 numbered articles pasted in a scrapbook from issues of RURAL, Harvard. (Brooklyn Historical Society).